Wa
Sugar Girls

'This vivid and richly readable account of women's lives in and around the Tate & Lyle East London works in the Forties and Fifties is written as popular social history, played for entertainment. If it doesn't become a TV series to rival *Call the Midwife*, I'll take my tea with ten sugars.'

– Bel Mooney, *The Daily Mail* (Book of the Week)

'Delightful, a terrific piece of nonfiction storytelling, and an authoritative and highly readable work of social history which brings vividly to life a fascinating part of East End life before it is lost forever.'

– Melanie McGrath, bestselling author of *Silvertown* and *Hopping*

'Be sure to read *The Sugar Girls* – top social and female history, beautifully researched and written.'

– Heidi Thomas, *Call the Midwife* screenwriter

'An unlikely page-turner, synthesising a pacey narrative from what we assume must have been a bottomless well of memories and anecdotes from the surviving sugar girls. It reads like a novel. By the end, we half-wished we'd lived through those impoverished, crater-strewn days.' – Londonist

'Do have the tissues close at hand when you get to the final chapter for the wrap-up of this remarkable, warm-hearted story . . . [a] wonderful book.' – London Historians

PRAISE FOR

GI Brides

'Apart from the strength of the individual stories, one of the richest things about this book is the detail ... More life stories of their generation need to be recorded, because we owe them so much and can learn from their ethos of grit and hard work.'

– Bel Mooney, *The Daily Mail*

'This is a treasure box of testimonies from a very different world, and one that will soon slip from living memory. Kudos to the authors for capturing these memories for posterity, and in such a readable, touching way.' – Londonist

'A captivating and pacey read, thoroughly researched and told with clear-eyed honesty.' – *Family Tree* magazine

'Beautifully written, it manages to seamlessly combine oral history with well-researched social history. The retelling of the excitement, romance, fears and hardships the GI brides experienced is engaging throughout ... An immensely readable history of real people.' – London Historians

'Packed with emotion, as well as shocking insights into war-torn Britain ... compelling and illuminating reading.'

– *Richmond Magazine*

'Beautifully rounded portraits ... delightful and touching.'

– *The Daily Mail*

The Girls Who Went to War

An extraordinary true story of heroism, heartache and happiness in the women's forces of the Second World War

DUNCAN BARRETT
& NUALA CALVI

HARPER
element

HarperElement
An imprint of HarperCollins*Publishers*
1 London Bridge Street
London SE1 9GF

www.harpercollins.co.uk

HarperCollins*Publishers*
1st Floor, Watermarque Building,
Ringsend Road
Dublin 4, Ireland

First published by HarperElement 2015
This edition published 2021

1 3 5 7 9 10 8 6 4 2

A catalogue record of this book is
available from the British Library

ISBN 978-0-00-846119-5

Printed and Bound in the UK using
100% Renewable Electricity at CPI Group (UK) Ltd

FSC
www.fsc.org
MIX
Paper from
responsible sources
FSC™ C007454

This book is produced from independently certified FSC™ paper to
ensure responsible forest management.

For more information visit: www.harpercollins.co.uk/green

For
Cathleen Alexander (ATS, 1941–1946)
Anne Barrett (ATS, 1943–1944)
and in memory of
Jane Bekhor (WAAF, 1941–1943)

Preface

In the summer of 1940, Britain stood alone against Germany. One by one, the other Allied nations – France, Belgium, Holland, Norway, Denmark and Poland – had all surrendered, and America and the Soviet Union were yet to join the war. But for all the brave talk of fighting the enemy on the beaches, the country was outgunned – and outmanned as well. The British Army stood at just over one and a half million men, while the Germans had three times that many, plus a population almost twice the size of Britain's from which to draw new waves of soldiers.

Clearly, in the fight against Hitler, manpower alone wasn't going to be enough.

During the First World War, all three branches of the British military had formed a female auxiliary service, but the new organisations had been mothballed soon after hostilities came to a close. In the build-up to a second global conflict they were hastily recalled to life, and it was now that the women's forces really came into their own.

Initially, both the Army and the RAF were supported by the Auxiliary Territorial Service, or ATS, but two months before Britain declared war on Germany in 1939, the Women's Auxiliary Air Force (WAAF) split off and became a separate organisation. Fulfilling an equivalent role in relation to the Navy was the Women's Royal Naval Service. Among the women's forces, the WRNS was considered the 'senior service', just as the Navy was among the three male forces. Its members – thanks to its unwieldy acronym – were known as 'Wrens'.

In fact, settling on a suitable name for the organisation had proved quite a minefield. It came close to being christened the Women's Auxiliary Naval Corps, until someone realised that the abbreviation 'WANC' might provoke jibes from the sailors its members worked alongside.

Of the three services, the WRNS was generally regarded as the classiest, and was by far the hardest to get in to, unless you had the right naval connections. Being a Wren was seen as rather glamorous, in part thanks to the distinctive navy blue uniform, which had been designed by the celebrated couturier Edward Molyneux. While the WAAF and ATS outfits featured belted waists and pleated pockets that were unflattering on the hips, the WRNS jacket was straight and streamlined, and the officer's tricorne hat was much admired. To top it off, the Navy girls were even allowed to wear black silk stockings – when asked why he had permitted such extravagance, the First Lord of the Admiralty joked, 'The Wrens like the feel of them, and so do my sailors.'

By the time war was actually declared in September 1939, all three of the women's services had been deluged with applicants, and tens of thousands of young women were soon donning their distinctive new uniforms – khaki for the ATS, Air Force blue for the WAAF, and navy for the WRNS. When conscription for women was introduced in the National Service Act of 1941, the ranks of the services were swelled further, as many girls chose the rigours of military life over hazardous work in a munitions factory or the hard labour of tilling the fields with the Land Army. There were some who refused to be drafted – 257 female conscientious objectors found themselves imprisoned as a result of their principles – but most girls reported for duty reasonably willingly and did their best to fit into life in the forces, however alien the military environment might seem to them.

In many ways, the girls in uniform were aspirational figures, and during the war their image was appropriated by advertisers keen to appeal to young, independent-minded women. But they were far from universally popular. Old sweats in the military were often mistrustful of their new colleagues, and anxious about sharing facilities with them. One veteran RAF officer told the BBC of his horror at the thought of 'petticoats' on his air base, and General Eisenhower himself was initially opposed to working alongside women, although the competence and professionalism he saw at his HQ in London were enough to make him change his mind.

Some men, whether military or civilian, feared that girls in uniform were getting ideas above their station. 'The menace,' fumed one magazine editor, 'is the woman who thinks she ought to be flying a high-speed bomber when she really has not the intelligence to scrub the floor of a hospital properly, or who wants to nose around as an air-raid warden and yet can't cook her husband's dinner.' Others complained that servicewomen were encroaching into previously male-dominated spaces – most shocking of all, they were seen accepting drinks from strangers in pubs.

The government attempted to calm the male population with a pamphlet that asserted reassuringly, 'The girls look healthy and happy, and clearly most of them will make better wives and mothers and citizens, if only because they have had some physical and mental training.' But many British people – men and women alike – were unconvinced. The confidence that many girls exuded when they put on a military uniform was seen by some as unladylike, and they were frequently accused of having loose morals – in fact many civilians fervently believed that women in the forces were little more than prostitutes. In popular slang, the letters ATS were said to stand for a number of lewd expressions, from 'Any time, Sergeant!' to 'American Tail Supply'. Army girls were referred to colloquially as 'officers' groundsheets', while WAAFs were labelled 'pilots' cockpits' and the girls in the Navy were the butt of a popular expression – 'Up with the lark and to bed with a Wren.'

The tabloid press didn't help matters. 'TOO MANY MISFITS IN THE ATS AND WAAF,' thundered the *Express*, while the *Daily Mail* ran a poll on what their readers hated most about the war, in which 'women in uniform' came top.

Such was the strength of feeling among the public that Parliament set up a committee to look into the alleged moral failings of the women's forces. In August 1942 the social reformer Violet Markham reported confidently that the accusations levelled against the girls were groundless. Although some servicewomen had been discharged for illegitimate pregnancies – in the ATS this was known as 'going para 11', after the section of the rulebook that dealt with such cases – the illegitimate birth rate in the services was in fact lower than among the civilian population at the time, and the rate of venereal disease among servicewomen was half that among men.

It seems particularly unfair that so many civilians looked down on the girls in uniform, since the part they played in winning the war was a crucial one. Without the contribution made by the WAAF, for example, the Royal Air Force would have needed an extra 150,000 men – a figure all but impossible to muster. And although the girls of the three forces were forbidden by Royal Proclamation from personally firing deadly weapons, they were closely involved in many of the key events of the war, and frequently found themselves in harm's way. In 1940, ATS ambulance drivers serving with the British Expeditionary Force in France were caught up in the frantic rush to evacuate at Dunkirk. Four years later, WAAF medical orderlies were among the first women to return to Europe after D-Day – when their air ambulances landed in Normandy just a week after the invasion, they were hailed as 'Angels of Mercy'.

Many servicewomen won medals for their bravery in terrifying circumstances – among them Daphne Pearson, who dragged a pilot out of his crashed plane just before a bomb exploded, hurling herself on top of him to shield his body from the blast. Others made critical contributions to Allied operations, such as Constance Babbington Smith, the first person to locate the launch sites of Hitler's deadly V1 flying bombs. Girls from all three forces worked under top-secret conditions at Bletchley Park, helping to shorten the war by at least two years – Churchill later referred to them as 'the geese that laid the golden eggs but never clucked'.

Then there were the courageous young women who shed their military uniforms when they were transferred to the Special Operations Executive, a spy network whose operatives were trained to kill with guns and explosives, and whose life expectancy in occupied Europe could be measured in weeks. Among them was former WAAF Noor Inayat Khan, who, after her comrades in the field were arrested, found herself the only link between a resistance network in Paris and the Allied command in London. In time she too was captured and taken to Dachau concentration camp, where she was executed with a bullet to the head.

Throughout the course of the war, around two thousand WAAFs, Wrens and ATS girls lost their lives in the service of their country. Some died on their bases around Britain, the victims of enemy bombing raids. Some were buried in foreign fields far away from home – in Cairo, Kuala Lumpur or Tel Aviv. Others were lost at sea, among them the 23 Wrens who drowned when the SS *Aguila* was sunk in the first U-boat attack on an Allied shipping convoy.

Overall, more than half a million women served in the armed forces during the Second World War. This book tells the stories of just three of them – one from the Army, one from the Navy and one from the Air Force. But in their stories are reflected the lives of hundreds of thousands of others like them – ordinary girls who went to war, wearing their uniforms with pride.

1

Jessie

The morning of Sunday 3 September 1939 was a sunny one, and Jessie Ward was out digging potatoes in the garden of her family's house in the little village of Holbeach Bank, Lincolnshire. A petite girl with big blue eyes and dark hair, she looked far younger than her 17 years, but despite her slight build her mother always made sure to keep her busy with chores. That particular day Mrs Ward was looking after a sick friend's little girl, so Jessie had even more to do than usual.

Just after 11 o'clock that morning, Mr Ward called his wife and daughter into the living-room, where they found him listening intently to the bulky wooden wireless set. There was a crackle, and then the clipped tones of Neville Chamberlain rang out of the machine. 'This morning,' he announced, 'the British Ambassador in Berlin handed the German Government a final note, stating that, unless we heard from them by 11 o'clock that they were prepared at once to withdraw their troops from Poland, a state of war would exist between us.'

Jessie saw her mother and father exchange an anxious glance.

'I have to tell you now,' the Prime Minister continued, 'that no such undertaking has been received, and that consequently this country is at war with Germany.'

Mr Ward leaned forward, holding his head in his hands. 'It can't happen again,' he muttered. 'It just can't.' Jessie knew that her father had spent much of the last war watching his fellow soldiers in the Royal Warwicks being gassed and slaughtered in front of him, and had witnessed his best friend being shot in the head.

'Well, we'll probably be invaded, being so close to the coast,' said his tiny wife, matter-of-factly. 'I'd better take Tina back to her mother. Jessie, you'll have to do the Sunday dinner.'

'Yes, Mum,' Jessie replied, as the little girl began to howl. Whether it was because of the imminent invasion, or because she was missing dinner, Jessie wasn't sure, but she was surprised to find that she herself felt nothing at all. Unlike her father, she had little idea of what war might bring, since the last one had ended four years before she was born.

Jessie went back out into the garden, and nodded over the fence at Mr Crawford, the elderly man who lived next door. 'Do *you* think we'll be invaded?' she asked him.

'Oh, don't worry,' he told her. 'Even if we are, the Germans aren't going to hurt the likes of us.'

Jessie's father came marching out into the garden just in time to catch Mr Crawford's remark. 'You silly bugger!' he shouted. 'You're the first ones the Nazis'll get rid of. Your wife is blind and you're an old man!'

'They wouldn't do that,' Mr Crawford protested weakly.

'They would,' retorted Mr Ward. '*I* know the Germans. They wouldn't waste food on people like you!'

Jessie was shocked – not so much by her father's anger, or by the grim prophecy in his words, but at the fact that he had said 'bugger'. She realised she had never heard him swear before.

In fact, it was rare to hear Mr Ward raise his voice at all, other than where Germans were concerned. He was a kindly man, whose health had never been the same since he had returned from the trenches 20 years earlier. It didn't help that he had to work six days a week, hammering away in his little cobbler's shop – and keeping it open until 9 p.m. most nights for the sake of the local farm labourers. Most of his customers only had one pair of dilapidated old boots to their name, but Mr Ward would work miracles on them, knowing that their owners couldn't afford to buy new ones.

While Jessie's father was out working all hours, his wife had free rein to boss their only daughter around. Fanny Ward was small, pretty woman, but her demure exterior belied a sharp temper, and Jessie had learned from a young age never to displease her. Every time she dropped a ball of wool she was winding or accidentally broke a cup in the kitchen, she was bound to get a clout round the ear.

Whenever she could, Jessie escaped to her grandmother's house to play on their beaten-up old piano. She had inherited a talent for music from her father's side of the family, and when she sat and played her cares seemed to melt away, the music transporting her to a realm of pure joy. Mr Ward was proud of his daughter's musical talent, and put aside a shilling a week to pay for her to have lessons.

The only thing that came close to playing, as far as Jessie was concerned, was dancing. As she grew older, she and her best friend Joan started attending the dances that were held every week at the little church hall in Holbeach Bank. She knew she was a good dancer, and she enjoyed showing off her skills, but her mother made sure that her confidence never went to her head. 'Do I look all right, Mum?' Jessie asked her one night, as she was about to head out. 'You'll do,' Mrs Ward replied. 'But who's going to be looking at *you*, anyway?'

When Jessie left school her piano playing proved a useful source of income, as she began giving lessons to the village children. But most of her time was still dictated by her mother, who kept her busy helping with knitting for the local wool shop, doing the gardening, cleaning the house, cooking and running errands.

There wasn't much to look forward to in Holbeach Bank, beyond one day marrying a boy from the village and moving out – and to begin with, the advent of war didn't make much difference to the sleepy community. Most of the local lads were farm labourers, so they were exempt from conscription, and the village was so tiny that no one thought it worth installing air-raid shelters.

But for Jessie's father, the new war brought with it a new sense of purpose. He was thrilled when he heard on the wireless that men up to 65 were needed to help defend their country, as part of the Local Defence Volunteers or 'Home Guard'. Now Mr Ward spent his spare time back in uniform, practising his marching and going out on night patrols, armed with an old First World War rifle. Wherever he went, he walked about with his chin up and his back straight as a rod. The neighbours joked that if you cut him, his blood would be khaki.

But Jessie's father's new pastime meant that she was left alone in the house with her mother more than ever, and she began to grow desperate for something that would take her away. One day, she spotted an advert for a waitress at a little truckers' cafe on the road to Holbeach proper. It was hardly glamorous, more of a 'greasy spoon', but Jessie jumped at the chance to get out of the house, hurrying to the cafe and offering her services.

'Are you sure you want the job?' asked the woman who ran it, looking at the slip of a girl in front of her. 'We get some pretty tough types in here, you know.'

'Oh, that doesn't bother me,' Jessie replied. If she could put up with her mother, she was sure she could handle a few truckers. The other woman didn't look quite convinced, so Jessie suggested helpfully, 'If you like, you can serve the posh customers, and I'll look after the tough guys.'

'You're on,' said the woman, hastily handing Jessie an apron as a group of burly-looking men came in through the door.

On the evenings when Mr Ward was at home, the family always gathered to listen to the BBC's 9 p.m. bulletin and hear the latest news of the war. In May 1940 they all sat in shock as they heard that the British Expeditionary Force was being evacuated from Dunkirk. An armada of fishing boats, crabbers, trawlers, shrimpers and yachts had answered the call for assistance, bringing back hundreds of thousands of exhausted soldiers while the Luftwaffe pounded them from overhead.

The new Prime Minister, Winston Churchill, told the country that the evacuation was a 'miracle of deliverance', but Mr Ward wasn't so easily convinced. 'We ran away from those Jerrys with our tails between our legs,' he said, shaking his head sadly.

Back on home soil, the effects of the evacuation were soon felt around Holbeach, as the battered British Army regrouped and replenished itself. Soon soldiers started to be seen around the village, and a nearby stately home called Bleak House was requisitioned by a Royal Artillery regiment.

Jessie knew the house well, since her friend Joan was the niece of the caretakers there, Mr and Mrs Hedqvist, who encouraged Jessie to come and play the grand piano in the drawing room whenever she liked. 'We don't see much of the soldiers really,' Mrs Hedqvist told her when she turned up to practise one day. 'They're mainly just using the kitchens and the dining room for their officers' mess.'

As Jessie approached the magnificent piano, Mrs Hedqvist sat down on a chair and took some knitting out of a little bag. She often liked to knit while Jessie played, and the regular klick-klacking was almost as good as a metronome.

Jessie began to run through a few scales. Then, when she felt she was properly warmed up, she moved on to a piece she had recently learned, a nocturne by Chopin in G minor. She was pleased to find that she could get through the whole thing without the sheet music – and even more pleased, when she reached the final notes, to hear applause echoing around the drawing room.

Jessie looked over to Mrs Hedqvist, but the caretaker was still busy with her knitting. Then she turned and looked behind her, where she discovered the source of the clapping. A young soldier was standing by the doorway, clearly enraptured by the music. 'That was wonderful,' he exclaimed, beaming at Jessie enthusiastically.

'Oh – hello!' Jessie replied, her cheeks flushing red. 'I'm glad you liked it.' The soldier was a couple of years older than her, with dark hair and a beautiful smile, and Jessie found him very attractive.

The young man approached the piano. 'I don't suppose you take requests?' he asked her.

'Well, what do you like?' Jessie said. 'If I don't know it, you can always hum the tune and I'll try to pick it out.'

'How about "There'll Always Be an England"?'

'Oh, that's easy,' Jessie told him, launching into the popular tune. But what seemed easy to Jessie obviously impressed the young soldier. As she played, she looked up now and then, and every time she saw him grinning from ear to ear, clearly enchanted by her performance.

Jessie had come to Bleak House intending to practise her classical pieces, but that afternoon she found herself playing a host of popular tunes instead as the young man requested one song after another. Soon they were both so lost in the music that they had completely lost track of time, and it was only when a grandfather clock in the corner of the room began to chime that the young man suddenly came to his senses. 'Oh my goodness,' he said. 'I'm supposed to be on duty!'

He dashed for the door, shooting Jessie another quick smile as he went.

Jessie remained seated at the piano for a moment. 'That was charming, my dear,' Mrs Hedqvist commented, giving her an encouraging smile.

Jessie had almost forgotten that the older woman was still in the room. 'Oh, thank you,' she replied, as she stood up and brought the lid down over the keys. But somehow she wasn't quite sure that it was the music which Mrs Hedqvist had been charmed by.

The following day, Jessie was on her bike, riding home from her job at the greasy spoon, when she saw the young soldier cycling towards her on the other side of the road. 'Oh, there you are,' he called as he spotted her, wheeling around until they were side by side.

'Hello again!' Jessie said. 'What are you doing here?'

'Looking for you, of course,' the soldier replied cheekily. 'I've just been round to your house and your mum said you'd be coming along this way.'

He must have got my address off Mrs Hedqvist, Jessie thought. She couldn't help smiling.

'Would you mind if I cycle with you?' the young man asked politely. 'I thought you might like some music on your way home.' As they pedalled away, he began singing 'Wish Me Luck As You Wave Me Goodbye', one of the songs Jessie had played for him the day before. She noticed that he remained perfectly in tune throughout, and his delight in the music shone through just as it had in the drawing room at Bleak House.

'That was lovely,' Jessie told him when he came to the end of the song.

'I'm glad you liked it,' he replied. 'I take requests too, you know.'

Jessie laughed. 'All right, how about "Run Rabbit Run"?' she suggested.

The man launched into a spirited rendition of the song, and for the rest of the two-and-a-half-mile journey, he kept her entertained with one tune after another.

In between songs, Jessie learned that the young man's name was Jim Winkworth, and that he had worked in the kitchen of a top London restaurant before joining the Army Catering Corps. 'I'm in charge of the food for all the bigwigs,' he explained.

'Well, I suppose you could say I work in catering too,' Jessie replied, 'but we mostly serve truckers, not Army top brass!'

'Oh, I'd swap with you any day,' Jim told her. 'You'd be surprised at the table manners of some of the majors and colonels.' But it was clear when he talked about the fancy dinners they laid on for the officers at Bleak House – with the finest crystal and silverware the grand stately home had to offer – that he loved his job very much, and took great pride in getting every detail just right. 'When I was out in France, we'd have killed for a pantry stocked as well as the one they have here,' he told her wistfully.

'You were in France?' Jessie asked, surprised.

'Oh, yes,' Jim replied. 'I was sunk twice on the way back from Dunkirk, but both times I got pulled out of the water. In the end I came back on a little fishing boat.' He grinned at her. 'I guess I must have just been born lucky.'

'Most people would call being sunk twice pretty bad luck!' Jessie pointed out.

'Well,' Jim shrugged, 'there's plenty of men who didn't make it back at all.' After a moment's silence, he began to sing again. Clearly whatever horrors he had seen had only made him more determined to embrace the joy of life.

When they got to Holbeach Bank, Jessie invited Jim in for a cup of tea, and soon he was entering her parents' little house for the second time that afternoon.

'Oh, he found you then?' Mrs Ward commented dryly as Jessie ushered the young man into the kitchen.

'Yes, Mum,' Jessie replied, hoping her mother wasn't going to be rude to him.

'So, Jim, where do your family come from?' Mrs Ward asked, as she plonked the teapot down on the table, gesturing for Jessie to pour the tea.

'To be honest, I have no idea,' he told her. He explained that he had spent his childhood in a Dr Barnardo's orphanage in Hastings and had never found out who his parents were.

As she listened to the sad story, Jessie's heart went out to Jim, but his words had a different effect on her mother. 'I'm not keen on that one,' she told Jessie, after the young man had set off back to Bleak House. 'He's got no family, no background. You don't know who he is.'

'Neither does he, Mum,' Jessie reasoned. 'You can't hold that against him.'

But Mrs Ward shook her head firmly. 'You don't want to get involved with him,' she said.

Jessie took little notice of her mother's advice, however, and soon Jim was stopping by at the greasy spoon several times a week to see her. They spent hours at a time cycling around the countryside together, pausing every now and then for a kiss and a cuddle, until it was time for him to accompany her back home.

Jim hadn't failed to notice Mrs Ward's coolness towards him. 'I don't think your mother likes me,' he told Jessie one day, as they were cycling back to Holbeach Bank.

'Oh, don't worry. She doesn't like anyone!' Jessie replied, trying to make light of the situation.

But Jim was uncharacteristically serious. 'You know, it's hard for me to meet new people,' he told her. 'They always want to know about my family.'

'Well, I don't care who your parents are,' Jessie declared. 'And anyway, the way some families are, you're probably well off without one!'

But despite Jessie's words, Jim was determined to win her mother over. One evening, he turned up at the little house in Holbeach Bank bearing an enormous fillet of smoked salmon. 'Don't worry, I haven't stolen it,' he told Mrs Ward when he saw the suspicious look in her eye. 'We over-ordered at the officers' mess and it was going to be thrown in the bin.'

'Well, in that case, I suppose we'd better eat it,' Jessie's mother replied, taking the fillet off to the kitchen.

When the food was served, even Mrs Ward had to admit that the salmon was delicious, and fresher than anything the family had eaten since the start of the war. But her frostiness towards Jim didn't thaw one bit.

Mr Ward, on the other hand, clearly enjoyed having a soldier in the house. 'You know, the cooks are the most important people in the Army,' he declared over dinner, looking over approvingly at Jessie's guest. 'When I was in the trenches, they were the ones who kept our peckers up. As Napoleon said, an army always marches on its stomach!'

After Jim had left at the end of the evening, Jessie's father turned to her. 'I like that young man,' he said. 'And I'm glad that he's an Army lad, not one of those stuck-up Navy or Air Force types.'

But despite the wonderful salmon, the expression on Mrs Ward's face made it clear that her opinion of Jim hadn't altered one bit.

Jessie soon discovered that Jim was forming his own views about her mother as well. 'You know, you take too much notice of her,' he announced one day while they were out cycling. 'You shouldn't let her boss you about so much.'

'Well, there's no point arguing with her,' Jessie told him. 'It only makes things worse.'

'Maybe,' Jim replied. 'But don't let her keep you under her thumb.'

The more time Jessie spent with Jim, the more she felt herself falling in love with him – but her feelings were of no concern to the Army. One day, out of the blue, orders went up at Bleak House announcing he was being transferred to Sleaford, 25 miles away. There were no more romantic bike rides after work, and Jessie found she missed Jim terribly.

Fortunately, he was billeted with a kind local vicar who allowed him to use the phone once a week. He would write to Jessie and let her know what time he would be calling, so that she could queue up at the phone box in the village for a quick snatched conversation. It was wonderful to hear his voice, even only briefly, but afterwards she always returned home glumly, knowing it would be another seven days before they could speak again.

Before long, Jim was sent even further away, to Woodhall Spa, where they could no longer even talk on the phone. Now Jessie lived for his letters, which arrived faithfully every other day. He was a natural writer, and the two of them filled pages and pages with heartfelt reminders of their love.

When Jim wrote one day and asked Jessie if she would marry him, she knew instantly that her answer was yes. But she also knew that her mother would do her best to talk her out of it.

Jim's words echoed in Jessie's mind: 'Don't let her keep you under her thumb.' She picked up a pen and quickly wrote back accepting Jim's proposal, making sure the letter was signed, sealed and posted before she went in to tell her parents the news.

'Jim's asked me to marry him – and I've said yes,' she announced excitedly, when she found them together in the living room.

Mrs Ward shot an annoyed look at her daughter, but she could see it was too late to change her mind. Instead she said coldly, 'Well, you'll have to wait until the war's over. It would be very unwise to marry before then.'

Jessie was determined not to give too much ground. 'We'll have to wait and see,' she said boldly.

Her father grinned at her. 'I don't mind what you do love, as long as you're happy,' he said.

A few weeks later, when Jim was granted a day's leave, he and Jessie met up in King's Lynn. There he presented her with the most beautiful ring she had ever seen – it was made of platinum and encrusted with tiny diamonds.

As much as Jessie was thrilled about her engagement, it made life at home even more difficult. Her relationship with her mother was frostier than ever, and she realised that, even if she did defy her and marry Jim while the war was still raging, with the Army moving him around constantly, she would still be stuck at home until he was finally demobbed.

It didn't look like the war would be over any time soon, either. When they gathered around the wireless in the evenings, Jessie and her family heard reports of aerial bombings in London, Birmingham, Liverpool and other big cities, including nearby Peterborough. A few bombs had even landed near Spalding. 'Those blooming Germans are walking all over us,' Mr Ward fumed.

Jessie was beginning to wonder what *she* was doing to help with the war effort. All she did was spend her days serving beans on toast. Surely there was something more she could do – perhaps even something that would have the added bonus of getting her out of Holbeach Bank.

Ever since Dunkirk, stories had been circulating about the brave ATS girls who had travelled to France with the British Expeditionary Force. Some had heroically escaped after having been captured by the Germans, while others had endured terrifying dive-bombing by the Luftwaffe. Their efforts had proved that the women's forces deserved to be taken seriously, and now a massive recruitment drive was underway.

Jessie had seen the posters and advertisements up around the village, calling for girls to join the ATS – 'YOU ARE WANTED TOO!' they proclaimed in large, bold letters, alongside an image of a young woman marching in uniform. Jessie liked the idea of joining the Army, like her father, and when she wrote to tell Jim about her idea he was supportive. But she had a feeling that if she spoke to her mother, she would try to put a dampener on her plans.

When a friend who lived ten miles away in Boston invited Jessie to come and visit her for the weekend, she realised it was the perfect opportunity for her to join up without any interference. She took the bus into Grantham, where she knew there was an ATS recruiting office, and was ushered into a hall where a male Army sergeant was seated behind a desk. He took down her name, address and date of birth, and told her she would be hearing from them shortly.

'I've signed up for the ATS,' Jessie told her parents, as soon as she got back home after her holiday.

Mrs Ward didn't even look up from her knitting. 'Well, the Army ought to teach you what hard work is,' she muttered.

'I don't mind working hard,' replied Jessie. After all, her mother had been treating her as a domestic drudge for years.

Mr Ward, of course, was over the moon at the thought that he was going to have a daughter in khaki. 'My Jessie's going to win us the war, you know,' he began telling anyone in the village who would listen.

Now that she had made the decision to join up, Jessie's excitement was growing, but it soon began to be mingled with impatience. She had volunteered in December of 1941, and had been rated 'A1' at a medical exam in Grantham just before

Christmas, but she was told that it wouldn't be until the new year that the Army would get around to calling her up.

At long last, one crisp January morning, an official-looking envelope arrived on Jessie's doormat. She tore it open to find a railway warrant and instructions for getting to an ATS training camp at Leicester the next day. She was to bring just one small suitcase, containing two pairs of pyjamas.

Jessie didn't own any pyjamas, so she rushed into Holbeach to buy some, stopping off along the way to let her boss at the greasy spoon know that she was leaving to join the Army. 'Well, I can't argue with that!' the woman said, wishing her luck.

The next morning, Jessie was up bright and early, ready to begin the journey to Leicester. To Mr Ward, it was a red-letter day, although his wife treated it just like any other. As far as she was concerned, Jessie might have been setting off for her usual shift at the cafe, not leaving home for the duration of the war.

Right now, though, nothing could dampen Jessie's spirits, and she walked the two and a half miles to Holbeach Station fizzing with excitement. At the station, she presented her railway warrant and boarded a train to Spalding, where she had been instructed to make a connection that would take her to Leicester.

As she got on the second train, Jessie spotted a couple of girls she recognised from her medical in Grantham, and soon they had introduced themselves and were chatting away. One of them, Mary, was tall and slim, and carried herself with an air of quiet confidence. The other, Olive, was more cuddly-looking, with glasses and an infectious laugh.

As they got to know each other, the girls talked about their reasons for joining the ATS. Olive, it turned out, had signed up after a love affair turned sour. 'I just got so fed up that I had to leave!' she told Jessie and Mary with a giggle.

When they arrived at Leicester station, the girls were met by a railway transport officer, who pointed them in the direction of a fleet of ATS lorries. They clambered up over the tailgate of one of the vehicles, along with a group of other young women. They were all anxiously clutching little suitcases, with the same expression of bewilderment on their faces. They didn't exactly look like an Army in waiting.

When the girls finally arrived at the barracks it was well into the afternoon, and they were led into the canteen for a late lunch. Jessie went up to the counter to get her food, and was surprised to find a familiar face serving her. It was Peggy Hogg, a girl she remembered from school, who was now on permanent staff at the camp as an ATS orderly.

'Fancy seeing you here, Peggy!' Jessie exclaimed, as the girl slopped a portion of mashed potato onto her plate. 'I didn't know you were in the Army.'

'Oh yeah, I've been here a year now,' Peggy replied with a sigh.

As Jessie returned to her seat, she couldn't help feeling a little sorry for her old schoolmate. Wasn't joining the ATS supposed to be about doing something important and exciting? Yet here was Peggy still at a training camp a year after she had signed up, with nothing more thrilling to do than doling out slop.

When they had eaten, the new recruits were led to the stores to be issued with their kit. A woman took one look at Jessie's diminutive form and declared, 'Size one in everything, and if it's still too big you can take it in yourself with your hussif.'

The 'hussif' – or 'housewife' – was a sewing kit issued to every member of the services, and was just one of a bewildering array of items that Jessie soon found herself piling into a large Army kitbag. First there was the basic ATS uniform: shirt, skirt, tunic, tie and cap, along with stockings, suspender belt and bra – plus three pairs of voluminous khaki bloomers, which were known throughout the ATS as 'passion killers'. Jessie found that two of hers were broadly speaking wearable, but the third for some reason stretched from above her bosom to below her knees.

Next came two pairs of heavy lace-up shoes, plimsolls, a top and shorts for physical training, a field dressing, knife, fork, mug and spoon (collectively known as 'irons'), towels, hairbrush, comb and toothbrush, plus special brushes and implements for polishing shoes and buttons.

On top of all this, every girl was handed a gas mask, complete with a haversack to carry it in, and – last but by no means least – a supply of sanitary towels. The cost of providing these had been met by the generous Lord Nuffield, the founder of Morris Motors – and as a result they were known unofficially as 'Nuffies'. Little did he know that in addition to their intended purpose, they were used by resourceful girls in uniform for everything from cleaning buttons to straining coffee grounds. Those with loops were even fashioned into makeshift eye-masks, popular with night-shift girls trying to catch 40 winks in the daytime.

By the time they were all kitted out, the new recruits were ready to retire for the evening, but first they had to face the dreaded Free from Infection parade, or FFI. Lining up one by one, the girls were asked to pull their knickers down as the doctor inspected them for parasites and venereal disease, before their armpits were checked for lice, their hair gone through with a nit comb and their chests and backs examined for rashes. For the sorry few who failed the nit-comb test, the treatment offered a further humiliation: their hair was cut short and covered in a thick black paste made from coal tar, paraffin and cottonseed oil, before being wrapped up in a turban.

Finally, once the FFI was over, Jessie and the other girls were issued with a pair of sheets each and led to the large wooden dormitory huts, each containing 30 hard iron beds, which were to be their home for the coming weeks. Each bed had a mattress made up of three separate square parts or 'biscuits', as well as an uncomfortable-looking straw bolster for a pillow, and three grey blankets for warmth.

Jessie was disappointed to find that she wasn't sharing a dorm with Olive or Mary, who were both in the next hut along. Instead, she was bunking with a group of strangers, who, judging by their accents, hailed from every inch of the country, from Lands End to John o' Groats. The cacophony of different voices was quite something, but it was the Londoners who really stood out to Jessie. Whether cut-glass or Cockney, they all sounded so confident and loud, and beside them she felt like a bit of a country bumpkin.

The next morning, Jessie packed up her civilian clothes in her suitcase so that the Army could post them home to her parents, and dressed in her new ATS uniform for the first time. Then she and the other girls in her hut grabbed a quick breakfast in the canteen before they were introduced to one of the staples of basic training: drill practice.

The girls lined up on the parade ground as a red-faced male sergeant strode up and down in front of them. From the sour expression on his face, he obviously wasn't too impressed with what he saw. 'When I call "Attention!" I want you to bring your left foot in to your right,' he announced. 'Ready? Atten-shun!'

Jessie instantly snapped to attention, her back as straight as a pole. Thanks to her father's example, she had a pretty good idea of what military posture looked like.

'As you were,' the sergeant shouted. 'Now, ri-i-ght turn!'

Jessie pivoted 90 degrees to her right and sharply brought her feet back together. But, looking ahead of her, she could see some girls were facing the wrong way.

'Don't you know your right from your left?' the sergeant shouted at them, exasperated. The confused girls giggled, and awkwardly shuffled round to face the front.

'Now, when I say, "By the left, quick march," you're going to leave on the *left* foot with the *right* arm up,' the man told them. 'Forget what your mothers told you and make sure you open your legs.'

There was barely time to take the information in before he bellowed, 'By the le-e-ft, qui-i-ck MARCH!'

The girls began moving forward as the sergeant bellowed, 'Left! Right! Left! Right! Left! Right!' Thanks to her dancing experience, Jessie found it easy to keep in time, and to make sure her arms were swinging alternately with her feet. But not all her colleagues were finding the training so straightforward. The basic marching movement was too much for some of them to grasp, and they were waddling forward with arms flailing out randomly.

Their posture didn't exactly match Jessie's straight-backed bearing either. 'Stop slouching, and keep your legs open,' the sergeant bellowed at the group. 'What are you, a bunch of pregnant virgins?'

In the face of such a nonsensical insult, the new recruits struggled not to laugh.

When they weren't drilling, the girls spent much of their time at the training camp in lectures, scribbling down notes in little exercise books. There were talks on the history of the local regiment in Leicester, and on the basics of Army discipline. 'You won't be *asked* to do something, and you won't be *told* to do it either,' they were informed. 'You'll be *ordered*, and you'd better know the difference.'

Among the many topics covered in the lectures was the uncomfortable subject of venereal disease, or 'VD'. Many girls who had yet to learn the facts of life were shocked at being told about the virtues of 'French letters', and even the more worldly wise were horrified by the grisly photographs of syphilitic sores that flashed up on a giant screen in front of them. But for the ATS, sexually transmitted diseases were no laughing matter. National rates of gonorrhoea and syphilis had more than doubled since the start of the war, and it was estimated that one out of every 200 ATS girls had already been infected.

Of all the lectures that Jessie attended in her first week of training, the one that made the strongest impression on her was a talk about Anti-Aircraft Command. To begin with, the Royal Artillery's 'ack-ack' gun-sites had been strictly male environments, but the drive to free up men for fighting roles abroad was seeing the formation of a number of mixed heavy gun batteries. The prime minister's daughter, Mary Churchill, had been among the earliest ATS girls to join one of them.

The Army was keen to boost recruitment among the current cohort of ATS trainees, and as the girls sat and listened, the speakers pressed home the importance of the guns in defending Britain's cities against German bombers. 'When you're asked what job you'd like to do in the Army,' they told the hut full of young women, 'we want as many of you as possible to request ack-ack.'

Jessie was very much taken with the idea of serving on the guns. She had joined the ATS keen to do something meaningful for the war effort, and helping to shoot down German planes sounded a lot more exciting than answering the telephone or working as a kitchen orderly like her old school-mate Peggy. And the idea that, like Jim, she would be serving in the Royal Artillery appealed to her too. She decided then and there that when the time came, she would put her name down for ack-ack.

After a week of daily drill, even the most uncoordinated recruits had begun to master the basics of marching, and were able to about-turn at a moment's notice, salute to the side while still moving forwards, and halt without piling into each other. Now that she wasn't the only girl capable of keeping in rhythm, Jessie was enjoying the regular practices more than ever. She might be petite, but she felt like a small cog in a very powerful machine, and the sound of a hundred feet hitting the ground together was exhilarating.

Jessie was also growing used to the regimented nature of Army life, which infused every hour of her time at the training camp. In the mornings the girls had to dismantle – or 'barrack' – their bedclothes, stacking them up in perfect piles. Then they were subjected to kit inspections, in which each item had to be laid out in a prescribed pattern. At night, they had to polish their shoes and tunic buttons until they shone.

Every moment of the day was accounted for – the girls were told when to wake up and when to go to sleep, even when to visit the communal washing facilities, or 'ablutions', where they were allowed to shower three times a week. The lack of privacy there was just part of the ATS way of life – a reminder that, like every item of kit, the girls' bodies belonged to the Army.

The one small touch of individuality they were allowed was a little shelf above each bed, where they could place a few personal items. Jessie had proudly displayed a photograph of Jim, and she saw that many of the other girls also had pictures of their sweethearts back home.

Despite the busy training schedule, Jessie wrote to her fiancé every couple of days, but she was kept so busy that she barely had time to miss him. In the evenings the girls in her hut would stay up singing and chatting together until lights out at 10.30 p.m., and if they weren't cleaning and polishing their uniforms while they did it, they were doing embroidery. There was a concession in the barracks that sold the patterns, and Jessie was working on a tablecloth.

If the first part of ATS training was about instilling a respect for Army discipline, the second was for sorting the wheat from the chaff. The girls lined up in an exam hall to sit a series of intelligence and aptitude tests, with questions on general reasoning and mathematics. There they were asked to write an essay about their lives before they had signed up, to assess their spelling and grammar.

When the written exams were out of the way, they were given eye checks to establish how far they could see, and a steady-hand test where they had to avoid setting off a buzzer. Then there were memory and visual recognition tests, in which cards showing various German planes were flashed in front of them and they had to try to remember which was which.

By the time Jessie was led into a little room and asked what trade she would like to be considered for, her head was spinning, but she confidently proclaimed, 'Ack-ack, please.' A corporal made a note on a clipboard and sent her on her way.

Finally, at the end of their time at the training camp, the girls all gathered to be assigned to their postings. As a corporal read their names off a list one by one, they waited anxiously to hear what their future in the Army would be. Some trades, such as cook, were so unpopular that girls had been known to go to extreme lengths to get out of them, as evidenced by the occasional dollop of mustard in the morning's porridge.

Since Jessie's surname was Ward, she was one of the last to hear what role she had been assigned to. Mary and Olive had already been told they were going to an ack-ack training camp in Berkshire, and she crossed her fingers, hoping that she would be setting off with them.

Finally, the corporal came to her name. 'Private Ward,' she called out. 'Anti-aircraft.'

At that moment, Jessie couldn't have been happier. She was joining the artillery, and would soon be giving the Germans what for.

2

Margery

When Margery Pott announced that she had joined the Women's Auxiliary Air Force, her family couldn't help laughing. Surely, they thought, she must be pulling their legs – but the serious look on her face told them it was no joke.

'Fancy Margery doing that!' was all her sister Peggy could say, a remark that accurately captured the view of the whole family. It was, in fact, a view that Margery privately shared – she was the last person in the world who anyone would expect to join up.

If anyone should be answering the call to war, it ought by rights to be Peggy. A tomboy three years older than Margery, she had always been the fighter of the family. When Margery was a little girl and her best friend Daisy had knocked her to the ground, it was Peggy who had rescued her, marching up and giving her attacker a good walloping.

Growing up, Peggy had always been there to protect Margery, but she had also been a tough act to follow. She loved nothing better than cycling to the local forest and camping out overnight, and her favourite films were action-packed Westerns. Margery was too scared of insects and the dark to join her sister on her expeditions, and their mother didn't let her go to the cinema in case the cowboy movies gave her nightmares.

As the youngest of three daughters, Margery was the baby of the family, and Mrs Pott kept her wrapped in cotton wool, forbidding her to ride Peggy's bike for fear that she would fall off and hurt herself. Little did she know that Peggy had already taken it upon herself to give her little sister lessons in secret.

Mrs Pott had a lot on her plate, since she also had her husband's failing health to worry about. His emphysema, which had prevented him from fighting in the last war, was only worsening thanks to the dust he inhaled in his job as a maltster, turning the roasted barley every day. Mrs Pott kept a spittoon for him to cough into each morning, and poor Mr Pott would hack and hack until he brought up large lumps of phlegm. But at least his employment meant that the family got to live in the maltster's house, which meant they were the only ones in the little rural village of North Wallington to have running water.

When Margery began secondary school, she felt more in her sister's shadow than ever. 'Oh, Peggy was ever so good at games,' were the words that greeted her when she first arrived on the school playing field. Margery, who had never been particularly good at anything physical, felt her heart sink. In her academic lessons she always did well, but she was convinced she was nothing special.

By the time Margery left school at 15, Peggy had already moved out to train as a nurse. But when she urged her little sister to follow suit, their mother was horrified, and soon Margery had been dissuaded. Instead, she took evening classes in accountancy and found herself a job close by, in the back office of the local baker's.

At Pyle & Son Margery spent her days perched at a high desk, scribbling away in the accounts ledger. She was ruled over by the head clerk, a woman named Miss Pratt, who was always on the lookout for ink blotches. Miss Pratt quickly discovered Margery's pliant nature and began adding to her list of official duties. Soon the poor girl was required to clean the offices each morning, light the fires, type up the menus for the bakery's cafe and even wait tables, in addition to the bookkeeping she had been hired for.

One day, when Peggy popped in to see Margery, she was furious to find her stacking up goods for the delivery round. 'My sister is a ledger clerk,' she fumed. 'She shouldn't be packing buns!' But her outburst made no difference in the long run. When one of the horses escaped from its cart on the way back from the delivery round, it was Margery who was sent to catch it, and then to the chemist to fetch the ointment she was expected to rub into the animal's sore knees.

The unsatisfactory situation reached a new low one day, when Miss Pratt flew into a rage and called Margery a nincompoop for failing to fetch the dog's dinner. Margery wasn't normally one to stand up to authority, but even she could see it was time to leave.

She got as far as the shop next door – a musty old draper's called Dodge's, where she took a job as a cashier instead.

As Margery made her small stand against the tyrannical regime of Miss Pratt, the world was facing up to tyranny of a different kind. The first notable impact of the war on the quiet life of North Wallington was the sudden appearance of hundreds of sailors, when a naval training college, HMS *Collingwood*, opened up in nearby Fareham.

Soon, there were more reminders of the drama unfolding beyond the village. In the evenings, the sky was all too often lit up by an eerie glow, as German bombers pounded Portsmouth and Gosport. One night, the operating theatre at Peggy's hospital was hit, and the doctors and nurses had to form a line, passing buckets of water along in a desperate attempt to put out the fires.

A brand new air-raid shelter had been built just across the road from the maltster's house, but Mr Pott's health just wasn't up to the cold, wet conditions there, so when the sirens sounded the whole family remained at home, hoping for the best. Margery was secretly glad – she was more frightened of going out in the dark than she was of the bombs, and the thought of being trapped in a crowded public shelter made her shudder.

The war brought with it new job prospects as well, and soon Margery's friend Daisy had begun working at a munitions factory in Gosport, filling shell cases. But the idea of factory work filled Margery with dread. She'd had a horror of machines since her childhood, when she and Peggy had ridden the Gosport ferry and been taken below deck to view the engine room. Margery's sister had been thrilled at the sight of the enormous machines, but she had found the whole experience terrifying.

Daisy seemed pleased with her new factory job and the relatively high wages it offered. But, after a few weeks, Margery noticed that her friend's blonde ringlets had acquired a strange ginger tinge, and soon her usually pretty face had turned yellow. A few days later she heard from Daisy's mother that she had been off work sick, and when she went to visit she was shocked by the change in her. Daisy's entire body had gone a deep shade of orange, and now even the whites of her eyes were coloured with it. 'We reckon it's the TNT from the factory,' her mother told Margery, wringing her apron at Daisy's bedside.

Over the coming weeks Daisy slowly clawed her way back to health, but her illness only made Margery more terrified than ever at the thought of working in a factory. Yet to her dismay there was talk of young women being conscripted – not only into the armed forces but into munitions factories like the one in Gosport as well. In April 1941 the Registration for Employment Order was passed, requiring Margery, like all other young, single women, to register with the Ministry of Labour. Since she was now 20, she was in the catchment age for the impending call-up.

Margery was frantic. Throughout her young life, joining the military could not have been further from her mind – yet if she didn't volunteer now, the choice of whether to join the services or be put into a factory would be taken out of her hands. There was nothing for it: she would have to enlist.

She was relieved to discover that she was not alone – another girl at the draper's called Winnie was facing the same dilemma. But which force should they choose – Army, Navy or Air Force?

'The WAAF uniform's a nice colour,' remarked one of their colleagues over lunch one day, pointing to a recruitment ad in the magazine she was reading. The illustration showed Air Force girls in smart blue uniforms, dancing with dashing pilots. Before long, Winnie and Margery had hatched a plan to get the bus to Portsmouth together that weekend and volunteer for the WAAF.

At the recruiting office Margery's brief interview seemed to go well, and a WAAF sergeant said they would be pleased to take her, thanks to her experience in accounts. 'You'll be hearing from us soon,' she assured her.

Sure enough, it wasn't long before both Margery and Winnie awoke to find a brown envelope on their doormat. Inside was a letter ordering the girls to report to Portsmouth the next day at

7 a.m. From there, they would be taken to London for a medical exam.

Now Margery was gripped by a new fear – what if she failed the medical? She remembered with a jolt a broken tooth that she had been meaning to get fixed. Could that be enough to keep her out of the WAAF? She wasn't sure, but she had no intention of taking the risk. Something had to be done – and quickly.

Before long, Margery was sat in front of the local dentist, begging him to remove the offending tooth. The man was a little put out at being asked to perform such a last-minute operation, but he yanked and pulled with his pliers until finally it was extracted.

That night, as she tried to pack her tiny overnight bag while cradling her painful jaw, Margery received some unsettling news. Winnie's aunt had died unexpectedly, and since she was already motherless and the only girl in the family, her father had decided that he needed her at home to run the house. Winnie wouldn't be coming with her to London after all – instead Margery would be facing the Air Force alone.

It was a little after 5 a.m. the following morning when Margery caught the bus to Portsmouth. She was wearing her best suit – a pale blue jacket with matching skirt and blouse, which she hoped would make a good impression on the WAAF. As the vehicle trundled along the sleepy country lanes, she wondered where she might ultimately end up. She had never been away from home before – or really, gone anywhere at all, other than a few trips to Dover and Deal to see her relatives. Yet in the Air Force she would have no say in where she was stationed, and she might be sent far, far away from the familiar world of North Wallington.

On the train from Portsmouth to London, Margery sat with a small group of equally nervous-looking local girls, some a little older than herself and some younger. As they rushed towards the capital, a WAAF sergeant told the girls that if they passed the day's medical exam they would be sent for three weeks' basic training in Gloucester, but if they failed they would be going straight home again. Margery was wracked with nerves at the thought of flunking the medical, and more thankful than ever that she had got rid of her broken tooth.

At the imposing Victory House in Piccadilly, Margery's cohort was swept into a sea of new recruits being processed that day. The building was a hive of activity, with line after line of women queueing to see various doctors, each of whom specialised in a different part of the human anatomy. First Margery joined a queue of girls waiting to have their hearts and lungs tested – as they reached the front, they were asked to breathe in and out while a man with glasses listened intently for any rattles or murmurs. Margery was worried that her racing heart would let her down, but to her relief she passed and was moved on to the next line. There, she queued for more than an hour before her limbs were stretched and examined and her knees and elbows knocked with a little hammer to test her reflexes. Then there were the eye doctors, ear doctors, foot doctors – every kind of doctor imaginable – and all of them intent on weeding out substandard recruits. Yet to Margery's continual surprise and relief, time after time she was passed as fit and healthy.

Whenever she joined a new queue, Margery was sure that the doctor at the front would ask to inspect her teeth, but hour after hour went by and no one did. Finally, after a long and weary day with just a cup of tea and a sandwich to sustain them, she and the other girls from Portsmouth were all passed as fit and told they would be boarding the train to Gloucester.

Margery was overwhelmed with relief that she had passed her medical. But on her way from Victory House to Paddington Station, suddenly a new thought dawned on her – she had undergone the painful dental work for nothing.

It was getting on for midnight by the time the girls finally arrived at No. 2 WAAF Depot at Innsworth, near Gloucester, the central training facility for new recruits. Having opened only a few months before, the base now managed an intake of almost 3,000 girls a week, and ran like a well-oiled machine.

After the hours of queueing for medical examinations, followed by a lengthy journey, the girls were beginning to feel desperate for a hot dinner and a warm bed, but first there was more processing to be done. They were required to submit to the indignities of the FFI inspection and then to gather their kit from the stores, before making up the beds in their dormitory huts, alternately top to toe to limit the chances of infection. By the time they were finally taken to the mess, Margery was ravenous, but to her disappointment the long-awaited dinner consisted of just a spoonful of watery minced beef and lumpy mashed potato.

As the girls were finishing up their food, one of the kitchen hands came round with a large bucket and Margery saw that she was ladling something from it into their enamel mugs. 'What's in there?' she asked her neighbour.

'Tea,' the other girl replied with a smile.

Margery was horrified. After all the unfamiliar, exhausting experiences of the day, the thought of having what should have been a reassuring, homely cuppa doled out from a bucket somehow felt like the last straw.

Finally, the tired recruits were led back to their wooden huts for the night, and collapsed gratefully onto their hard iron beds. But now Margery, like many of the other girls, found that the sleep she had longed for was eluding her. The three square 'biscuits' that she had been given for a mattress had a tendency to separate every time she rolled over, and the hard bolster on which her head rested creaked under even the slightest movement. It was a miserable end to a difficult day, and Margery felt more wretched than ever. She thought back to that glossy picture she had seen in her colleague's magazine, which now seemed very far from the reality of life in the WAAF. She had volunteered out of fear, without really thinking about what she was letting herself in for. Now she began to wonder: What on earth had she done?

That night, Margery wasn't the only one whose mind was falling prey to such dark thoughts. After the constant bustle of a busy day, now, in the dark and quiet, the girls were suddenly hit by the reality of the decision they had made. She could hear a little sniffle coming from a few beds away, and before long it had turned into stifled sobbing.

Margery tiptoed out of bed and hurried over to her distressed neighbour, who she found weeping into her blanket. The two girls clung to each other in the dark, but before long the noise of crying had set off a third new recruit, and she too came over to sit with them, weeping helplessly. After a while everyone else began sitting up in bed too, and the tears flowed freely all around the hut as the girls shared their fears and feelings of homesickness.

'Well, at least we're all going to suffer together!' said one of them, doing her best to laugh. Suddenly, there were smiles in the hut as well as tears, and the girls began to feel calmer, buoyed by their new-found camaraderie. Eventually, even the hard bolsters and irritating biscuits could no longer stop them from slipping into a much-needed sleep.

But for poor Margery a good night's rest was not on the cards. A few hours later, she awoke to the taste of blood. Her gum was throbbing where the tooth had been needlessly yanked out the previous day, and when she put her hand up to her mouth it came back sticky and red.

Alarmed, Margery ran over to knock for the sergeant who was sleeping in a private room at the end of the hut, and spluttered an explanation of what had happened. The woman rushed with her across the camp to the sick bay, but on their way they were stopped by a man on guard duty. 'Halt! Who goes there?' he demanded, flashing a torch in their direction. As soon as he saw Margery, his jaw dropped in horror, and he stiffened as if he was about to raise the alarm.

'It's all right, there hasn't been an accident,' the sergeant informed him. 'She just has a problem with her tooth.'

The guard nodded, relieved, and the two women hurried on.

In the sick-bay, a night-time attendant was on duty. In her time, she must have dealt with all manner of gruesome medical problems, but in the middle of the night, half asleep, she was unprepared for the grisly sight which staggered in. For the last few hours, Margery had been tossing and turning in her uncomfortable bed, and the blood which had seeped out of her mouth was now smeared all over her face. Her hair was thick with the stuff too, and a fresh, dark trickle was oozing down her chin. The poor medic took one look at her and passed out.

Luckily the sergeant had quick reflexes, even in the early hours of the morning. She caught the girl before she hit the floor, narrowly preventing her from becoming the second casualty of Margery's rushed dental work.

'I'm so sorry,' the embarrassed attendant stammered, when she came round a few seconds later.

'Don't worry,' the sergeant told her. 'It's her fault for looking so gory.'

Once the sick-bay attendant had recovered a little and drunk a glass of water, she began plugging up the bleeding hole in Margery's mouth. But after such a mortifying start to her career in the WAAF, Margery only wished there were a hole big enough to swallow her up entirely.

Throughout their training at Innsworth, the new recruits were kept so busy that there was barely time for homesickness, and Margery found that the time flew by faster than she had expected. From the moment each day began, with reveille at 6.30 a.m., to the time they collapsed onto their little iron beds at 10.30 p.m., the girls were constantly chivvied around by sergeants and corporals. Everywhere they went they were marched in groups known as 'flights', whether that was to meals, physical training, gas and fire drills, sports practice, injections, lectures on the history of the RAF, classes in first aid and hygiene, or drill practice. But for those who found the routine gruelling there was no prospect of running home to mother – new regulations had recently been passed making the WAAF and the ATS officially part of the armed forces, meaning that absentee recruits could now be charged with desertion.

Before the girls knew it, their three weeks of training were up, and Margery and her hut-mates were separated as they went off to master their various trades. A number of them groaned as they learned that they were destined to be cooks and orderlies, enduring some of the longest working hours in the WAAF. Others heard they would be joining a whole host of different trades, working as admin clerks, teleprinter operators, nursing orderlies, mechanical transport drivers, parachute packers, balloon repairers, dental hygienists, wireless telegraphy slip readers, film projectionists and armament assistants.

As the war progressed, technical trades were beginning to open up to women too, as shortages in manpower compelled the RAF to experiment with a larger female workforce – among the new roles on offer were those of instrument repairers, spark-plug testers and charging-board operators, and in time women would be repairing planes and servicing radar equipment too. Although WAAFs were never actually allowed to serve as aircrew, a small number were lucky enough to receive a transfer to the Air Transport Auxiliary, where more than 100 'Attagirls' got the chance to pilot repaired Spitfires and Hurricanes from factories and maintenance units to airfields around Britain.

Thanks to her experience in bookkeeping, Margery was assigned to Pay Accounts. There was scarcely time to say good-bye to the girls from her hut before she and around 60 other young women were marched off and put on trains headed for Wales, where they were to begin their intensive training at an accountancy school in a little seaside town called Penarth.

Although most of the girls in Penarth were billeted together in hostels, Margery found herself staying all on her own, in the house of a middle-aged widow called Mrs Poole. The woman might have needed the money that the WAAF paid her for housing and feeding its overspill, but the arrangement was clearly less than ideal as far as she was concerned. 'I hope you're not going to be like the last lot,' she remarked when the lorry dropped Margery at her doorstep. 'Out till all hours, then loafing around in the daytime when they were supposed to be at their classes. I had my fill of them, I did.'

'Oh, don't worry,' Margery assured her, 'I wouldn't do anything like that.' Since childhood, she had always been terrified of getting in trouble – her sister Peggy had teased her for being a 'Goody Two-Shoes'.

Mrs Poole proceeded to tell Margery about the numerous rules of the house – how often she was permitted to use the tin bath and with how many inches of water, what time she was expected to be in by at night and when she was required to stay out. Although the landlady would feed Margery breakfast and dinner every day, between those two mealtimes she was barred from the house altogether.

The last rule proved a tough one for Margery, and after her course finished in the afternoon she often found herself at a loose end, roaming the seafront alone, whatever the weather, until dinnertime came around and she was allowed to return home for some of Mrs Poole's potato cakes or rabbit stew.

Margery had arrived in Penarth expecting to train for pay accounts, but she soon found herself assigned to equipment accounts instead, along with about 60 other girls. It didn't take long for her to learn the reason why – apparently the equipment accounts course was incredibly tough, and a large number of recruits who had recently attempted it had flunked out. The WAAF had decided to add an extra week of lessons for their replacements, in an attempt to improve the pitiful pass rate. But if Margery and her colleagues still failed to make the grade, they would be remustered and might end up in the kitchens or cleaning out the latrines after all.

Margery soon discovered for herself why the course was considered so difficult – it required a seemingly impossible feat of memory. There was a different form for every conceivable eventuality involving the issue of items in the Air Force, and the girls were expected to learn the official number of each of them. Form 674 was used to request a new item, but if the item in question was replacing an old and worn out one then a 673 was required instead. A 500 was needed for anything purchased from a private contractor, in which case a 531 would be required to issue the invoice, with the item ultimately paid for on a 600. The list of numbers seemed to be endless, and as well as memorising them all, the girls also had to learn how many copies of each form were required, and where each copy had to be sent. On top of that, every nut, bolt and screw, every piece of clothing, every item of food that went through the Air Force stores, had its own number as well, and these too had to be committed to memory.

Poor Margery had never been particularly good at rote learning, and her head was soon swimming. She worked diligently as ever, but the instructor was less than inspiring, simply reading out the information in a monotonous voice while the girls scribbled away frantically in their notebooks. After a few weeks, a sergeant was sent to check up on the class, and was horrified at their lack of progress. The instructor was promptly removed and a new one put in his place, but the sudden change didn't exactly inspire confidence.

At least Margery's days of living at Mrs Poole's alone were over. One day she returned from her course to find a new arrival who had been billeted on the widow as well. She was a large girl with terrible bucked teeth, which she revealed in their full splendour as she greeted Margery with a big grin. 'Oh, jolly good show,' she said, holding out her hand. 'I'm Oriole. Daddy named me after his ship.'

Margery had never felt like a pretty girl herself, but she couldn't help feeling sorry for poor Oriole. Not only had she been lumbered with the name of a seafaring vessel, but she had a face that would struggle to launch a gravy boat, let alone a thousand ships.

With her clipped vowels and naval connections, Oriole seemed like the kind of girl who should have been in the WNRS rather than the WAAF. But Margery appreciated having someone to pass the time with before she was allowed to return to Mrs Poole's for her evening meal. More than 150 miles away from her home in North Wallington, and with no older sister to look out for her, she had begun to feel terribly lonely.

It was Oriole who first introduced Margery to the delights of the local NAAFI – the Navy, Army and Air Force Institute. The NAAFI canteens and shops were becoming an increasingly familiar sight across Britain, offering forces personnel of the lower ranks a place to get cheap food and a hot drink. At last Margery had a place to go for a nice cup of tea once her classes finished, rather than traipsing along the seafront in the rain.

One day, Margery was sitting in the NAAFI with Oriole after a long and dreary afternoon in the classroom when an Army chap took a seat on the bench opposite them. As he warmed his hands over a steaming mug of coffee, he asked her, 'Got any ciggie coupons, love?'

Margery looked up, startled. She and her friend didn't usually attract the attention of the servicemen.

The man was a good ten years older than her, of medium build, with dark hair. There wasn't much that was remarkable about him, except for a strong Lancashire accent, but he had a friendly face and that was something Margery was sorely missing.

'I think I might have – hold on a minute,' she said, rummaging in her pockets until she found her cigarette ration card. Since she didn't smoke, she was happy to hand it over.

'Don't you want anything in return?' the man asked, surprised.

'Oh no, it's all right,' Margery told him.

'Aw, go on,' he pushed her. 'How about a nice choccy coupon? That'd be a fair swap, wouldn't it?'

Margery smiled shyly. 'Yes, please,' she said, taking the chocolate coupon gratefully.

The man seemed to interpret their little transaction as permission to stop and chat. Before long he had introduced himself as James Preston and was nattering away about the Army catering course he was doing in Penarth. He had an easy, Northern warmth, and Margery suspected that he, too, must be lonely and just keen to find someone to talk to while he was so far away from home.

Usually Margery kept on eye on the clock until 6 p.m. every evening, when she and Oriole were permitted to return home, so it came as a surprise when her friend pointed out that they were in danger of being late for dinner. 'Better get moving, old thing,' Oriole told her cheerfully. 'Mrs Poole's potato cakes wait for no woman!'

But before Oriole could drag her away from the NAAFI, Margery had agreed to meet James for coffee there the following day – and soon the afternoon chats had turned into a regular arrangement. For the first time since she had arrived in Penarth, Margery had begun to feel less cut adrift. All day long, as she studied the relentless lists of items and their numbers, she looked forward to the time she would be spending in the NAAFI with James.

*

With the end of Margery's course looming, the need to study only increased, as she became more and more anxious that she might fail the dreaded test. Night after night, she went over the long list of forms and parts until her eyes were swimming with numbers. But the thought of having to write home and admit to her family that she had fallen at the first hurdle in the WAAF, and imagine them laughing at her ambitions again, was unbearable.

Finally, the dreaded day arrived, and Margery and the 60 other girls who had trained alongside her turned over their exam papers. She summoned all her brain power to the task of recalling as many of the wretched forms and parts as she could, as well as the various processes and procedures she had learned. But by the time she reached the final page of the exam, she had only been able to answer less than half of the questions.

The following day, the girls were ordered to line up in alphabetical order on the seafront. One by one, their surnames were called out, and their results were read off in front of everyone. Margery cringed as a good few of the As, Bs and Cs in the group were told that they had failed to reach even the remarkably low pass mark of 40 per cent. It was an agonising wait until the sergeant finally made it down to the letter P. 'Pott,' she barked, '40 per cent exactly. Pass.'

Margery blinked her eyes in the early morning sunlight. She couldn't believe it – somehow, she had succeeded where so many others had failed. Despite her terrible memory and her crippling nerves, she had scraped through.

The poor girls who hadn't been so lucky soon heard their fates. One of them was furious when she found out she was being sent to train as a cook. 'I wanted to be in accounts!' she cried miserably. But it was no use – once the Air Force had made up its mind, the decision was final.

Meanwhile, the girls who had passed the test were marched off for a series of inoculations. Feeling heady after her unexpected victory, and exhausted from the stress of the past few weeks, Margery fainted before she even saw the needle.

The next day, the girls were issued with railway warrants to take them home, so that they could spend a bit of time with their families before they had to report to their new postings. Margery was sorry to say goodbye to James Preston, but he had taken her service number and promised that he would write. The two months she had spent in the WAAF was the longest she had ever been away from home, and she felt desperate to get back to North Wallington again.

After a long train journey, Margery walked up the lane to the old maltster's house, carrying her grey kitbag over her shoulders. The neighbours came out of their houses to get a look at her in her uniform, and when her parents opened the door she could see a glimmer of pride in their eyes.

Margery felt proud of herself too, she realised with a start. Nobody was laughing at her now.

3

Kathleen

Although thousands of girls up and down the country were joining up for the fight against Germany, not many of them could claim to have actually seen Hitler in person. But Kathleen Skin, a 19-year-old nanny from Cambridgeshire, was something of a rarity. In August 1939, she was staying at a hotel in Cologne when it was visited by some very high-profile guests.

Kathleen was on her way to a church summer camp in Denmark, and was staying in one of the hotel's cheapest rooms, up by the servants' quarters in the attic. One evening as she was returning to her room, a housemaid came up to her and whispered, 'Do you want to see the Führer?'

'What, here?' Kathleen replied, astonished.

'Yes,' the girl said, excitedly. 'He comes tonight for dinner. You can look from up here, but do not let anyone see you.'

'All right,' Kathleen said, taking up a good viewing position at the top of the stairs. She was eager to catch a glimpse of the man whose name was on the lips of everyone in Europe.

Peering down the stairwell, Kathleen watched as a little man in uniform strode into the hotel, accompanied by a large entourage. A quick glimpse of his famous toothbrush moustache was enough to convince her that it really was Hitler. It was strange to think that such a small, unimpressive-looking person could be holding the whole world to ransom.

After a couple of moments, the official party was whisked into the dining room. Kathleen crept back to her bedroom, pleased that she would be able to go home and tell her family that she'd actually seen the German chancellor.

Since childhood, Kathleen had always been gripped by a lust for travel. She had learned to read at an early age, and had devoured *Robinson Crusoe* and *Swiss Family Robinson*, dreaming of one day visiting such exotic lands herself. She loved nothing more than listening to her father tell stories about his adventures in India when he was a young man in the Army, or her mother's tales of growing up in South Africa, where her Danish grandparents had moved during the gold rush.

Kathleen's parents had met when William Skin was on his way back to Britain to be demobbed. While he was passing through Cape Town, a naval revolt had broken out, and he and his fellow soldiers had found themselves ordered to disembark and take over, until replacement sailors were sent out by the Navy. While he was there he had joined the local glee club and been enchanted by the red hair and green eyes of the lovely Amelia. He had promised to return and marry her as soon as he left the Army, but their romantic plans were scuppered by the outbreak of the First World War. Mr Skin was one of the first to be sent over to France, where his trench was so badly shelled that the stretcher-bearers left him for dead. It was only when a burial party came around to collect the dead bodies that they realised he was still alive and rushed him to hospital.

In time, Mr Skin had recovered sufficiently to be able to walk again, but the muscles and tendons in one leg were so badly damaged that he was left with a strange lolloping gait. He had lost the sight in one eye and his hearing had been affected too. He was convinced his beloved would no longer want him in his current state, but Amelia insisted he return to Cape Town and marry her, despite her parents' protestations that she was shackling herself to an invalid.

Mr Skin brought his new wife back with him to England and their family soon began to grow, but with just his pension from the Army to live on, feeding their five children grew increasingly hard. Throughout Kathleen's childhood, the family moved from village to village around Cambridgeshire, always going where the housing was cheapest. Wherever they went, they were seen as eccentrics. Mrs Skin scandalised the local women by allowing her daughters to wear trousers, while her husband was the only man they knew who was happy to push a pram for his wife.

Kathleen had inherited her mother's striking red hair and green eyes, as well as her gift for performance. She and her sisters would compose poetry and plays that they put on for the village children, and her older sister Lila kept her friends in the playground enthralled with tales of how she was really a princess, forced to live in poverty until she could one day return to reclaim her palace.

The Skins' house was always a favourite with the local kids, thanks to the unusual and imaginative games the family played. But one day when the other children had all left, Mr Skin turned to Kathleen and asked, 'Why don't you go home as well?'

'I am home, Dad,' Kathleen replied, wondering if her father was playing some kind of joke.

'No, you're not,' her father insisted. 'You're not one of mine.'

Kathleen did her best to shrug off the strange remark, but it wasn't long before her father was exhibiting other odd behaviours. Mr Skin had imparted a love of nature to his children, dragging them out of bed in their pyjamas to witness flocks of migrating birds coming over from Africa, or to count falling stars. But now he began talking to the birds as if they could understand him, and disappearing for hours on end, no one knew where. When he was found one day wandering the roads with no idea who he was, the whole family was forced to acknowledge that something was seriously wrong, and Mr Skin allowed himself to be taken to Fulbourn mental hospital.

X-rays eventually revealed that the shell that had almost killed Mr Skin in the war had left bits of shrapnel scattered throughout his brain. The peculiar effects came and went – for months at a time he would be perfectly fine and was able to return home to his family, but then the madness would begin again, and he would have to go back to the asylum.

Kathleen was a bright girl, but her educational prospects had been limited. Her older sisters Maevis and Lila had gone to grammar school, but by the time her turn came around there simply wasn't the money to send her – even though she had won a part-scholarship from the council. Instead, she attended the local technical school, where even her teachers admitted that her academic abilities were wasted. Kathleen found many of the classes there dull, but she did enjoy the weekly childcare lessons. She loved bathing the tiny babies and learning about their development, so when she left school she decided to become a nanny.

Kathleen had been working for a doctor's family in West London when the opportunity came up to visit Denmark with the church summer camp. Her employers had willingly given her the time off, and she spent an enjoyable few days swimming in the sea and learning to sail a dinghy.

On her way back through Germany, she stayed with a family in Kiel who her father had befriended after the war, in the belief that if old enemies could bury the hatchet it might help prevent another major conflict. They had three strapping blond blue-eyed boys, the oldest of whom, Konrad, was about her age.

One day, the boys invited Kathleen to come with them on an organised march through the local countryside. 'It will be great fun,' Konrad told her enthusiastically. Never one to turn down a chance for adventure, Kathleen agreed, joining the three lads as they set off in matching brown shirts with swastika armbands.

They met up with a group of younger boys and girls who Konrad explained were Deutsches Jungvolk – the junior section of the Hitler Youth. As the march progressed, they were joined by more and more young people, until Kathleen found herself among hundreds of German youngsters all dressed in Nazi uniforms.

The march culminated in a huge rally where everyone performed the Hitler salute together. For a British girl, far from home, it was a strange and unsettling spectacle to witness.

When the boys brought Kathleen back to their house that evening, their father was waiting for her anxiously. 'You must pack your bags now,' he told her. 'It is time for you to leave.'

'But I've still got a few days' holiday left,' she protested.

'No, you must go now,' the man insisted. 'You cannot be in Germany.'

He found a friend with a car and took the bewildered girl to the Dutch border, where he gave her instructions to catch a ferry back to England.

Two days later, German forces invaded Poland. Kathleen had scarcely got back to British soil before her country found itself at war with Germany.

The family Kathleen was working for had fled London for Wales, anxious to get their baby daughter out of harm's way. She joined them again in the small seaside town of Tenby, where they were staying with the doctor's elderly mother. In addition to her other duties, Kathleen now found she had to wait on the demanding old lady as well.

Kathleen wished that her job could take her to somewhere more exotic than Wales, but she had always loved the ocean, and enjoyed the sea view from her new room. She soon made friends in Tenby among the nannies of other well-to-do families who had evacuated themselves from London. She looked forward to the afternoons, when they would go for long walks together, pushing their prams along the sea front.

The girls often went up to Saundersfoot, a pretty village with a harbour a little way up the coast. One day they arrived to find that it was crawling with soldiers. 'What on earth's going on?' one of the other nannies wondered.

'Why don't we find out?' said Kathleen, going straight up to the nearest man in uniform. 'What are you lot doing here?' she asked boldly.

'We're here to practise our shooting,' the man told her proudly. 'We're training with the Royal Artillery.'

As he finished speaking, Kathleen heard the sound of guns in the distance. A round was being fired out to sea.

'Ooh, listen to that!' remarked Kathleen's friend excitedly. But as they pushed their prams along the seafront that afternoon, the girls found the sight of the handsome soldiers far more distracting than the noise of the guns. There were plenty of young officers about, and as they passed the young ladies they smiled and touched their hats, aware of the effect their uniforms were having.

When Christmas came, Kathleen used her time off to go home and keep her mother company. Poor Mr Skin would be spending the festive season in the asylum, and by now all but one of the children – Kathleen's youngest brother Lance – had joined the forces. Her eldest sister Maevis was in the ATS, her brother Cecil had joined the RAF and her sister Lila was in the WRNS, working on a naval base at Scapa Flow. Mrs Skin, meanwhile, had taken a job as a nurse at Addenbrooke's Hospital in Cambridge, which allowed her to pay the rent on a little house on Pembroke Street, not far from Lance's school.

'Hello, Mum,' Kathleen said as she arrived home for the holiday, giving her mother a big hug. 'What do you want to do while I'm here?'

'I'd love to go and hear the carols at King's,' Mrs Skin told her. She had always loved classical music but the family finances rarely stretched to the kind of concerts she had enjoyed while growing up in Cape Town.

On Christmas Eve, Kathleen and her mother joined the queue outside King's College Chapel, hoping to get a place for the three o'clock service. They were among the last to be admitted, but managed to find a pew near the back.

As the organist began playing the introduction to 'It Came Upon a Midnight Clear', three soldiers squeezed up next to them. They only had one hymn sheet between them, and the man next to Kathleen was humming along, obviously unable to see the words. She tapped his arm and offered to share her hymn sheet, and he began singing more confidently. He had a beautiful voice which rang out above those of everyone around him.

Throughout the service she was aware of the man looking at her now and then, and when it came to an end, he turned to speak to her. 'I didn't know you lived in Cambridge,' he said. 'I've seen you down in Saundersfoot, haven't I?'

The man was tall and blond, a good six or seven years older than Kathleen. Now that she looked at him properly, she recognised him as one of the handsome young officers whose presence had brightened up her daily walks with the other nannies. 'Yes,' she said. 'I work in Tenby as a nanny. My name's Kathleen.'

'Lieutenant Arnold Karlen, at your service,' the man said, offering her his hand.

'Kathleen, who is this young man?' asked Mrs Skin, craning round to see what was going on. Kathleen introduced Arnold to her mother, and saw her look approvingly at his officer's uniform. 'Well, Merry Christmas lads,' she said to the three soldiers. 'Won't you let us give you a cup of tea? We're only a minute away from here.'

Kathleen was a little surprised at her mother inviting three strangers into their house, but with her only adult son away with the Air Force, Mrs Skin was keen to extend her hospitality to some other young men away from home at Christmas.

Soon the three soldiers had piled into the little house on Pembroke Street, and Mrs Skin was boiling the kettle. Kathleen went into the kitchen to help and saw that she was spreading a very generous amount of butter onto the young men's slices of bread.

'Mum, are you sure you can afford to give them that much of your week's ration?' she asked anxiously.

'Oh, don't worry,' her mother replied, hastily piling up the bread and adding some slices of Christmas cake to the tray as well.

The soldiers took the food gratefully, complimenting Mrs Skin on the cake. 'So where are you boys staying?' she asked them.

'We've pitched our tents on a playing field at The Leys School,' replied Arnold. Kathleen sensed that he was the leader of the little group. His friends, John and 'Ding-Dong' – Kathleen later learned that his surname was Bell – always seemed to wait for him to speak first, treating him with an air of respect.

'A tent's no place to be spending Christmas!' Mrs Skin exclaimed. 'Will you at least get a proper Christmas dinner?'

'Oh, there'll be a good dinner – especially for the men,' Arnold replied with a laugh. 'On Christmas Day us officers have to serve them, and I'm sure they'll make the most of it!'

'It must be so difficult being in charge of all those people,' Kathleen remarked thoughtfully.

'It certainly can be!' Arnold replied. Before long, he had Mrs Skin, Kathleen and her awed little brother Lance laughing at his tales of life as a newly commissioned officer, and the trials and tribulations of trying to keep the rank and file in order. He was a natural storyteller, and as he spoke he seemed to hold the room in the palm of his hand. Kathleen, who was quite a performer herself, felt she had never met anyone quite so charming. She was utterly entranced, and she could see that her mother was too.

Before they knew it, an hour had passed and the men were due back at their campsite. 'Well, thank you, Mrs Skin – this has been delightful,' Arnold said, taking her hand. Then he turned and flashed a look at Kathleen, adding, 'I hope we see each other again.' Her heart leapt at his words.

'Our door's always open!' Mrs Skin called after the three soldiers. When they had gone, she turned to Kathleen and exclaimed, 'Well, what a lovely young man! I think he took quite a shine to you.'

Kathleen smiled. For the rest of the evening she could think of nothing but the handsome blond officer, and the following day, as she helped her mother prepare the Christmas lunch, her mind kept wandering back to all the little things he had said, how clever and funny he had been, and how unlike other men she had met. She had been on the odd date with boys her own age, but in comparison to Arnold they seemed like awkward, clumsy kids. He was a man of the world, the kind of man who could show you adventure and excitement, and she longed to see him again.

As it turned out, Kathleen's wish was granted sooner than she could have hoped. On the afternoon of Christmas Day she was sitting by the fire with her mother and her brother Lance, when suddenly the front door opened a few centimetres and three soldiers' caps came flying into the room, landing on the floor by their feet. Kathleen and her mother looked at each other in surprise.

'It means, "May we come in?"' a familiar voice called from behind the door.

'Oh yes, of course!' Mrs Skin cried, jumping up from her chair to welcome the three young soldiers back into the house.

'We come bearing gifts!' said Arnold, offering up an enormous parcel of food which he explained was left over from their Christmas dinner.

'Oh, you shouldn't have!' said Mrs Skin, but after the meagre meal she had managed to scrape together that day the gift was more than welcome.

Soon everyone was tucking into the unexpected treats, while Arnold again regaled them with jokes and stories. His friend John had been in an orchestra before the war and had brought along his oboe and a tin whistle, and in between Arnold's amusing tales he kept the little group entertained with music. The Skin family's rather quiet Christmas had suddenly turned into quite the party. But for Kathleen, it was the moments when Arnold threw her a lingering look that felt most special.

Before the soldiers left, they mentioned a football match that was being held at the boys' school the following afternoon, and Arnold asked if Kathleen would like to attend.

'Oh, I'm sure she'd love to, wouldn't you?' Mrs Skin piped up, before her daughter even had a chance to reply.

Boxing Day was cold and frosty, and by the time Kathleen and the lads arrived at the football pitch she was already shivering. As they stood watching the game, Arnold silently took her hand and put it inside the pocket of his greatcoat. It was a small gesture, but it told her that she belonged to him now, and to Kathleen nothing had ever seemed so romantic.

When Kathleen returned to Tenby she was delighted to find that Arnold's battery had been sent back to Saundersfoot for further training, and they began meeting on his nights off from the firing camp. They took walks together along the sea front or sat kissing on one of the little benches looking out to sea. They told each other all about their families and their childhoods, and Kathleen learned that Arnold's father had come over from Switzerland to take a job as a top chef at a five-star restaurant in London. He had fallen in love with an English rose and had three boys by her, all of whom were now in the forces.

Arnold was just as charming and romantic as he had been in Cambridge, and when Kathleen was alone with him he made her feel like the centre of the universe. 'You know, I think we're meant for each other,' he told her one evening, gazing at her with his piercing blue eyes.

Kathleen felt the same. She barely knew Arnold, yet she had no doubt in her mind that this was true love. Her every waking moment was filled with thoughts of him.

But Arnold's battery was only in Saundersfoot for a short time, and soon they were posted to Scotland. 'I'll write to you all the time, my darling,' he promised Kathleen. 'Don't forget me.'

Soon letters began arriving that were even more romantic than Arnold had been in person. He wrote that his heart yearned for Kathleen, that he longed to see her beautiful face again and stroke her lovely red hair. Kathleen treasured every missive, as if they were the most precious objects in the world.

Since she had first come to Tenby, Kathleen had felt as though the war was far away, but now she began to see signs of the horrors happening in the rest of the world. Strange things began washing up on the beach next to the house – sailors' hats, foreign money and parts from naval and merchant vessels that had been sunk by German U-boats. One day she discovered a whole crate of oranges, which she and the other nannies shared among their children. Another time half a dozen boxes of toothbrushes appeared, and she took them down to the port authority in the town. She knew items of interest had to be reported, particularly if they had numbers on them that could be traced back to specific ships.

But one afternoon, a haul washed up that no one wanted to go near. Kathleen and the baby had just had lunch when she looked out of the window to see a strange tangled mess sprawled along the beach. She went outside and began to walk down the stone steps to get a closer look, but as she got nearer she realised with a start that there were around 20 human bodies strewn across the sand, all in a state of partial decomposition.

Struggling to keep down her lunch, Kathleen ran back upstairs, put the baby in her pram and rushed to the port authority to report the gruesome discovery. That afternoon the corpses were wrapped up and discreetly taken away, but Kathleen was left sickened by what she had seen.

A few weeks later, Kathleen witnessed another sight that she was unable to forget. Thanks to its large docks and nearby oil refinery, Swansea was a prime target for the Luftwaffe, and on 19 February 1941 it was hit by a ferocious bombing campaign. Over three days, 800 high explosives and more than 35,000 incendiaries fell on the city, causing raging fires, destroying its ancient centre and killing and injuring hundreds of people.

The blaze could be seen for miles around, and as Kathleen stood watching it from Tenby she felt her heart fill with fury. She knew then and there that her days as a nanny were over. She had to get out and join the fight.

She had seen a newspaper advertisement calling on women to join up with one of the three armed forces. With her love of the sea, Kathleen was particularly attracted to the idea of the WRNS, and she hoped that joining the Navy might offer the chance to visit some of the exotic places she had read about as a child. It didn't hurt that, of all the women's forces, the WRNS had by far the most stylish uniform.

Kathleen wrote to the address given in the paper, and soon received some forms to fill in. A week later she was invited to attend an interview at her local recruiting office. There she was grilled by a man and woman dressed in the smart blue uniforms of naval officers. They asked her about her health, qualifications and any relevant experience she might have – as well as some rather surprising queries about boyfriends and personal hygiene.

Kathleen answered the string of questions as best she could, doing her best to impress upon her interviewers how desperate she was to do her bit for her country. There was no getting around the fact that the skills she had picked up nannying weren't exactly transferable to anything she might be expected to do as a Wren, but her obvious enthusiasm must have won them over. 'All right, we'll try you out,' the woman announced at last. Kathleen couldn't have been more thrilled.

'You'll have to pass a medical exam,' the Wren officer continued, 'but I'm sure you'll have no trouble there. If you're used to running around after young children you must be reasonably fit.'

The medical was to take place at a local doctor's surgery in Tenby, and Kathleen asked her employer if she could have a few hours' off to attend. She knew that competition for the WRNS was tough, and the medical standards for entry were high – generally only those passed as Grade I were accepted.

Kathleen was in good shape and she performed well in the physical tests, bending down, spinning around and walking along a chalk line to prove that she did not easily get giddy, and assuring the doctor that she wasn't prone to seasickness. By the end of the examination, she felt confident that she had passed, and eagerly awaited her results.

At last the doctor came out to see her. 'Grade I,' he told her approvingly, looking up from a clipboard he was holding.

Kathleen jumped up from her seat, smiling, but the man put his hand out to stop her. 'I'm afraid I can't pass you, though,' he said.

'Why not?' she demanded.

'You're too thin,' the doctor replied. 'The minimum for the WRNS is six stone, and you're a few pounds under. I'm sorry.'

He turned and walked away with his clipboard under his arm, leaving Kathleen utterly gobsmacked. She had passed all the fitness tests, she had proved her worth. Yet for the sake of a few pounds her dream of serving in the Navy had been thwarted.

Dejectedly, Kathleen returned home and began preparing the baby's dinner, staring longingly out of the window at the sea.

4

Jessie

When Jessie wrote to tell Jim that she'd volunteered for Anti-Aircraft Command, he was concerned. 'Why on earth did you do that?' he replied anxiously. The idea of his diminutive fiancée working on an enormous ack-ack gun, trying to shoot German planes out of the sky, sounded both absurd and distinctly dangerous.

Jessie wrote again, explaining that she wanted to do something tangible for the war effort – something that she could see was really making a difference. She hadn't signed up for the Army just to be stuck behind a desk.

As it turned out, however, before Jessie was going to be allowed anywhere near a gun she first had to spend a whole month studying the theory behind her new trade. She and her friends Olive and Mary were soon on their way to Arborfield Camp, near Reading, for an intensive ack-ack training course.

Arborfield was a permanent Army camp, much bigger than the barracks at Leicester where the girls had done their basic training. When they arrived they were marched straight to the stores and issued with battle dress for their new roles in the field.

Jessie had never owned a pair of trousers before, and putting them on for the first time felt strange. But even more peculiar were the long johns the girls were given to wear during long cold nights on the gun-sites. Then there were thick woollen men's socks that were far too big for Jessie's size-three feet, and leather boots with gaiters that had to be polished every night. It was beginning to seem as if the Army really was turning the girls into men.

The girls were told they would be forming a new ack-ack battery known as 518, joining a regiment that already included three other mixed-sex batteries: 483, 484 and 485. They were to train alongside male gunners who were also fresh recruits – the Army made sure not to mix girls with seasoned soldiers, who they knew might be more prejudiced against the sexes working together.

But even so, some of the men at Arborfield had low expectations of the women. 'You wait – there won't be a girl in sight when the guns go off,' one of them predicted, as they all sat down to dinner in the mess hall.

'We'll see,' Jessie replied confidently. She had already come to realise that much of the male bravado around the camp was just that. Soon after arriving at Arborfield, the new recruits had been inoculated against tetanus and typhoid, lining up in alphabetical order with their hands on their hips while a medic worked his way along the line. Since Jessie's surname was Ward she'd had plenty of time to watch as half a dozen men fainted at the sight of the needle, while the female recruits had barely batted an eyelid.

As Jessie got to know her fellow ack-ack girls she discovered that many of them had good reasons for wanting to shoot down German planes. That night, as they made up their beds in their Nissen hut, they shared the reasons they had volunteered for the guns. A small, sparky corporal called Elsie Windsor explained that she had been a parlourmaid in Coventry during the Baedeker raids. 'I saw the planes going right over our house,' she said, 'and there was no sound of gunfire. I just couldn't understand it. Why were we sitting there and taking it without putting up a fight?'

A Liverpudlian private called Lily, meanwhile, had been inspired to enlist after she was bombed out for the third time and her fiancé was taken prisoner by the Germans. But the saddest story of the night came from a girl called Gladys, who told the others about living through the terrible Hull Blitz. She and her family had been sitting round the fire one evening when their house had suffered a direct hit – the next thing Gladys knew, she was in the middle of the road, with her mother's corpse draped across her legs and her baby nephew dead in her lap. 'That's why I'm doing this,' she told the other girls bitterly. 'For revenge.'

As the girls talked, Jessie noticed a pretty blonde private in the bunk next to her who was pulling at the thread in some embroidery. 'That's nice,' Jessie told her. 'I've been working on one too.' She pulled out the tablecloth she'd started, and they compared notes.

After a bit of chat, the girl introduced herself as Elsie Acres. 'So why did you join up?' Jessie asked her. 'Did you lose somebody too?'

'My fiancé and my brother, both at Dunkirk,' Elsie said sadly.

'Oh, I'm sorry,' Jessie replied, feeling a little guilty. There she was with a fiancé lucky enough to have been rescued twice on the way back from France, while this poor girl had lost two people at once.

'Well, there are plenty worse off than me,' Elsie said thoughtfully, as she went back to her embroidery.

*

The next day the ack-ack course began in earnest, and the girls began wrapping their heads around the fundamentals of optics, magnetism, wind thrust and geometry. Although compared to boys their age they had generally been taught little mathematics at school, the instructors, who were used to classes of men, made no concessions. Jessie had always been top of her class, but even she found it a struggle to keep up.

Once they had got to grips with the theory, the girls learned about the different roles they would be performing on the gun-site, as well as the equipment they would have to use. On the lawn outside the classroom hut, Jessie had noticed a large metal device mounted on a rotating base. The height-and-range finder, as it was known, was an 18-foot-long horizontal cylinder, from which two eyepieces protruded like microscopes. The girls were told that the strange contraption was used to determine how far off an enemy plane was.

Then there was the Sperry predictor, a large black box covered in dials, knobs and levers, which, by rotating to follow the target, was capable of calculating the correct length of fuse so that a shell would explode as close to a plane as possible. Finally, less high-tech but no less important, were the Bar and Stroud binoculars used by the sharp-eyed girls selected to work as spotters. These required little instruction to use, but they had to learn about the optics all the same.

The only jobs on the gun-site that girls weren't allowed to perform were actually loading and firing the guns, thanks to a Royal Proclamation which expressly forbade women from combat roles – so that was where the men of the battery came in.

Aside from the technical training, the ack-ack girls spent hours every day on aircraft recognition, learning to distinguish between the tiny silhouettes of dozens of different German planes. Each night, Jessie and Elsie Acres swotted up for the next day's lessons together, testing each other over their embroidery.

And while their brains were getting a workout, their bodies were subjected to the rigours of the military as well. There was daily drill practice, and physical training sessions at the crack of dawn each morning.

The men and women at the camp exercised together, which wasn't always easy – at five foot one and just seven stone, there was little chance of Jessie successfully performing the 'wheelbarrow' with a male partner she could barely lift off the ground.

The PT instructor was a prim and pretty corporal by the name of Birchett, who was perhaps a little too fond of her airs and graces. Her favourite expression was 'Over and up, girls!' and she delivered it in shrill, clipped tones which always inspired giggles.

One day, when Corporal Birchett arrived for training, Jessie couldn't help herself. 'Over and up, girls!' she shouted, in a pitch-perfect impersonation. Her ear for music had made her an excellent mimic, and the parade ground was soon ringing with peals of laughter.

But Corporal Birchett was not amused by Jessie's performance. 'Private Ward!' she shouted, her usual unflappable demeanour wavering a little. 'Go and see the orderly sergeant at once.'

As dressings down went, Jessie's was not exactly a harsh one. The orderly sergeant, Molly Norris, was a rather cuddly woman whose quiet, gentle demeanour had earned her the nickname 'Aunt Molly'.

'Oh dear, oh dear,' she said, doing her best to suppress a little smile as Jessie explained what she had done. 'Well, I suppose I'll have to put you on cookhouse duties for the rest of the morning, won't I?'

Jessie soon found herself hunched over a large metal sink, doing the dishes for a camp of 300 people. Without any washing-up liquid this was no mean feat, but for Jessie – who had grown up as her mother's domestic dogsbody – the punishment was pretty easy to bear. In any case, she reasoned, it was worth it just to escape the dreaded early morning PT session.

After a few weeks, Jessie learned that the men and women of 518 mixed battery were being split into four sections – A, B, C and D – which would take turns operating the guns once the unit was fully operational. She and Elsie Acres, the blonde girl who slept in the next bunk, were excited to discover they had both been put in 'C' Section, which meant they would be working together. Even better, the two girls had both been chosen for the height-and-range finder, the strange bulky piece of equipment they had seen outside the classroom on their first day. It was considered one of the most elite jobs on the gun-site. 'There'll be no smoking or drinking for you,' one of the instructors warned them. 'You'll need steady hands and quick reactions.'

But before the girls got down to the serious business of equipment training, which was to take place at a practice firing camp in Weybourne in Norfolk, there was some fun to be had first. The end of the theory course was traditionally celebrated with a concert in the NAAFI, performed by the members of the new battery. Word soon got out that Jessie played the piano, and when the others heard that she could accompany any song on request, without the need for sheet music, she suddenly found herself in demand.

Some of the performers were less tuneful than others, but a girl called Lillian almost brought the whole battery to tears with a beautiful rendition of 'The White Cliffs of Dover'. The men, meanwhile, made them all cry with laughter, dressing up in drag and singing 'Kiss Me Goodnight, Sergeant Major' in screeching falsetto voices. Not to be outdone, one of the girls attempted to black up with shoe polish for her own comedy number, only to regret it later when she discovered it took seven baths to get the sticky stuff off her face.

As Jessie looked around the NAAFI that evening, full to bursting with men and women tapping their feet and singing along to the songs she was playing, her heart swelled with happiness. Growing up under her mother's roof might not have been easy, but in the Army she had found a new family – and one where her talents were appreciated.

For the next stage of ack-ack training, Jessie and the other girls travelled to the seaside town of Sheringham, where they were billeted at the Grand Hotel. But the building conspicuously failed to live up to its name – the rooms had been stripped of all furnishings apart from beds and a small wooden chest for each girl's belongings, and although they had access to bathrooms with beautiful marble-topped sinks, they were rationed to five inches of bath water per week. To check that no one was exceeding the quota, officers would frequently barge in on them unannounced.

The gun-site itself was a few miles away at Weybourne – it was right on the coast, so that the shells could be fired out to sea. When the girls left the hotel at six in the morning and piled sleepily into the back of an Army lorry for their first day's practical training, it was still dark outside. They had been issued with an extra thick one-piece denim uniform to wear on the gun-site, but as the chill winter air crept in through the canvas around the lorry they were still bitterly cold.

But all thoughts of physical comfort evaporated the moment the team arrived on the gun-site. Jessie gazed at the huge guns in the glint of the breaking dawn, feeling a thrill of excitement rush through her. There were four of them, lined up majestically on a raised platform, like great cannons pointing out to sea. Behind them she could make out the height-and-range finder and the predictor – as well as a large, dome-shaped object called a kinetheodolite, which was used to record practice firings so that trainees could review how they had done.

On the order of their commanding officer, Captain Rait, the mixed group of ack-ack personnel took their stations. There were five men to each gun, six girls gathered around the predictor, and two spotters. Jessie and Elsie Acres took up their positions on the height-and-range finder, looking through a pair of eyepieces on one side of the long metal tube. Opposite them stood a young woman called Jean, who was their reader. When they signalled to her that a target was locked in, she would call out the distance displayed on a little dial in front of her.

High up in the sky, Jessie could see the target approaching – a small British plane towing a long red-and-white sleeve. Surely that can't be too hard to hit, she thought, as she watched it glide along in a perfect straight line.

When the aircraft came within range, one of the spotters called out its bearing, and Captain Rait shouted 'Engage!' Jessie and Elsie rotated the height-and-range finder until they could see the plane through their little eyepieces, and began furiously adjusting their instruments until the images were perfectly lined up.

'Read!' Jessie shouted, as soon as she could see the plane clearly.

'Read!' Elsie echoed moments later.

Jean read off the height of the plane, and the predictor girls began combining it with their own data. As they studied the dials of the giant box, it rotated to follow the plane through the sky. Then one of them shouted, 'Fuse one-eight!'

'Set!' called out the men, as the shells were loaded into the guns.

When all four were ready, Captain Rait bellowed, 'Fire!' The whole procedure had taken place in a matter of seconds.

The noise that followed the captain's command was indescribable, louder than anything Jessie could ever have imagined. She felt the wind rush against her face, and her nostrils filled with the smell of cordite. Moments after the sound of the guns firing came a loud clanging noise as the metal shell cases fell onto the concrete.

Looking up at the sky above her, Jessie saw four puffs of black smoke were the shells had exploded. She gazed at the little plane, still dragging the red-and-white sleeve behind it. There was no sign that they had made any impact.

Through her ringing ears, Jessie could hear Captain Rait call, 'Stand down.' Feeling rather shaken, she followed the others into a little hut, where the kinetheodolite images were being processed.

'Predictors – you were at fault this time,' a stern gunnery instructor told the group, pointing out how a tiny error in one of their readings had caused the guns to miss their target. The predictor girls listened sheepishly, feeling they had let everyone down.

But as 'C' Section practised firing over and over again that day, each time it was someone else's turn to be in the instructor's bad books. By the time the sun set and Jessie and her colleagues piled onto the lorry to head back to the Grand Hotel, the girls were hoarse from shouting out their readings, and their hair stank of cordite. But after countless attempts, they still hadn't so much as grazed the red-and-white sleeve.

Captain Rait had some reassuring words for his team, however. 'It's not all about scoring direct hits,' he told them, as they trundled back to Sheringham. 'As long as we come close enough to a Jerry plane to spook the pilot, he won't be able to target his bombs accurately.'

Over the next few weeks, the exhausting routine on the gun-site was repeated day after day, and bit by bit Jessie and her colleagues improved – until finally, one afternoon, they managed to punch a hole right through the red-and-white sleeve. The thrill of success was indescribable, but it turned out to be short-lived – the rest of that day they were unable to repeat the great achievement, and however hard they trained, direct hits proved to be the exception rather than the rule.

As the girls of 518 mixed battery got to know each other better, they began to acquire affectionate nicknames. A girl with brilliant red hair became 'Ginger', while a tall girl was inevitably christened 'Lofty'. Jessie's diminutive height meant she was known around the camp as 'Short-arse', and Elsie Windsor's quick temper saw her labelled 'the Spitfire'. Two sisters called Thelma and Olga Twig, meanwhile, were simply called 'Twig' and 'Twiglet'.

After the exhausting demands of practising on the gun-site, the evenings came as a welcome respite, and the men and women of the battery looked forward to letting their hair down in the NAAFI. Jessie's piano playing had proved such a hit during the concert at Arborfield that now she found herself roped into joining a new band. Lilian Booth, who had so impressed at the concert, was their singer, while a handsome, fair-haired Scottish gunner called Stan played the trumpet.

Stan, as it happened, had recently initiated 518 battery's first romance – and with none other than Elsie Windsor. As a corporal, Elsie had been commanding the ATS guard at the Grand Hotel one night, when a girl cried out suddenly, 'There's a man trying to break in!'

'All right, you grab him and I'll hit him round the head,' Elsie had told her. But as she was preparing for action, in had walked Stan, asking innocently, 'Is there any cocoa going?'

After that inauspicious introduction, Elsie and Stan had begun courting. Since they were in different sections, their time off didn't always coincide, but by pooling their cigarette coupons they were able to bribe Stan's sergeant to ensure that they could spend a bit of time together.

While Jessie was in Sheringham, she was able to arrange a date of her own. Jim was also stationed in Norfolk at the time, and they agreed that he would come and meet her in the lobby of the Grand Hotel. It was several months now since they had last seen each other, and when Jim first caught sight of Jessie in her ATS uniform, the look of shock on his face was unmistakable. Although he had been supportive of his fiancée joining the Army, actually seeing her in khaki threw him a little. 'I'm … not sure the uniform suits you,' he admitted, when Jessie asked what was on his mind.

'Well, tough!' she replied, with a laugh. 'You'll just have to get used to it.' Then she added, gently, 'Don't worry, it's still me underneath.'

Jessie and Jim spent a blissful day together, wandering along the sea front and exploring the little seaside town. After months of making do with just his letters, it felt wonderful to finally hold him again, and to hear the words 'I love you' spoken out loud. That evening Jessie returned to the Grand Hotel feeling like she was walking on air.

After a month at the practice camp, Jessie felt ready to put her skills to the test in a genuine raid. But before the men and women of 518 mixed battery departed for their first proper posting – a gun-site outside Sheffield – they were sent home to spend a weekend with their families.

Jessie and her friend Elsie Acres caught the same train from Leicester station, and as they settled down in one of the carriages they heard a couple of men coming along the corridor. 'I wouldn't go in there,' one of them told the other as they passed the girls' compartment. 'It's full of those bloody ATS tarts.'

For a moment, Jessie felt a little shocked, but when she and Elsie caught each other's eye they both burst out laughing.

Back in Holbeach Bank, Jessie's mother was as cold as ever, but her father couldn't have been more pleased to see her, and he pestered her incessantly with questions about ack-ack. 'Dad! You know I'm not allowed to tell you,' she replied, doing her best to satisfy him with tales of life in the huts or the NAAFI instead.

Although it was nice to see her father, Jessie spent most of the weekend looking forward to getting back to her friends in the battery, and she arrived in Sheffield on Monday morning buzzing with excitement. 'Well, here we are – the ATS tarts!' she declared, when the girls all gathered for breakfast in the canteen. After Elsie Acres had explained the origin of the phrase, everyone soon began using it.

The camp had been built in a beautiful hilly area about four miles away from Sheffield city centre. It was a basic set-up, with just the guns and a few wooden accommodation huts that stood about 20 feet away. Although the battery had arrived there ready for action, to begin with the Germans seemed reluctant to send any targets their way. Several times Jessie and her friends were woken in the night by the alarm that indicated an imminent raid, but after an hour or more of shivering in the cold, the order was always given to stand down without any guns being fired.

The girls had plenty to keep them occupied, however. There were regular kit inspections and lectures on aircraft recognition, as well as an hour's drill practice every day on the parade ground. And then there were the fatigues – a series of odd jobs that the girls were expected to perform around the camp when their section wasn't needed at the gun-site. In the evenings, Jessie would check a board in the guardroom to find out her duties for the next day – which could be anything from peeling potatoes to cleaning out the latrines.

One of the least popular fatigues was guard duty, which meant sitting up at night in the sentry box and shouting, 'Who goes there?' at anyone coming or going in the dark. Jessie soon found that she was lucky to get a straight answer, particularly if there had been a dance that evening, and often her queries were met by such jokey responses as 'Fred and Ginger' or 'Hitler and Mussolini'.

Most of the girls found guard duty tedious, and struggled to stay awake with no one to talk to, but Jessie rather enjoyed the quiet solitude. She whiled away the hours reciting poems she had learned at school in her head, or quietly humming her favourite songs.

*

One night, Jessie was fast asleep in her Nissen hut when the piercing call of the alert siren jolted her back to consciousness. She leapt out of bed and threw her greatcoat over her pyjamas, forcing her bare feet into her boots. Then she dashed out of the hut and ran to the gun park as fast as she could.

By the time she reached the height-and-range finder, Elsie and Jean were already in position, and something about the intense atmosphere at the gun park told her this was no false alarm. She cast her eyes up to the sky, watching the beams of the searchlights criss-crossing above her.

Suddenly she saw it – three little shining dots, flying in formation. As they passed directly through the glare of the beams, they flashed silver for a second, and Jessie could make out the outlines of German aircraft.

'Engage!' Captain Rait bellowed, and the girls on the gun-site flew into action. Jessie and Elsie swivelled the height-and-range finder until they had the lead plane in their sights.

'Read!' Elsie shouted.

'Read!' Jessie yelled.

'Seven-nine-hundred!' Jean shouted, squinting at her little dial. At once, the predictor girls began working their magic, turning knobs and pulling on levers as the giant box rotated on its base. After what felt like an age, one of them called out, 'Fuse two-four!'

Jessie watched anxiously as the shells were loaded into the guns. The moment they were ready, Captain Rait boomed 'Fire!'

In the stillness of the night, the noise of the guns was like a thunderclap, but by now everyone was too used to it to flinch. As the shells burst thousands of feet above her head, Jessie stared at the lead German plane, hoping to spot some sign of damage. If the damned thing would only burst into flames it would be the most wonderful feeling in the world.

There was no dramatic explosion, no flaming fireball dropping from the heavens. But as Jessie peered at the little plane, silhouetted in the piercing beam of the searchlights, she saw it swerve slightly from the straight line it had been cutting through the night sky. That was it – they had forced the pilot to deviate from his course, and everyone knew what that meant. Without a clear 30-second run-up before he dropped his bombs, there was little chance that they would land on target.

The men and women of 518 mixed battery were far too professional to cheer or applaud, but silently everyone shared in the thrill of that moment. A few seconds later, the German planes passed out of the searchlight beams and disappeared back into the inky black. 'Stand down, everyone,' Captain Rait said soberly.

Jessie made her way back to the dormitory hut, her heart still pounding with excitement. 'That was good, wasn't it?' she said to Elsie, as they crept back to their beds in the dark. She was just tucking herself in when a strange thought crossed her mind – was she developing a thirst for blood, she wondered.

But the worry didn't linger for long. After the exhilaration of her first real-life raid, Jessie felt utterly exhausted, and soon she had fallen into a deep and satisfying sleep.

5

Margery

Having passed the dreaded test in equipment accounts, Margery waited anxiously for her posting to come through, wondering where on earth she would end up. By now, the Air Force had women working at stations the length and breadth of the land, from Cornwall to the Outer Hebrides. Some girls were serving as far afield as New York and Washington DC, while a small team of radio operators were about to set off for a post in Cairo.

But as it turned out, Margery's new workplace was distinctly unexotic. She was ordered to report to RAF Titchfield, just four miles down the road from her home in North Wallington – so near, in fact, that she was expected to make her own way there, without any assistance from the Air Force.

It was a scorching summer's day, and by the time Margery arrived at the camp, struggling under the weight of her heavy kitbag and clutching her respirator and helmet, her blue uniform was soaked with sweat and she was looking distinctly dishevelled. A guard on the gate glared at her before asking dismissively, 'What are you, one of the new cooks?'

'No,' replied Margery, blushing. 'I'm here for Equipment Accounts.'

When he heard the last word, the guard's attitude seemed to change a little. 'Name and number?' he asked, slightly more civilly.

'Pott, 294,' replied Margery.

The man stared at her, a smile playing at the corners of his mouth. 'Say that again, would you?' he asked.

'Pott, 294,' she repeated.

The man turned to a fellow by his side and bellowed, 'Sergeant, this woman is being rude to me!' Then the two of them burst out laughing.

All her life, Margery had put up with jokes about her name, but the endless repetition hadn't served to make it any easier. She wasn't one to answer back, and in any case she wouldn't dare to confront a guard, so she stood patiently, wiping the sweat from her brow, until finally the laughter died down.

The guard, whose face was by now as red as Margery's, ushered her through the gate, and soon a WAAF sergeant came to collect her. 'You can drop your kitbag in the dormitory hut,' she told her, 'and then I'll show you to the office.'

Margery followed the other woman to a large wooden hut, similar to the one she had slept in during her initial training at Innsworth. There were 30 metal beds arranged along the two sides, with double lockers in between them. She left her things on an empty bed and then followed the WAAF sergeant back outside.

On her way to Equipment Accounts, Margery got her first proper look at the camp that was to be her home for the foreseeable future. It was a large site, where several hundred men and women worked side by side in seemingly endless rows of wooden huts. There were residential huts for the airmen and WAAFs who lived on the base, offices for administration and pay accounts, the camp police station and armoury, and a series of large mess buildings, with separate huts for officers, NCOs and other ranks. To Margery it seemed like an entire wooden city.

The Equipment Accounts office looked out over a wide parade ground, on the other side of which was the most striking feature of the camp: four giant aircraft hangars. RAF Titchfield was a maintenance station for Number 12 Balloon Centre, employed when the enormous inflatables, which were sent up from various sites in the area to disrupt low-flying German bombers, required repairs. In the vast hangars at Titchfield the fabric of the balloons would be checked for tears and stitched up by WAAFs handy with a sewing machine, before they were painted with three coats of silver 'dope' to prevent any hydrogen gas from leaking out. The girls charged with this unpleasant task spent their days inhaling the noxious fumes from the paint, and were given a special ration of milk as compensation.

The camp was also a training site for balloon-operating teams, and in a field off to one side Margery could see one of the huge inflatables being filled with gas. Lying on its side on the grass, it looked like a giant beached whale, but as Margery watched, the crumpled surface began to ripple and grow taut, until the magnificent 60-foot balloon slowly started to rise off the ground.

Although girls had been hard at work maintaining the balloons since the Battle of Britain, it was only recently that the WAAF had agreed to try out all-female teams to actually fly them. These 'Young Amazons', as they were known unofficially, were chosen for their physical strength – their training involved weight-lifting, as well as mastering the inflation procedure, splicing the ropes that held the balloons down and operating the winches that kept them anchored. The girls worked in teams of 12, whereas it was seven for all-male groups, but it was a tough job and many women ended up hospitalised with ruptured stomachs.

Compared to the work of the balloon girls, Margery's job in Equipment Accounts was pretty low-risk, and the heaviest lifting she would have to do was heaving ledgers around the office.

But that didn't make her feel any less nervous as the WAAF sergeant led her up to the door.

She entered to find half a dozen young women, along with a handful of men, nattering away at their desks almost as if they were in a mess hall, not an office. For a moment, Margery was a little taken aback. This wasn't the strict Air Force atmosphere she had grown used to during her training.

A male flight sergeant stood up and approached her. He was an ugly-looking fellow in his mid-thirties, tall and thin with dark hair. 'Oh, you must be the girl from the course,' he sneered. 'I suppose you're here to show us all how it's done.'

Margery didn't quite know how to respond to that. She nodded awkwardly and allowed herself to be led over to an empty desk, where she began familiarising herself with the ledgers she would be working on.

The job of Equipment Accounts was to keep track of things ordered from the camp stores – everything from cups and saucers to guns and ammunition. But it wasn't long before Margery realised that her new colleagues had very little understanding of the procedures they were meant to follow. Since none of them had gone through the official training course, they had got used to muddling through with a mixture of common sense and improvisation.

Each item ordered at Titchfield would be registered on a form and signed by the officer responsible, but as Margery flicked through the paperwork, she began to notice a number of strange irregularities. Many of the forms in her ledger had been marked up with unfamiliar acronyms, 'NIV' and 'OI'. Had she missed something in her accounts training, she wondered.

Nervously, Margery went up to the flight sergeant's desk. 'What do the letters NIV mean?' she asked him.

'Not in vocab,' the man replied dismissively.

Margery was puzzled. She knew that every item, even down to the tiniest nut or screw, had a vocab number, which was supposed to be used on all paperwork. The idea of an item not being in vocab went against everything she had learned during her training. 'What about OI?' she asked, anxiously.

'Over-issued,' replied the flight sergeant, without looking up from his own work.

Now Margery was really confused. 'I don't understand,' she told him. 'How can you issue something you haven't got?'

The man fidgeted in his chair, before mumbling, 'Well … you know … it doesn't really matter.'

His reply only made Margery feel more worried. Clearly something had gone badly wrong in Equipment Accounts. If they were audited, she realised, they could all find themselves in hot water. 'Would you like me to go over to the stores and try to sort it out?' Margery suggested helpfully.

But her boss was less than appreciative of the offer. 'Suit yourself' was all he said.

The girls in the stores were not much more interested in Margery's problem than the flight sergeant had been, but after a bit of pleading, she persuaded them to consult their own records. It didn't take long for her to work out where the irregular entries were coming from – if someone took a form down to the equipment store and hadn't bothered to look up the vocab number, they would write 'NIV' in its place. The 'OI' was a way of covering their backs – as without the correct number, stock in the stores would no longer match up with what was written in the ledgers.

Back in the office, Margery didn't say anything, but she was secretly horrified at the state of the department's paperwork. From then on she made it her mission to put everything in order, beavering away at the ledgers and heading down to the stores every time she found an 'NIV', and begging the girls there to look it up for her.

The warrant officer who presided over the stores, however, was none too happy with someone from Accounts coming in and asking inconvenient questions. Around Titchfield, he was known as a bit of a bully, who delighted in tormenting new recruits, especially female ones. One day, when he saw Margery come into his department for the umpteenth time that week, he bellowed across the room, 'Not you again, Pott!'

After her days working at the baker's, under the reign of the terrifying Miss Pratt, Margery was used to putting up with rough treatment from those in authority. But right now her heart swelled against it. After all, she was the one striving to put the books in order, despite the lackadaisical attitude of her colleagues. To bawl her out publicly just for making a bit of an effort seemed so unfair.

'Who does that man think he is?' Margery muttered to a girl standing next to her.

The words had slipped out before she could stop herself, but she realised, to her horror, that the warrant officer had heard them. 'What was that?' he demanded, striding over and fixing her with an angry stare.

Margery gulped – but there was no going back now. 'I said, "Who does that man think he is?"' she replied, before adding, 'Sir.'

She could hardly believe that she had done it. Ordinarily, Margery wouldn't say boo to a goose – she was the last person to stand up to authority.

Suddenly the implications of her uncharacteristic outburst began to dawn on her. She was for it now, she felt certain – her career in the WAAF was about to come to an ignominious end with a court-martial for insubordination.

But to Margery's surprise, instead of yelling at her, the warrant officer burst out laughing, evidently tickled pink at her unexpected forthrightness and honesty. 'I like it when one of the girls shows a bit of gumption,' he told her, once he had caught his breath. 'It doesn't happen to me all that often.'

Margery was stunned at the sudden change in the man's attitude. But she was beginning to feel a little more confident now, so she asked him boldly, 'Why do you talk to people like that?'

The man thought for a moment, and then gave a rueful smile. 'Well,' he admitted, 'I suppose I like seeing them quake.' Then he turned around, still laughing, and went on his way.

After that, Margery never had any trouble from the warrant officer again. When she saw him in the stores he was always courteous, and sometimes even downright friendly. She certainly hadn't gone down there looking to assert herself, but in doing so she had learned a valuable lesson: sometimes, if you stood up for yourself, people respected you more.

While Equipment Accounts was not exactly a beacon of high standards, everywhere else around RAF Titchfield things were run very much by the book. Unlike Penarth, where Margery had been free to wander along the sea front for hours at a time, here she was truly subjected to the rigours of Air Force discipline. There were regular parades, drills and route marches, and every day the camp flag was raised and lowered in military style.

The airwomen's days began at 7 a.m., when a corporal yelled through the door of their hut, letting them know that it was time for physical training. After they had run around the camp a few times in just their shorts and shirt tops, beds had to be stripped and stacked to exacting specifications. Only then were the girls lined up in flights and marched off to breakfast.

Once they'd eaten, the half-dozen young women in Equipment Accounts would form another flight to march over to the office, even though it was just the other side of the parade ground. The rigorous military discipline continued throughout the day – the lax atmosphere within the office itself excepted – until the dormitory lights were switched out by the duty corporal at 10.30 p.m. sharp.

As the months rolled by and the weather turned colder, nights spent in the wooden dorm huts, where one window was always left open, whatever the weather, grew increasingly miserable. And it wasn't much warmer in Equipment Accounts either. When the flight sergeant saw the girls shivering at their desks, his solution was to order them to take their tunics off, roll up their sleeves and run around the camp. The girls certainly returned warmed up – but also dripping with sweat, which they struggled to keep from blotting their ledgers.

The huts were not only cold but dark as well, and the dwindling daylight hours made it increasingly hard for the girls to read the paperwork in front of them. They complained bitterly to each other and encouraged Margery, who as 'the girl from the course' carried a certain dubious authority, to mention the problem to a WAAF officer on their behalf. But to Margery's dismay, when the unimpressed officer turned up at the hut and demanded to know if anyone else felt the same way as she did, suddenly the cat seemed to have got her colleagues' tongues. Margery was carted off in an ambulance to get her eyes tested at the nearest hospital, returning with a very ugly pair of steel spectacles. They were distance glasses, so they made no difference to her work in the dimly lit office, but the sight of her wearing them gave the rest of the girls a good laugh.

One thing that brightened Margery's days at Titchfield was the arrival of the latest letter from James Preston, the Army cook from Lancashire who she had met during her training in Penarth. He had recently been posted to a camp on the Isle of Dogs in London, and for Margery his long, artfully written letters brought every detail of his experiences there to life. Tearing open the latest missive to find page upon page of his beautiful handwriting always brought a smile to her face.

It was James who had helped allay Margery's loneliness during her time in Wales, but at Titchfield she made her first proper friend in the WAAF – a Geordie woman in her mid-thirties called May Strong, who more than lived up to her name. May was the corporal in charge of Margery's dorm hut, and slept in a private room at one end of it. Before the war, she had worked as an office manager at a paint factory in Haltwhistle, a coal-mining town not far from Newcastle. She had a natural self-assurance and authority, combined with a talent for leadership, and all the girls in the hut looked up to her – none of them more so than Margery.

One evening, when one of Margery's hut-mates was suffering with a bad cold, May announced that she knew just what to do. 'A tot of whisky would cure this,' she proclaimed. Then turning to Margery, she said, 'Come on, we can get some at the Joseph Paxton.'

It wasn't exactly an order, but somehow Margery didn't feel she could say no, so she grabbed an empty bottle and accompanied May to the pub in the nearby town of Locks Heath.

'Can I have a whisky, please?' Margery asked the woman behind the bar. She was just fumbling for the money to pay for the drink when May announced loudly, 'And a sherry for me, if you don't mind.'

The woman put the drinks on the bar, and Marjorie poured her shot of whisky into the bottle she'd brought with her. 'Bottoms up!' May declared, knocking her sherry back in one go.

Suddenly, the doors of the pub burst open, and a couple of sailors rushed in, making for the bar in a hurry. As they waited for the landlady to serve them, they struck up a conversation with the two WAAFs. The men had worked themselves up into quite a state, and it didn't take long for the girls to find out why. 'Our barracks has been under attack!' one of them declared dramatically.

Margery stared at the sailor in horror. Had German forces finally landed in England?

But the man's explanation soon reassured her. In fact, they had suffered only the ignominy of an invasion by British Army units, who, as part of a training exercise, had burst into their camp and taken them prisoner in the middle of the night.

The unexpected visitors had clearly made a strong impression on the sailors. 'How would you like to wake up and see their ugly, blacked-up faces?' one of them asked Margery indignantly.

Clearly the galling experience had left the men intent on drowning their sorrows – and as far as they were concerned anyone who wasn't Army was welcome to join them. 'Let's have some drinks all round!' one of them shouted as the landlady came over. Then he turned to Margery and May, and asked, 'What can I get for you two ladies?'

'Ooh, I'll have another sherry if you don't mind,' May told the sailor merrily.

The landlady nodded and began fixing May's drink. 'And another whisky for you?' she asked Margery.

'Oh no, I couldn't,' Margery protested.

'Well, that's what you had last time,' the woman pointed out.

After much encouragement from May and the sailors, Margery finally accepted a shot of whisky for herself. Cautiously, she took a little sip, wincing as it burned her throat on the way down. But despite the discomfort, on such a cold night she found the heat of the liquor quite appealing.

As the evening wore on the men grew merrier and merrier, and it was late by the time Margery and May finally made it back to camp and offered their medicinal tot of whisky to the ailing WAAF. By then an unlikely friendship had already sprung up between them.

After that, Margery spent most of her free time at Titchfield with May, and when she went back to her parents' house at the weekends, which she often did since it was so near, she began inviting her new friend to come with her. For May, who was stationed more than 300 miles away from her own family, the Pott residence soon came to feel like a home away from home.

For her part, May took Margery very much under her wing, requesting special permission for her to take the spare bunk in her room at the end of the hut, which was normally reserved for non-commissioned officers. Margery wasn't sorry to leave the cramped 30-bed dorm for somewhere a little more private, nor for the chance to spend more time chatting to May. They got hold of a little electric stove and made cocoa on it in their enamel mugs. As they sat up late into the cold winter nights, Margery told May all about her friendship with James Preston, and showed her the beautiful letters he had written her.

What Margery really wanted was to see James in person again, but, to her disappointment, whenever he got leave he always seemed to rush back home to Lancashire rather than suggesting they spend it together. It was now many months since they'd first met, but Margery had been forced to make do with nothing more than his letters.

Then one day, James wrote and suggested that Margery come and visit for the weekend. He had made friends with a family in Poplar, in the East End of London, not far from where he was posted on the Isle of Dogs, and they had offered to put her up for the night.

Margery was thrilled at the thought of seeing James again, and the weekend proved as wonderful as she could have hoped. The two of them spent hours just walking and talking, until it felt like they must have trekked around the entire city. But whether they were sharing tea and buns at St Martin in the Fields, or chatting on a bench in one of the beautiful Royal parks, James always seemed to have something witty and interesting to say. There was no one whose company Margery enjoyed more, and as he waved her off at Waterloo Station, she wondered how long it would be before she saw him again.

Back at Titchfield, the exchange of letters continued, but again whenever James was granted leave, he always seemed to rush straight back to Lancashire. Eventually, Margery decided to take matters into her own hands, writing to James and asking if he would like to come and spend an evening with her family in North Wallington. A few days later, she received a reply in his usual perfect handwriting, saying that he would be delighted to come and visit.

They fixed a date for the following weekend. James would get the first train down on Friday afternoon when his shift in the kitchens was over, and Margery would meet him at her parents' house once she had finished in the office. Her sister Peggy was also planning to be home for the weekend, so it was a chance for James to meet the whole family.

On Friday evening, Margery rushed home from Titchfield as fast as she could, but when she got there James was nowhere to be seen. 'Did he miss the train?' she asked her mother anxiously.

'No, he arrived bang on time,' Mrs Pott told her. 'He's just taken Peggy down the pub.' Then, seeing the look of disappointment on Margery's face, she added, 'They said they'd be back in time for dinner.'

Margery waited patiently for James and her sister to return. When they finally did, it was clear that they'd been getting on famously – there was an easy rapport between them, as if they'd known each other for years. 'Don't worry, I was just looking after him for you,' Peggy told Margery with a little laugh, as she led James into the house.

James had clearly made a good impression on Peggy, and as the Potts sat down to dinner he began to work his magic on the rest of the family as well. Once again, Margery was struck by his gift of the gab – as he regaled the family with tales from his Army camp in London, he soon had Mr and Mrs Pott as rapt as both their daughters had been. By the time everyone retired to bed that evening, Margery felt satisfied that James had charmed the whole family.

But the following morning, when Margery was alone with her mother in the kitchen, Mrs Pott said something that shocked her. 'I don't think you should bring James back here again,' she announced gravely.

Margery was stunned. She was sure that James had been the perfect house guest – courteous, charming and friendly. Only the night before, her mother had been hanging on his every word. How could she have changed her mind so quickly?

'I've just got a feeling about him,' Mrs Pott told her daughter, lowering her voice a little. 'I think that he's a married man.'

Margery couldn't believe it. 'What makes you say that?' she asked her mother in astonishment.

'Trust me, love,' Mrs Pott replied. 'I just know.'

That morning, Margery and James went out for another long walk together. He was as witty and blithe as ever, but with her mother's words playing on her mind, she found it hard to relax in his company. She couldn't believe that her mum's intuition was correct, but when she thought about it she realised that she had never asked James about his family back in Lancashire. In all their long conversations together, when he had seemed to discourse on every topic under the sun, the subject of his home life had somehow never come up.

Several times that morning, Margery almost asked James the question that had burned itself into her consciousness, but again and again she couldn't quite bring herself to do so. When the time came for her to see him off at the railway station, however, the anxious look in her eyes was impossible to miss. 'What's wrong, Margery?' he asked her, as he stepped up onto the train.

Margery hesitated, looking down at the platform. 'It's – it's just my mum,' she said, falteringly. 'She told me she thinks that you're married.' She looked up at James, half expecting him to laugh in her face.

But instead he held her gaze. 'Does she?' he asked.

'You could show me your pay book,' Margery suggested. 'That way I can tell her I've seen it and I know that you're not.'

'No,' James replied slowly, 'I'm afraid I can't do that.' Margery stared at him. 'You see, it does say I'm married,' he told her.

As the train's giant wheels slowly started to turn, Margery felt as if the air had been sucked out of her lungs. She couldn't think of anything to say.

The train began to pull out of the station. 'I'll write to you, Margery!' James called.

Margery stood and watched, dumbstruck, as he disappeared from view. She had never felt so stupid in her life. How could her mother have realised in one evening what she had failed to pick up on in all these months? Now she finally understood why James had been so reluctant to spend his leave with her, why he had always rushed back to Lancashire at the first opportunity. For all she knew, there was a whole family up there that he had never told her about.

By the time Margery arrived back at Titchfield, the shock was beginning to subside a little, but as soon as May Strong clapped eyes on her she could tell that something was wrong, and she insisted that Margery tell her the whole sorry story.

Margery talked her friend through everything that had happened, before concluding, 'Well that's it then, I suppose. There'll be no more of his lovely letters to look forward to.'

May put an arm around Margery and hugged her tight. 'Oh, I think there will be,' she replied wisely. 'And the best thing you can do is keep on reading them. Then you'll see how easy it is for men to write pretty letters, when what they say doesn't mean a thing.'

Sure enough, May turned out to be right. James continued writing to Margery, almost as if nothing had happened. She forced herself to read every beautifully written word, although the task no longer brought her any pleasure. But she didn't respond, and after a handful of ever shorter missives, he finally gave up the correspondence altogether.

Although she felt hurt by the way James had treated her, and humiliated at the thought that she had been so keen to introduce him to her family, Margery was convinced that she had learned another valuable lesson. From now on, she told herself, she would take anything a man told her with a heavy pinch of salt. As far as she was concerned, all men were to be considered married until proven otherwise. She had no intention of feeling like such a fool ever again.

6

Kathleen

Being rejected by the WRNS had been a bitter disappointment for Kathleen, but she wasn't going to let it stop her doing her bit for the war effort. If the Navy wouldn't take her now, she reasoned, she would just have to find something else to do until it was ready for her.

She had seen posters in town calling on women to join the Land Army – 'for a healthy, happy job' as they put it. The pictures showed girls standing in golden fields of corn, tilling the soil, gathering hay and tending to cute farm animals. The life of a land girl looked distinctly appealing, and even if the work was hard, the camaraderie would surely make up for that.

Kathleen handed in her notice with the family she was nannying for in Wales, telling them she was going back home to Cambridge. She was sorry to say goodbye to the little girl she had been looking after, but she felt it was for the best. The child was beginning to grow so attached to her that many people seeing them out together assumed she was her mother.

Once she got home, Kathleen lost no time in presenting herself at a recruiting centre, where she was interviewed by a rather superior woman who wanted to know if she had a farming background.

'Well, I used to help my father grow vegetables in the garden,' she replied, hopefully.

'Horticulture for you then,' the woman declared. 'You'll get your call-up soon, so be ready.'

A week later, Kathleen was on the train to Bury St Edmunds, ready to take up her first posting. She arrived at the station to find a rather luxurious-looking car waiting for her, along with a chauffeur who introduced himself as Bradley. 'I've been sent to collect you,' he explained.

Kathleen got in, wondering what kind of farm had its own chauffeur. They headed out into the countryside for a while, before turning up the gravel drive of a grand mansion, whose once carefully manicured gardens had been given over to food production.

A dumpy woman with rosy cheeks and white hair met Kathleen at the door. She looked awkwardly at her, as if she didn't quite know how to address her. 'I'm Mrs Jones, the cook,' she said, shaking Kathleen's hand and half-curtseying at the same time. 'I'll take you up to yer room.'

'Thank you,' Kathleen replied, following the other woman into the house. She admired the magnificent entrance hall and the broad, sweeping staircase carpeted in red velvet. Kathleen had imagined the land girls would all bunk together in a barn, sleeping on bundles of hay, yet it sounded as if she was to have her own bedroom, right inside the grand house itself.

Kathleen's room turned out to be at the very top of the building, and it was small but tastefully decorated. 'You've got a lovely bathroom along here,' Mrs Jones said, showing her into a large room with decorative tiles around the walls and the deepest bathtub she had ever seen. 'Well, I'll leave you to get settled,' she told her.

'Thank you,' replied Kathleen. 'Just one thing – where are all the other land girls?'

'There ain't none,' the cook replied. 'You're the first we've had.'

Kathleen couldn't help feeling disappointed. She had imagined herself making friends in the Land Army, going to dances with the other girls in the evenings and sharing confidences late into the night. Yet here she was, entirely on her own. It didn't help that the servants seemed unsure how to treat her, since her status was somewhat unclear. She certainly wasn't on the same level as the aristocratic family of the house, yet she wasn't really one of the staff either.

That evening Kathleen's dinner was sent up to her on a tray and she ate it alone in her room. But after she had finished, she decided to head downstairs and try to break the ice. In the basement she found the servants' sitting room, where some of the maids were drinking tea. As she entered, they instinctively jumped to attention.

'Oh, please don't get up,' Kathleen insisted. 'I thought maybe I could join you for a while.'

The maids looked at her a little uncertainly, but one of them, a pretty ginger-haired girl a few years younger than Kathleen, gestured her towards a chair. 'Course you can,' she said. 'I'm Minnie. How d'you do.'

Kathleen introduced herself and sat down opposite Minnie. 'Do you play cards?' the girl asked her.

Kathleen nodded.

'How about Beat your Neighbour out of Doors?'

'I've never heard of that one!' Kathleen laughed.

'Don't worry, I'll teach you,' Minnie said, doling out the cards to Kathleen and the other girls. Soon they were all engrossed in the game, their former awkwardness forgotten.

Kathleen liked Minnie, and she soon discovered that the two of them had a lot in common. Minnie's father had been stationed with the Army in India, just like Kathleen's dad, and she had spent her early years living abroad.

As they played, Kathleen couldn't help noticing that one of the other kitchen maids' hands were badly disfigured, the fingers stuck together and the thumbs missing. 'My mum fell off her bike when she were pregnant with me,' the girl said, seeing her staring.

'Oh, I'm sorry,' Kathleen replied. 'How awful.'

The girl shrugged. 'Stopped me bein' called up, though, so that's somethin'.'

Mrs Jones wandered in from the kitchen. 'You lot better let Miss Skin 'ere get to bed,' she told the other girls. 'She's got to be up at 'alf five to help Mr Shaw, you know.'

Kathleen was shocked – that was even earlier than in her old job as a nanny. But there was no time to protest, as Mrs Jones gave her a candle to take up with her.

'Oh, this arrived in the post for you,' the cook added, handing her a parcel. 'I reckon it must be your uniform.'

The next morning Kathleen was awoken by a knock on her door, and one of the maids came in with a cup of tea for her. It was still dark outside as she struggled into her new uniform – a fawn shirt, green V-neck pullover, brown corduroy breeches and long socks up to her knees. It was hardly a glamorous combination, but worst of all were the shoes – brown leather so hard that it felt like she was putting her feet into clods of iron.

Down in the kitchens Kathleen found Mrs Jones, who showed her the way to the gardens. Dawn was just beginning to break, and as Kathleen stepped outside she spotted a tiny old man with a bald head motioning to her to follow him. She guessed that the gnome-like figure must be Mr Shaw, the gardener.

The old man led Kathleen into an orchard of apple trees, where every spare inch of ground had been planted with vegetables. 'Shu' geh,' he called back over his shoulder.

Kathleen looked at him blankly.

'Shu' geh,' he repeated, more emphatically.

'I'm sorry, what does that mean exactly?' Kathleen asked, confused.

The little man walked slowly back over to the gate and pulled it shut behind her. '*Shu' geh*,' he repeated for a third time, clearly exasperated.

Mr Shaw hailed from Yorkshire and made no concessions to Southern ears like Kathleen's. But as he showed her around the gardens, she realised he was a kind soul really. He had a daughter her age in the ATS, he told her, and he and his wife worried about her terribly.

Mr Shaw explained that thanks to the war he now grew everything from potatoes and turnips to broccoli, cabbages, kale, sprouts, carrots and mangold wurzels, all of which were sold at market in town. There were also apple, pear and plum trees, as well as bushes of gooseberries, raspberries and redcurrants. 'Now, you jus' do what ye can,' he told Kathleen, handing her a spade and looking at her skinny frame uncertainly. 'I don't expect too much of ye.'

At Mr Shaw's instruction, Kathleen set to work digging and planting, determined to prove to him that she was more than capable of the job she had been sent to do. But after an hour or so her brow was dripping with sweat and she felt ravenous.

She was relieved when, at eight o'clock, they stopped for a breakfast of porridge. 'When do we finish for the day?' she asked Mr Shaw.

'Why, when t'sun goes down!' the old man said, with a chuckle.

Soon they were back at work again, digging and hoeing away until at last Mrs Jones rang the bell for lunch. Kathleen took her meal on her own, while Mr Shaw headed back to the gardener's cottage to eat with his wife.

By mid-afternoon Kathleen was utterly exhausted, but as Mr Shaw had promised there was no stopping until dusk fell. The vegetables had to be got ready for market on Monday, he told her, and with only a tiny old man and a skinny young girl to get it all done, it was going to be quite a task.

By the time Kathleen went up to her room that evening she was barely able to stand from the physical exertions of the day, and she woke the following morning feeling as if every muscle in her body had been pulled. It hurt just to walk down the stairs, but there was nothing for it except to head out to the gardens and start digging all over again.

The days at the grand estate passed excruciatingly slowly, and for Kathleen, who loved to talk and laugh, it was a lonely time. She was often left on her own for hours while Mr Shaw worked elsewhere in the grounds. Much of the time her only company was an old Suffolk horse called Patsy who, like the gardener, had seen better days.

One evening, Kathleen had just returned to her room to change out of her muddy clothes when there was a knock on her door. 'Come in,' she called, sitting down on the side of her bed.

Minnie came tumbling in excitedly. 'You've been asked to go to dinner,' she announced.

'Where?' Kathleen asked her, confused.

'Here, with the family,' the girl explained, grinning. 'They want you to join them in the drawing room first – for sherry!'

'Oh, right!' Kathleen exclaimed. She hastily put on her only decent-looking dress and followed Minnie downstairs into the grand drawing room.

There, the lady of the house, Mrs Ashbourne, and her youngest daughter were waiting to receive her. The mother was a tall and elegant woman and her daughter was pretty, although Kathleen thought she looked rather tired.

'So, you're our new land girl,' Mrs Ashbourne said, eyeing Kathleen with interest. 'How delightful. And how is old Shaw treating you – not too roughly I hope?'

'Not at all,' Kathleen answered. 'He's been very kind.'

'I'm *so* glad,' the lady continued. 'My daughter Jane here works as a nurse in the local hospital, you know. It's terribly hard work, but the young must do their bit for the war, I suppose.'

Jane looked up and gave Kathleen a feeble smile.

Looking around the room, Kathleen saw that it was hung with a number of old oil paintings depicting the family's ancestors. Mrs Ashbourne was delighted to talk her through them all, introducing each long-departed family member one by one. From what Kathleen could gather, the Ashbournes, along with most of the other wealthy families in the area, were Quakers. They had all made their money in manufacturing, and by now they had intermarried pretty thoroughly.

At dinner, however, it was Kathleen's family that was the object of conversation. The Ashbournes had never had anyone like her sit at their table before, and they were fascinated by every detail of her life when she was growing up. Story-telling was Kathleen's forte, and she warmed to the task, entertaining them with tales of her parents' romantic meeting in Cape Town and the struggles they had faced coming back to England, where they had survived on the rabbits they caught and skinned for dinner. The whole family hung on to her every word – in fact, the only difficulty she faced was trying not to giggle when the servants she had been playing cards with the night before winked as they served her potatoes.

After dinner, Kathleen snuck back down to the basement for a cup of tea with the maids and listened to them gossip about the family. 'They've got 12 children, you know, and at least two of them are doolally,' Minnie told her.

'They say the Ashbournes are running out of money,' the girl with the deformed hand chipped in. 'It was all invested overseas, and now they can't get it 'cos of the war.'

'And as for that Jane,' the head housemaid, a woman of about 40, added, 'I've heard she's in love with one of the wounded soldiers she's been treating down at the hospital – and it turns out he's a lorry driver in Civvy Street!'

'Ooh, I don't think madame would be too pleased about that!' declared Minnie. The group of women laughed together until their sides ached.

Kathleen enjoyed the chance to join in with the servants' gossiping, but she soon discovered that the head housemaid had a romantic secret of her own. That night, when Kathleen tiptoed down to the kitchen to fetch herself a glass of water, she found the woman perched on the kitchen counter with her legs wrapped around the postman.

Kathleen gasped, and the couple sprang apart in embarrassment. As the postman hastily picked his trousers up off the floor, she backed out of the room, blushing, and fled up the stairs.

*

Kathleen's own love life was continuing as well as could be expected with her boyfriend hundreds of miles away up in Scotland. She and Arnold continued writing to each other regularly, and she kept him up to speed with all the strange goings on at the grand house. But it wasn't long before she had a new and entirely unwanted admirer to deal with.

The fields neighbouring the Ashbournes' estate were owned by a young farmer who had recently inherited them from his father. He had several land girls working for him already, but when one of them fell ill he asked Mr Shaw if he could borrow Kathleen for the day to help harvest his Brussels sprouts.

'Aye, ye can 'ave the girl,' the old man replied, 'but only if ye promise not to overwork her. The poor lass is thin as a rake, you know!'

Kathleen set off, happy for a change of scene and hoping to get to know some of the other land girls. But she soon discovered she would be spending the day all alone in a ten-acre field, her only visitor being the farmer. The young man took a keen interest in the flame-haired girl who was picking his sprouts, and stopped to stare at her whenever he passed by on his tractor.

It didn't take long for him to find an excuse to come and talk to her. 'You be a pretty little thing to be getting your hands so muddy,' he remarked admiringly.

'Oh, I don't mind,' Kathleen replied, carrying on with her work.

'Got a boyfriend, have you?' the man asked her.

'Yes, I have,' said Kathleen, firmly.

'That be a shame,' the man told her wistfully. 'I been looking for a wife to run this 'ere farm wi' me.'

Kathleen said nothing, and eventually the man went away. But over the next few weeks he kept asking Mr Shaw if he could 'borrow' her again. The young man was clearly lonely and longed for someone to share his days with, but Kathleen soon grew sick of him pestering her.

One day, the young farmer took Kathleen with him into Bury St Edmunds, where he had some errands to run. She sat in the passenger seat of his van, wrapped up in her own thoughts and doing her best to avoid conversation.

Suddenly there was an almighty crash as the van collided with another vehicle. Kathleen was thrown from her seat and her head smashed straight through the windscreen, lodging there as the van came to a halt. Her neck was completely surrounded by glass, and it was cutting painfully into her skin. If she moved even an inch, she was sure it would sever an artery.

Before long the police were on the scene, carefully dismantling the windshield around Kathleen's head and freeing her from the prison of glass. She was rushed to the local hospital, where her cuts were bandaged up, but the accident left her with a ring of tiny scars around her neck.

Before long, the case came to court, and Kathleen was called as a witness. The young farmer was claiming that the other vehicle had come out of nowhere when he hit it, and she was asked what she remembered of the incident.

'I'm sorry, but I can't help you,' she replied. 'I just don't remember a thing.'

'You must have seen what happened,' the magistrate protested. 'You were sitting right up in the front!'

But Kathleen had been so busy daydreaming that she had no recollection of anything before the moment her head hit the glass.

The young farmer was duly fined for dangerous driving, and after Kathleen's failure to corroborate his account, he never asked her to pick his sprouts again. It was scarcely the easiest way to free herself from his unwanted advances, but it seemed to have done the trick nonetheless.

It was many months now since Kathleen had last seen Arnold, but his letters had kept her going through the long, hard days on the land. At last, when she went home to her mother's house in Cambridge for some leave, he was able to join her for a day. To Kathleen he seemed even more charming than she remembered, and her feelings for him were stronger than ever before.

Mrs Skin did everything she could to make her daughter's handsome officer welcome, using up an entire week's rations on a single magnificent meal. But it was when she finally went out on an errand that Arnold revealed the true purpose of his visit. 'My darling,' he said breathlessly, taking Kathleen in his arms, 'you know we belong together. Will you marry me?'

Kathleen felt as if her heart could have burst then and there. 'Yes, of course!' she cried, falling into his embrace.

Arnold drew a little box out of his pocket and handed it over to her. Inside was the most beautiful ring that Kathleen had ever seen, set with a stone of yellow citrine. He tried to push it onto her finger, but to her disappointment it just wouldn't fit. 'Oh dear,' he murmured. 'I suppose we're going to have to get it altered.'

'No – don't take it away,' Kathleen pleaded. 'I'll wear it around my neck on a chain. That way it'll always be with me when we're apart.'

Kathleen hoped it wouldn't be long before the two of them could be married, but to her surprise Arnold told her that he wanted to wait until the war was over. 'I'll never forget the woman who used to wash our steps and windows,' he told her. 'She had been wealthy once, but when her husband was killed in the last war she was left with two young children to support by herself. I wouldn't want that to happen to you, my dear.'

'Yes, of course, you're right,' Kathleen replied, trying to hide her disappointment. If it was up to her, she would have married Arnold then and there, but she was willing to abide by his decision.

After Arnold had left, Kathleen showed her mother the ring. 'I knew it!' Mrs Skin declared, ecstatically. 'I just knew that you'd be married before the year was out! Oh isn't he wonderful, Kath. What a lovely man you've found yourself! I'd better start seeing about your trousseau.'

'We're not getting married until after the war, Mum,' Kathleen protested weakly. But it was no use reasoning with her mother. Mrs Skin was already off to tell all her friends, and gather material for her daughter's bottom drawer.

7

Jessie

After Jessie's first exhilarating experience of a bombing raid, 518 mixed battery hadn't seen much action in Sheffield, and a decision was made to move them to a gun-site at Barrow upon Humber, just across the river from Hull.

An all-male battery had recently been stationed there, and when Jessie and her friends arrived they were greeted with an impressive piece of the men's handiwork: an enormous mural on the wall of the canteen, depicting Adam and Eve in what could only be described as their full splendour.

'Well, that would take your mind off the quality of the grub,' one of the gunners commented, as he marvelled at Eve's enormous breasts.

A sign writer was hastily summoned by a rather flustered ATS officer. 'I need you to paint some foliage over the … ah, intimate areas,' she told him.

The man dashed off to fetch a tin of green paint, but before he returned word had got round the camp, and soon the whole battery was jostling to get a look at the lewd artwork before it was censored.

It was a wonder the all-male battery had found time to paint while they were at Humberside, since the ack-ack guns there had been almost constantly in action, as Hull endured a devastating battering from the Luftwaffe. Over six months, hundreds of tonnes of high explosive had been dropped by the German planes, along with over 100,000 incendiaries. The number of homes destroyed or damaged had already reached five figures, and almost a thousand civilians had been killed.

It had been a tough time for the local anti-aircraft batteries, and the departing all-male crew were adamant that their gun-site was no place for women. 'You lot won't last long here,' one of them told Jessie as he piled into a departing lorry. 'Give it a month and you'll be begging to be posted somewhere else.'

Jessie had heard that kind of male bravado before, and had seen the men of her own battery eat their words when they realised that the women were every bit their equals. But, as she and her friends soon found out, nothing in their previous experience had prepared them for the job of defending Hull. There were alerts at all hours of the day and night, and they soon found that it was rare to sleep through until dawn without having to leap out of bed and run to the gun park. By the time the men and women had made that frantic dash for the seventh or eighth time in a single night, everyone's nerves were beginning to fray.

To make matters worse, often the team would rush out to the guns, only to be ordered to stand down without a single shell being fired. Planes flying above 12,000 feet were out of range, but there were also strict rules on where in the sky an enemy target could be engaged. Bombers approaching south of the Humber were fair game, but anything flying directly above the city was off limits, for fear that the guns might bring down a plane full of bombs on a populated area. As a result, Jessie and her colleagues spent a lot of time watching as the city across the river was engulfed in fire, unable to do anything to help.

As well as high-explosive bombs, the Germans were dropping plenty of incendiaries, and some of these ended up landing near the gun park. There was a lot of dried grass around, which the girls did their best to keep short, but one night, despite their efforts, a large patch caught fire. Staring down the eyepiece of her height-and-range finder, Jessie could see the blaze growing out of the corner of her eye. But since no order had been given to stand down, all she and the other girls could do was stay at their posts and hope whoever was on fire-picket dealt with it quickly.

More sinister than the incendiaries, though, were a new German invention: the butterfly bomb. These small metal contraptions would fall to the ground and then explode as soon as somebody picked them up. 'If you see something unfamiliar on the ground, whatever you do, don't touch it,' the ATS girls were warned in a special briefing. Across the river in Hull, dozens of curious children had already lost their arms to the new weapons.

On the gun-site, the longest nights seemed to go on for ever. One time, Jessie counted nine alerts between dusk and dawn, and none of them turned out to be a false alarm. Every few hours a new wave of bombers would come over, and she and her friends rushed over to the gun park to meet them. But despite their weariness, the moment captain Rait bellowed 'Engage!' everyone was focused and alert.

That night, the ack-ack guns fired more than ever, and since the Luftwaffe were flying almost directly overhead, a lot of the flak fell right back down onto the gun-site. As the shards of hot metal pinged off the girls' helmets, Elsie Acres turned to Jessie and said, 'This is bloody dangerous, you know!'

Despite the severity of the situation, Jessie couldn't help laughing. In all their time on the gun-sites none of the girls had ever really acknowledged the risks that went along with the job. But they had all heard the story of poor Nora Caveney, the first ack-ack casualty of the war. She had been hit by a German bomb splinter while working on her predictor, managing to stay on target long enough for another girl to take over, before falling to the ground and dying at her colleagues' feet. Throughout the whole incident, the guns had never stopped firing.

Then there were the poor searchlight operators who helped illuminate the targets for the ack-ack girls. Jessie had been out on the gun-site one night when the girls two fields away came under machine-gun fire from a German plane determined to put out their beams. Unlike the gun-sites, which gave off as little light as possible, the searchlights were easy to spot from the air, and were popular targets with the Luftwaffe. Yet when a group of searchlight operators begged the Army for a machine-gun so that they could fire back, they were refused, on the grounds that arming the girls would mean violating the Royal Proclamation that limited servicewomen to non-combatant roles.

While 518 mixed battery was far from the safest posting for a young ATS girl like Jessie, there were few jobs in the forces more thrilling than manning the ack-ack guns – and one direct hit was worth all the terror and exhaustion that preceded it. Jessie was still laughing at Elsie's comment about the danger they were in when she saw something that made her heart soar – a German plane with smoke billowing out of it. Before long, she knew, it would be dropping from the sky like a stone.

After the all-clear was finally sounded, the girls traipsed back to their Nissen hut, desperate to catch a few hours' sleep before they were woken again in the morning. 'You know,' Jessie told Elsie with a sigh, 'when I get demobbed I'm going to bed for three months!'

*

Jessie and her friends had grown used to seeing Hull from across the river, but after a few weeks she decided she wanted to get a closer look at the city they were protecting. From the nearby village of New Holland it was possible to catch a ferry across the Humber, and the 25-minute journey was rather lovely, especially just as the sun was going down in the evening.

But what Jessie saw in Hull itself was far from beautiful. After months of pounding by the Luftwaffe, the city had been utterly devastated, and the destruction was unlike anything she could have imagined. More than half of the housing stock had been either ruined or badly damaged, and as Jessie gazed aghast at the smashed houses and piles of rubble, at the giant craters where people's homes had once been, she found it hard to comprehend that such devastation was possible.

The battered city was a shadow of its pre-war glory, with many public buildings put out of use. The municipal museum had been wiped off the face of the earth, the General Post Office was gutted, and the City Hall and Guildhall had suffered direct hits. The grand department stores that once lined the main shopping thoroughfares had taken their fair share of knocks too – among them Hammond's, Edwin Davis and Thornton-Varley. Banks, churches, cinemas and even the Royal Infirmary were closed owing to bomb damage, while in the area around the docks, factories, mills and warehouses had been razed to the ground, and barges sunk to the bottom of the river.

For the people of Hull, though, it was the damage to domestic properties that hurt the most. As Jessie toured the blitzed streets, gazing up at fractured terraces, with house after house ripped open to expose what was left of its owner's belongings, her heart went out to them. Almost half the population had been made homeless at some point or other, but outside the city their suffering was almost unknown. To avoid giving the

Germans an opportunity to gloat, national newspapers never specifically mentioned Hull in print, only making vague references to raids on 'a north-east coastal town'.

But while their troubles were not widely spoken of, the locals were well aware of how much the anti-aircraft batteries were doing to protect them. As Jessie and her friends roamed the battered streets, they realised that the white ack-ack lanyards they wore on their uniforms were seen as a badge of honour in the city.

One night, when Jessie went out to the cinema in Hull, a woman came up to her in the queue and thrust a ticket into her hand. 'You have mine, love,' she insisted. 'It's the least I can offer after all you girls have done for us.'

Jessie accepted the ticket gratefully. After so many long nights out on the gun-site, it was nice to be reminded of who it was she and her friends were protecting.

In the ATS, leave was supposed to be granted every three months, but Jessie had been in khaki more than twice that long before the Army finally sent her home for a week's rest. She spent the time in Holbeach Bank feeling desperately bored, wishing she could be back with her friends in the battery. Her father continued to pester her with questions about the guns, although they both knew that she wasn't allowed to answer them. At her camp, every hut and office was plastered with posters proclaiming, 'Careless Talk Costs Lives' and 'What You Do Is Not For General Knowledge'.

Jessie did her best to keep her father satisfied with tales of the pranks she and the other girls had played on each other. 'One time they left my bed out on the football pitch,' she told him. 'I had to ask the guards to bring it back in for me.'

'Those cheeky buggers!' Mr Ward exclaimed. 'I hope you got them back for that.'

Jessie reassured him that she was as much of a prankster as anyone else in the battery. 'There's a girl in my hut called Mary Natress,' she told him, 'and one time we took her uniform, stuffed it with all her kit and laid it out on the bed. Then we put up a sign that read, "Here lies the body of Mary Natress, laid in state upon her mattress." You should have seen the look on her face when she came in!'

Mr Ward wheezed with laughter, the tears streaming down his face. 'Oh, what I wouldn't give to be back in the Army!' he said wistfully.

While she was on leave, Jessie decided to pay a visit to an old family friend who lived in Spalding. Mrs Billet had known the Wards for years, but when she opened the door and found Jessie on the threshold, she stared at her as if she were a stranger. 'Oh,' she remarked, aghast. 'You're in uniform.'

'Yes,' Jessie replied, not sure what else to say.

'Well, I don't agree with it, you know,' Mrs Billet declared. 'War is a wicked thing, and I've made up my mind not to have anybody in uniform in my house.'

Jessie was shocked at the woman's unexpected hostility. 'I'm proud of my uniform,' she protested.

'But you *kill* people!' Mrs Billet cried.

Jessie drew herself up to her full height, even if that was only five foot one. 'That's right,' she told the older woman. 'We kill them to stop them killing you. Which would you rather have?'

At that Mrs Billet was rendered speechless, and Jessie turned on her heel and left.

All the way home, she could feel herself fizzing with rage. Night after night she had manned the gun-site across the river from Hull to protect ordinary civilians like Mrs Billet, and at considerable risk to herself. She couldn't help hoping that the next time Spalding got raided, the annoying woman's house would be the first to get flattened.

When Jessie returned to Humberside after her week away from the battery, she found the situation there was worse than ever. The alerts were almost constant now and everyone was feeling the strain.

Despite their exhaustion, the girls were still expected to drill every morning, but one day Elsie Windsor reached the end of her tether. 'I've had enough of this!' she exclaimed suddenly, 'It's a load of rubbish!' Then she stormed off the parade ground in the direction of her hut.

The other girls gasped at Elsie's outburst, but someone quickly stepped in to fill her place in the ranks, and they carried on as if nothing had happened. No one wanted to draw attention to her behaviour and run the risk of getting her in trouble.

Elsie's quick temper was well known around the battery. When her boyfriend Stan told one of his mates that they were getting engaged, the other man was incredulous. 'You're not really marrying that Spitfire, are you?' he asked – to which Stan replied calmly, 'Aye, I am.'

One night, the girls were all sitting together in the NAAFI when Stan came over and whispered in Elsie's ear. 'Come outside,' he told her, 'I've got something to show you.' They went and sat on a little wall out the back, where he drew a ring out of his pocket.

But just as Stan was slipping it onto Elsie's finger, the alarm sounded. She flew off to her predictor, pushing the ring up over her knuckle as she ran. She hadn't had a chance to see it properly yet and was desperate to know what it looked like.

The girls were soon busy dealing with a wave of German bombers overhead, but once the fuses had been set and the guns started firing, Elsie's thoughts turned again to the ring. There was no light on the gun sight, but one of the predictor's many windows contained a tiny red bulb, and Elsie held her finger up to it, trying to see by the faint glow. It was useless, though – she couldn't make out a thing.

The moment the girls were told to stand down, Elsie rushed back to the NAAFI, where she finally got a proper look at the ring. It had been beautifully crafted into the shape of a little flower, and she couldn't have loved it more.

Jessie, meanwhile, had her own diamond engagement ring to admire, but unlike Elsie she rarely got to see her fiancé's face. It was hard enough getting any leave at all, and timing it to coincide with Jim's was almost impossible.

In September 1942, though, Jim managed to pull a few strings and they were able to enjoy a whole week in each other's company – the first time they had seen each other for more than six months. It was wonderful being together again, even if they had to stay under Jessie's mother's roof. But the reunion was over far too quickly – Jessie felt she had barely got home before she was packing up to return to Humberside again, wondering when she would next see her fiancé.

The situation was only going to get worse. Not long after Jessie arrived back at 518 mixed battery, she received a letter from Jim in which he told her that his unit would be shipping out soon, though they hadn't been told where. 'I want us to get married before I go,' he wrote.

Jessie remembered her mother's stern warning when she and Jim had first got engaged. It would be very unwise to marry before the end of the war, she had told her. But she could hardly deny Jim his wish now, when he was about to be sent far away.

Jessie was an independent woman now, she reminded herself, doing a job that really mattered. She had every right to get married when she wanted to, whether her mother liked it or not. She set about making the necessary enquiries and had soon arranged marriage leave for the beginning of December.

Since she was under 21, Jessie had to get her father's written consent to marry, and although she had decided to defy her mother's wishes, she didn't want to sneak around behind her back – so as soon as she arrived home to prepare for the wedding she brought the form into the living room where her parents were both sitting, and asked the old man from next door to come and witness it.

Mrs Ward sat silently while her husband signed the papers, but the look on her face revealed the burning fury she was feeling. Never before had she experienced such blatant defiance from her daughter, and Jessie couldn't help feeling a secret pleasure at her mother's reaction. Perhaps it would teach her a lesson, she thought – that she couldn't always get her own way. But in the days that followed, the atmosphere at home was far from pleasant, and Mrs Ward offered Jessie no help with arranging the wedding.

Jessie would have been happy to get married in her ATS uniform, but Jim begged her not to. 'Let's do it properly,' he wrote. 'I've got a suit I can send for.' So instead she searched her little wardrobe for something suitable. All she had were clothes from before she had joined the ATS, and being in the forces meant she wasn't entitled to the clothing coupons she would need to buy anything new. In the end, the best she could come up with was a black skirt that was several years old, a woolly jumper she had knitted herself, and her brown lace-up Army shoes.

The night before the wedding Jessie stayed with an aunt who lived near the church in Holbeach, while Jim was put up at her parents' house – 'You've got your own way, then,' Mrs Ward told her future son-in-law bitterly.

In the morning, Mr Ward came and knocked for his daughter, offering his arm with a melancholy smile. His happiness was tinged with sorrow at the thought that he was losing her for ever.

It was a frosty December morning but as they approached the old Norman church of All Saints, with its ancient porch and beautiful stained-glass windows, everything looked absolutely perfect. When Jessie and her father walked through the doors, Jim turned at the altar to smile at her – the same carefree smile that she remembered from their first meeting in the drawing room at Bleak House. After those blissful early days of cycling through the countryside together they had been separated for most of the time they had known each other, but their feelings had never wavered – and right now Jessie knew she loved Jim more than ever.

It was so cold in the church that Jessie had to keep her coat and hat on throughout the ceremony, but Jim didn't seem to care. He spent the whole time beaming from ear to ear, until finally Reverend Boswell announced, 'You may kiss the bride.'

After the wedding, there was no party being thrown back at the Wards' house, so when they left the church Jessie and Jim headed straight for the train station. Her father offered them his hearty congratulations, but her mother said nothing at all. 'Goodbye, Mum,' Jessie offered, but Mrs Ward turned away without even responding.

Once Jessie and Jim were safely on the train, he turned to her and said, 'You know, I think if your dad was a drinker he would go and get drunk about now.'

Jessie felt sorry for her father, knowing that he would be putting up with the frosty atmosphere at home on his own. But as she and her new husband sped away from Holbeach, their arms tightly wrapped around each other, nothing could dent her happiness. They had got what they wanted – each other – and that was all that mattered.

The newlyweds spent their week's honeymoon up in Leeds, staying with a couple Jim had been billeted with when he had returned from Dunkirk. Knowing he had no family of his own, they had taken the cheerful young soldier under their wing, and when they heard he was getting married they had written to offer him their spare room.

If Jessie had any qualms about turning up at a complete stranger's house for her wedding night they were soon laid to rest. She and Jim arrived to find a beautiful meal laid out for them in the kitchen, and his friends welcomed her into their home as if they had known her for years. After the fraught experience of staying with her parents in Holbeach Bank, the warm, lively atmosphere was a relief.

In Leeds, Jessie and Jim whiled away their days riding the tram into town, going window shopping, and wandering around the parks and gardens. When they got cold they would head into a café, where they perfected the art of making a single cup of tea last for hours. They had no money to spend, but in each other's company they felt truly rich.

When the time came for them to return to their respective Army camps, saying goodbye was even more of a wrench than usual. But at least they had a week's embarkation leave to look forward to before Jim was sent abroad.

Back in Barrow upon Humber, Jessie was touched to find that her fellow 'ATS tarts' had clubbed together to buy her a wedding present. It was a beautiful decorative mirror they had bought from Hammonds, one of Hull's finest department stores, which had been bombed out but was still trading from its basement. 'It's probably daft giving you something made of glass around here,' Elsie Acres told her, 'but we thought you might like it.'

Recently, Jessie had noticed a new spark in her friend's eye, and it didn't take long for her to find out why. Three years after losing her fiancé at Dunkirk, Elsie had finally found love again, with a sailor called Charles who she had met while he was on shore leave in Hull. Jessie could not have been happier for her.

Finally, Jim's embarkation leave came through, and to Jessie's relief her superiors agreed to grant her another week off to spend with him before he was sent abroad. With nowhere else to go, they returned to his friends' house in Leeds, and as before they spent their days mainly just wandering around the city and talking. In the evenings they made the most of the local picture-house, indulging Jim's love of movies. 'Who knows whether they'll have a cinema where I'm going!' he pointed out. He was convinced that he was being sent to North Africa, since his unit had been issued with a new uniform that included khaki shorts.

But while Jim wondered what his own posting might have in store for him, he worried about Jessie's safety after he was gone. She had told him about some of the horrors that the girls from the battery had seen in Hull, and he knew that her job on the gun-site was a hazardous one. The ATS had already lost a number of ack-ack girls to enemy action – in Great Yarmouth, 25 young women were killed when they suffered a direct hit during a German raid.

When Jim told Jessie of his fears, she was resolute. 'You know I wouldn't want a job in an office,' she told him, before adding, more gently, 'but I wish you wouldn't worry.' She was aware, though, that this was easy for her to say, since Jim's job as a cook was hardly dangerous.

When the time finally came for Jessie to see Jim off at the station, he pressed her to him like she was the most precious thing in the world. 'Just take care of yourself,' he pleaded, 'and be careful.'

'Don't worry, I will,' Jessie promised. 'However long you're gone, I'll be here waiting for you when you get back.'

Jim nodded and smiled at Jessie. Then he stepped onto the train, waving as it disappeared into the distance.

A few days later, the phone rang in the battery command post. 'Can I speak to my wife, please?' Jim asked the girl who took the call. 'I'm shipping out tomorrow and I want to say goodbye.'

'I'm sorry,' he was told, 'but we don't allow personal calls. I can let her know you rang.' She went off in search of Jessie to pass on the message.

'Can I speak to him?' Jessie asked her, when she was told that Jim had called. She didn't like the thought of him setting off without hearing her voice one more time.

But the other girl was adamant. 'I'm sorry,' she said, 'but you know the rules.'

*

After Jim's departure, Jessie did her best to throw herself back into life at the gun-site, glad that her work was so absorbing that it distracted her from the pain of separation. It was a tough job but she loved it, and she wouldn't want to be anywhere else.

It was just a question of waiting, she told herself. Who knew how long the war might go on – it could be another ten years. But she and Jim would sit it out, like all the other young couples up and down the country who were desperate for their lives together to begin.

Once Jim had arrived at his new posting, his beautiful letters began arriving several times a week. Although he couldn't reveal his location, Jessie guessed that he must have been right about going to North Africa. He often mentioned how warm it was outside – 'a bit too warm, though I never thought I'd say that!' as he put it in one letter – and he wrote vividly about the beautiful butterflies that fluttered around the camp. 'I wish you could see them,' he told Jessie.

Jessie spent her 21st birthday on guard duty, alone in the little sentry-box near the camp entrance. It was hardly the most festive way to celebrate the big day but she didn't mind, and when she returned to her Nissen hut that evening, she found her bed festooned with cards from her colleagues, not to mention an extra-long letter from Jim.

Among the birthday cards, Jessie found one from her father, and opening it she noticed, without much surprise, that her mother hadn't even bothered to sign it. Although Jessie always addressed her letters home 'Dear Mum and Dad', she hadn't heard from Mrs Ward since the wedding.

Jim, by contrast, wrote religiously every other day – which made it all the stranger that, after her birthday letter, Jessie didn't receive anything from him for over a fortnight. She knew that sometimes there were hold-ups with post from abroad and just hoped that her letters to him weren't being delayed as well. 'You know what it's like,' one of the sergeants told her, 'you'll probably get a whole bundle of them arriving all at the same time.'

One day, Jessie was sat writing to Jim at a table in the battery rest-room, a small wooden hut near the camp offices where it was possible to get a bit of peace and quiet. As she looked up from the sheet of paper in front of her, she caught sight of movement outside the window. It was one of the camp's regular dispatch riders, running towards the offices. That's strange, she thought – he normally comes in the morning. What could have brought him over at this time of day?

Jessie went back to her letter, but after a few minutes she was interrupted by the sound of the door opening. An orderly sergeant was standing on the threshold. 'Private Winkworth, you're wanted in the administration office,' she told her.

Jessie shoved her pen and paper into a pocket and followed the woman outside. What could anyone want with me? she wondered, hoping that she hadn't done anything wrong. 'Hello?' she called, as she stepped inside the office. 'I was told somebody wanted to see me.'

Another sergeant, who was seated at a desk, looked up at her, and Jessie noticed she had something in her hand. 'This letter came for you,' she said. 'The dispatch rider just brought it in.'

Jessie took the envelope, noticing as she tore it open that it was stamped 'Army Records Office'. She pulled out the sheet of paper inside and unfolded it.

'It is my painful duty to inform you ...'

Jessie's breath caught in her throat.

'... of the death in action of your husband, Private Cecil James Winkworth.'

Jessie stood rooted to the spot, her eyes fixed on the piece of paper in front of her. 'This can't be true,' she murmured. 'It can't be true.'

But there in black and white was Jim's service number, 1507435, and the details: 'Army Catering Corps, attached 67th Field Regiment RA'. There was no mistake – that was Jim all right.

Jessie forced herself to read down to the bottom of the page. 'His Majesty and the unit send their condolences on your loss,' the letter concluded. There was no further information on what had happened to Jim, but his date of death was listed as 25 April. That was Easter Sunday, Jessie realised – more than two weeks ago.

Suddenly, she was aware of a palpable silence in the room. She looked up slowly, and realised that everyone was watching her with concern. 'Excuse me a minute,' she muttered. 'I have to be on my own.' Then she walked out of the office and back to the rest-room, collapsing back down at the little desk where only minutes before she had been happily writing to her husband. She looked again at the words on the bit of paper in her hand, blinking at them in disbelief.

After a while, Jessie became aware of a grey-haired female officer entering the room. 'I'm terribly sorry, Winkworth,' the older woman said as she approached. 'I can't help, but here's a cup of tea for you.'

Wordlessly, Jessie took the cup and the officer went away again, shutting the door gently behind her.

When Jessie had drunk the tea, barely registering the taste of the hot liquid as it went down her throat, she wandered in a daze to her Nissen hut. It was empty when she got there, and she sat on her bed in complete silence.

After a while, the other girls began to shuffle in. From the looks on their faces it was obvious that they had heard Jessie's news. They took her with them to the canteen, but they couldn't persuade her to eat anything, so instead the little group just sat in silence. Many of the girls had lost loved ones to the war already, and they knew there was nothing they could say that would make any difference, but Jessie found it helped a little just having them around her.

Before long, the Army administration had kicked in, and Jessie was granted a week's compassionate leave. She set off on the next train to Holbeach Bank.

When Mrs Ward opened the door, there was a look on her face that her daughter had never seen before. 'I'm sorry, Jessie,' she said, as she ushered her into the house.

But as far as Jessie was concerned, it was too little, and far, far too late. 'Don't give me your sympathy,' she replied coldly. 'I don't want to know what you think, or whether you're sorry or not.'

Although her mother had warned her not to marry in wartime, Jessie was determined that she would never give her the satisfaction of thinking that she had been right. Marrying Jim had been the best decision of her life, even if they had only shared a couple of precious weeks together as husband and wife.

The next morning Jessie left her parents' house and went to stay with her aunt instead, until her week's leave was up and it was time to return to the battery.

8

Margery

After a few months, the shock Margery felt at discovering that James Preston was married had subsided. She still felt bruised by the whole experience, but her friend May Strong, who had been there for her at the time, was determined to distract her from ruminating on what had happened.

May was in her mid-thirties, which at the time was considered old for a single woman, but she didn't appear to have any concerns about not being married herself. Her main aim in life was to have fun, and to make sure that everyone around her was as happy as she was. One evening, when she saw Margery looking over one of James's old letters, she announced, 'Come on – there's a dance down in Portsmouth tonight, and I'm ordering you to go!'

The two of them got the bus into town together and spent the night dancing their socks off. Margery couldn't help laughing at the sight of her superior burning up the dance floor without a care in the world, and she enjoyed letting her hair down for a change too. But each time she danced with a man she made it very clear that she wasn't interested in anything further. After her experience with James, she had decided to treat all men she met as if they were married, whatever they told her.

The two WAAFs were having such a good night that they lost track of time completely, and when they arrived back at the bus stop they discovered, to Margery's horror, that they'd missed the last bus home to Titchfield.

'Don't worry, we'll hitch-hike!' May told her. 'If there's one thing I've learned, it's that cars always stop for a girl in uniform.'

Margery just hoped that her friend was right. It was getting later and later, and she didn't want to be put on a charge for missing the curfew.

May stuck her thumb out confidently, but a good ten minutes went by without anything stopping. Finally, a motorbike came roaring round the corner and screeched to a halt next to the two women. 'Hop on!' the driver told them.

'Don't mind if I do,' said May, eagerly clambering up behind the rider. 'Come on, Margery.'

Margery stared at the bike doubtfully. It looked terrifying, and neither of them had helmets. 'Have you ever done this before?' she asked May.

'No, but there's a first time for everything!' her friend replied. 'Come on!'

Gingerly, Margery followed her example and they sped off to Titchfield, making it back just in time to beat the curfew.

Gradually, May Strong's carefree attitude to life began to rub off on Margery. Breaking the rules didn't come naturally to her – not for nothing had her sister Peggy branded her a 'Goody Two-Shoes' – but she was beginning to realise that, if she didn't mind bending them a little, her job in Equipment Accounts offered certain perks. Everyone in the office was used to her leaving her desk several times a day to check up on some item in the stores, so she could easily disappear for half an hour or so without anyone batting an eyelid. She began making the most of her little excursions, dropping in on the lads in the Armoury, who were always willing to brew up a nice pot of tea, and then taking an illegal short cut back across the grass when no one was looking.

To her surprise, Margery found that she rather enjoyed the feeling of doing things she wasn't supposed to, and before long she began committing more minor offences. One night, when she wanted to go out but didn't have a pass, she decided to break camp, sure that with her wits about her she could get past the guard at the entrance without being noticed.

Margery wandered casually down towards the gate. As she approached the blast wall that ran alongside the guardhouse, she cast a furtive look around her, before kneeling down, as nonchalantly as she could, and pretending to tie her shoelace. She was pretty sure that no one had seen her duck down, and as she scuttled along behind the improvised air-raid barrier and out of the camp, she felt flushed with excitement. All that remained was to repeat the trick on her way back in and she would be home and dry.

Margery's scheme worked like a dream, giving her the freedom to come and go whenever she wanted, and over the ensuing weeks she repeated it many times. But one night, as she was striding purposefully towards her dormitory hut, having successfully sneaked back into camp, she heard a stern female voice call out, 'Pott!'

Margery stopped dead in her tracks and slowly turned around, meeting the stare of an intimidating-looking WAAF officer. 'You haven't booked in,' the woman told her accusingly.

'I haven't booked out either!' Margery replied, flustered. This at least had the merit of being true, although it didn't exactly help the situation.

The WAAF officer narrowed her eyes, but before she could say anything, Margery announced confidently, 'I'm on a 48-hour pass, you see, so I didn't think I needed to.' She felt rather pleased with herself for coming up with such a convincing lie on the spur of the moment.

The WAAF officer continued to stare at Margery, who somehow managed to hold her gaze. 'On your way then,' she said eventually, turning on her heel and marching off.

Margery breathed a sigh of relief, and rushed back to the dormitory hut as fast as she could.

With Christmas approaching, Margery was disappointed to learn that she was expected to remain at Titchfield over the holiday rather than spend the time at home with her family. Throughout her childhood, the Potts had always attended midnight mass on Christmas Eve – and although she couldn't be with them this year, she was determined to keep the tradition alive. With a little cajoling, she managed to convince a couple of girls from her hut to accompany her to the church in the local village.

The service was as magical as any Margery remembered, and as the girls came out afterwards, they were met by a scene so beautiful it could have been printed on a picture postcard. While they had been inside the church, it had begun to snow, and the little village was now frosted in white. The sky was dotted with a thousand bright stars, and a brilliant moon lit up the landscape in defiance of the blackout. Margery was struck by an overwhelming feeling that everything was right in the world.

'I think I know a short cut back to the camp,' she told the other girls. 'If we cut across these fields we'll be home in half the time.'

The others peered anxiously at the terrain in front of them. 'I don't know, Margery,' one of them said. 'What if we get lost out there?' The girl was a Londoner, and not used to being out in the countryside at night.

'Don't worry,' Margery told her. 'We'll be all right. Just follow me.'

As she strode out across the field, she was struck by how far she had come since the day she first put on her WAAF uniform. She had joined up as a timid young woman who followed where others led, fearful of what lurked around every corner. The old Margery would never have suggested walking home after midnight, with no more than the moon to light her way – but tonight it hadn't even crossed her mind to be scared.

When one of the WAAF corporals was transferred away from Titchfield, Margery decided to put in for a promotion. She knew the extra money would come in handy for her parents, since her father was now retired and they were living off his small pension. She had seen the way May Strong looked out for her girls and gained their respect without the need for harsh discipline, and she had found it inspiring. Perhaps that was something she could do, she thought.

The wing commander was sympathetic to Margery's family situation and agreed to send her off for training. As long as she passed the 'discip' course, he told her, the job was hers.

Margery was sent to RAF Cardington in Bedfordshire, the main training centre of RAF Balloon Command. The three-week course there included lectures every day, as well as practical demonstrations on subjects such as how to make a field kitchen. Margery doubted whether such skills would ever come in handy at Titchfield, but she applied herself conscientiously, determined to make the most of the opportunity she had been given.

The girls on the course drilled every morning, and took turns in leading the parade. For Margery this was the hardest part of the training, since she found it almost impossible to time her commands correctly – an order had to be issued just as the left foot was passing the right, so that everyone moved together on the next step. One day, when she was commanding the rest of her cohort, the instructor told her to give the order, 'About turn.' But as she stared at the dozens of feet marching in unison, Margery felt herself become transfixed, and she kept missing her chance to issue the order.

Before she knew it, her troops had marched off the parade ground altogether, and were progressing through a giant aircraft hangar, past a group of bemused engineers who had been hard at work repairing a damaged plane. The instructor was forced to go running after them, frantically shouting out the order himself to prevent them from marching into a wall. Margery stood and watched sheepishly as the group of girls emerged from the hangar, several of them stifling giggles.

But despite such a humiliating setback, Margery struggled through the rest of the course, and at the end of the three weeks she felt reasonably confident she had done all that could be expected of her. She and her friend May were both due some leave, and they had decided to spend it with May's family up in Haltwhistle, so together they took the train up to Newcastle.

When the call came confirming that Margery's promotion had gone through, the whole Strong family cheered as if she were one of their own. 'Here, why don't you take these, Margery,' said May's brother, who was also in the Air Force, handing over an old set of corporal's stripes. 'If you wear new ones, everyone'll know you've only just been promoted,' he explained, 'and you don't want that!'

Margery took off her jacket, whipped out her 'hussif' – the little pouch containing needle and thread which was part of every servicewoman's standard kit – and carefully sewed the stripes onto her sleeve. Then she put the jacket back on, and headed down to the local pub to celebrate with the Strongs.

'Well, that's it, then,' May announced, as she set a drink down on the table in front of Margery. 'I don't outrank you any more!' From the broad smile on her face it was clear that she was happy for her. When they had first met, Margery had very much looked up to May, but as her own confidence had grown, their friendship had matured into one between equals.

Unfortunately, though, fostering friendships wasn't one of the Air Force's priorities, and much to the two girls' disappointment May was soon transferred to a new posting. Margery had finally earned the right to her place in the NCO's room at the end of her hut, but from now on she would be occupying it on her own.

As a newly minted corporal, Margery had a whole new set of responsibilities at RAF Titchfield. In the dormitory hut, it was her job to ensure that everything was spick and span, ready for regular inspections, and to lead the flight of girls to breakfast each morning. She was also called on to patrol the camp at night, looking out for any naughty WAAFs who were out canoodling with their male colleagues, and at exactly 10.30 p.m. every evening she was the one who now turned out the lights.

In her time off, Margery generally went home to North Wallington to see her parents. Despite the fact that he had recently retired, Mr Pott's emphysema seemed to be getting worse, and Margery was now the only one of his three daughters who was living close by. Not to be outdone by her younger sibling in the Air Force, Peggy had joined the Army as a Queen Alexandra Nursing Sister, and had almost immediately been sent to the Middle East.

When Mr and Mrs Pott first saw the corporal's stripes on Margery's arm, the pride they felt was plain to see. 'You know, you look an inch taller these days,' her mother told her. Then she added, with a laugh, 'I suppose next you'll be wanting to go abroad like your sister.'

Margery wasn't sure if her mother had been joking, but as chance would have it, a few days later a notice went up on the board at RAF Titchfield calling for volunteers for overseas service. The list of trades required included Equipment Accounts.

Margery thought for a moment. Would it really be such a joke for her to go overseas like her sister, she wondered. After all, she was the one who had enlisted first, not Peggy – and she had been promoted to corporal. Already she had achieved so much more than anyone in her family had thought her capable of, and the decision to join the WAAF was one of the best she had ever taken in her life. Who was to say that this might not be an equally great opportunity?

Before she could talk herself out of it, Margery had put her name down.

A few days later, she was called into the Admin Office for an interview about her application. Before she went in, she read over the rules and regulations on overseas service, and was horrified to discover that WAAFs with elderly parents were not eligible to go abroad. Margery's father was well into his seventies, and scarcely in the best of health – if the Air Force discovered that fact she felt sure that they would strike her off the list.

As she walked to the office, Margery wrestled with her conscience. In her time at Titchfield she had grown more comfortable with bending the rules now and then, but out-and-out lying still didn't come easily to her. Eventually, she made a pact with herself: if they asked her directly, she wouldn't deny her father's age or his illness, but neither would she volunteer the information unprompted.

The interview turned out to be very straightforward, and to Margery's relief no questions were asked about her parents. She walked out of the Admin Office safe in the knowledge that she had made it through – Margery Pott was going to see the world.

She knew just how fortunate she was to have been accepted for overseas service. Although the Air Force was gradually beginning to send women to postings all over the globe, their numbers were small, and less than five per cent of WAAFs ever ventured beyond the British Isles.

While she waited for her orders to depart, Margery continued to see her parents as often as she could. But each time she returned to the maltster's house in North Wallington, her father seemed to have deteriorated a little more. Now every breath was accompanied by a low rattling noise and, unable to walk unaided, Mr Pott was confined to a wheelchair. Whenever Margery visited, she would wheel him out of the house and he would stare sadly out over the fields. One day, while they were admiring the view, he reached out to grab her arm and pleaded with her not to go abroad.

Margery was beginning to have serious doubts herself about leaving, but her mother did her best to reassure her. 'Don't you take a blind bit of notice of your father,' she declared. 'He's just worried about who's going to push his chair around.'

As the days and weeks wore on, and Margery waited patiently for her embarkation orders, Mr Pott got sicker and sicker. She was heading home to see him most nights after work now, cycling through the blacked-out lanes of North Wallington on Peggy's old pushbike. But by this stage he was too sick even to be wheeled along the road, so she just sat by his bedside playing cribbage with him.

Mr Pott's bed had been moved downstairs, and he was surviving almost entirely on a diet of raw eggs and whisky, which his wife was convinced was the only thing keeping him alive. She was determined not to let him go into hospital, convinced that he would die if he was taken away from home. But sitting by his side for hour after hour, Margery could see that her father was in terrible pain, and it was beginning to take a toll on his mind. Sometimes when she visited he seemed barely aware of who she was, and he would talk to her about things that weren't really there.

One time, Margery had arranged to stay at the house overnight so that her mother could get a proper rest for once. It was a warm evening, and she thought a bit of air might help her father's lungs, but under the black-out regulations no light was allowed to show after nightfall, so she let the fire in the grate go out, turned off all the lights, and then opened the windows, letting in a blissful cool breeze. In the pitch black, Margery couldn't see a thing, but she could tell that her father was in a particularly bad way. In between his desperate gasps for breath, she heard a furious ripping noise, and it took a few moments for her to realise what it was – Mr Pott was tearing his sheets to shreds. Since childhood Margery had been familiar with his strong, sinewy hands, the muscles developed from years of tying ropes at the brewery, but right now the thought of them ripping through the fabric of the bedclothes sent a chill down her spine.

For the first time in her life, Margery felt afraid of her father. Despite his sickness, there was strength in him yet, and his grip on reality was failing. If he suddenly reached out and took hold of her, she wasn't sure she would be able to get away.

Margery ran from the room, locking the door behind her, and went upstairs to find her mother. 'What's the matter?' Mrs Pott asked her anxiously, as she came into her bedroom.

'He's tearing the bedclothes to pieces, Mum,' Margery told her. 'He can't go on like this!'

But Mrs Pott was adamant. 'I don't want him going to a hospital,' she insisted.

Margery knew her mum's feelings on the subject, but it didn't seem right to do nothing while her father continued to suffer. 'I'm calling the doctor,' she announced defiantly. 'Wait here.'

Then she ran up the road to find a phone box, where she summoned the local doctor to come and help.

When Margery returned to the maltster's house, she found her mother wringing her hands. 'They'll take him into hospital, I know they will,' Mrs Pott cried. 'I can't be here to see that.' She picked up her coat and ran out of the house, leaving Margery all alone.

Margery went to sit by her father's bedside once again. He was still twisting the bedclothes between his fingers, but he was quieter now and she no longer felt so afraid of him.

When the doctor arrived, he regarded Mr Pott with a look of deepest pity. 'Your father should have gone into hospital a long time ago,' he told Margery, shaking his head sadly. 'They wouldn't have let him live like this. They'd have given him morphine for the pain and he would be gone by now.'

Margery nodded. She knew that what the man was saying was true. No one would want to carry on living in the state her father was in. 'I understand,' she told the doctor soberly.

There was just one problem. Thanks to the war, all the local hospital beds were full, and the only place that would take Mr Pott was an asylum. 'You and I both know he's not insane,' the doctor told Margery, 'but all the pain he's suffered *has* done something terrible to his mind.' He drew a form out of his bag and handed it over to her. 'I'm afraid I'll need a signature on this,' he said. 'I can't have him taken away without authorisation.'

Margery held the form in her hand, wavering for a moment. Having her father committed to an institution was a responsibility she wasn't sure she could bear. She had always been the baby of the family, yet now she was being asked to make the biggest decision the Potts had ever faced.

But then, there was no question in her mind that it was the right thing to do, that it was in her father's best interests. And if not her, who else was going to do it?

Margery took a pen from the doctor and added her signature to the form.

'You're doing the right thing,' he reassured her. 'It'll all be over soon, I guarantee it. Three days at the most, and he'll be at peace.'

A little while later an ambulance arrived, and Mr Pott was taken away. Margery watched in silence as the vehicle disappeared into the blackout.

*

In the morning, Margery awoke to find that her mother had returned to the maltster's house. 'It's done, then?' she asked her quietly.

Margery nodded. 'They took him in, Mum,' she told her. 'But don't worry, it's for the best.' She couldn't bring herself to mention the paperwork that she had signed.

That morning, Margery went to work in Equipment Accounts as usual, but as soon as her shift ended she cycled straight over to the mental hospital. 'Your father's this way,' one of the nurses told her when she arrived. 'Such a lovely old man, isn't he?'

Margery followed the nurse into a little room, where Mr Pott was asleep on a bed. For a moment she almost didn't recognise him. The staff at the hospital had shaved off his bushy moustache, and it made him look a good ten years younger. But there was more to it than that, and it took Margery a moment to work out what it was that seemed so different. For the first time in as long as she could remember, her father was totally free from pain. Margery could still hear the familiar rattling noise every time he breathed in or out, but the breaths were shallower now, and they didn't seem to require such a terrible effort.

The next day, Margery came to see her father again, and again he slept through her entire visit. But she didn't mind that she wasn't able to talk to him – it was reassuring just to see him sleeping so peacefully.

On the third day, she was working in the office at Titchfield when she received a phone call from her eldest sister, Jessie. Their father had passed away early that morning, just as the doctor had predicted.

Margery hung up the phone and sat rooted to the spot for several minutes, as the tears began to stream down her face. After a while, one of the other girls came and put a hand on her shoulder. 'You ought to go home, Corp,' she said gently.

'Oh no, I can't,' Margery protested, weakly. 'I need to get on with my work.'

'It can wait,' the other girl told her. 'Let me go and talk to the squadron leader.'

Margery was issued with a three-day pass, and sent home to be with her mother. By the time she got back to the maltster's house, Jessie and her husband had already arrived. At the funeral a few days later, the four of them were the only mourners. Jessie had paid for the grave, but there was no money left over for a headstone.

Margery never did tell her mother about the paperwork she had signed to admit her father to the asylum, but as she stood and watched him being carefully lowered into the ground, there was no doubt in her mind that she had done the right thing. He was out of his misery now, just like the doctor had promised, and mingled with her sadness at losing him was an overpowering feeling of relief.

Back at RAF Titchfield, preparations were underway for the departure of the girls who were going overseas. Given the circumstances, Margery could certainly have told them that she had changed her mind, that she wanted to be near to her mother at such a difficult time. But that would have felt like backing away from an opportunity, something she was no longer prepared to do.

None of the WAAFs who had volunteered for foreign postings knew where they were going, but that didn't stop friends and colleagues from cracking plenty of jokes on the subject. 'I hope you're good with chopsticks!' Margery's flight sergeant teased her at a leaving party thrown by the girls in Equipment Accounts.

Margery was rather surprised to discover that she was the only one from the office who would be going. Although several of the girls had talked about volunteering for the overseas positions, no one else had actually gone through with it.

The first stage of Margery's journey was to a dispersal camp near Birmingham, where the girls would be kitted out for their eventual destination. She had to change trains in London, and spent most of the journey up to the Midlands sitting next to a young woman who was clutching a small child in her arms, along with a bundle of ragged clothes. 'We just got bombed out,' she told Margery, by way of explanation.

'Oh, I'm sorry,' Margery replied. 'Where are you going?'

'I've got a sister up north, so we're gonna stay with her,' the girl told her. 'Only she don't know about it yet.'

Margery was touched by the sight of the poor woman, carrying all that was left of her worldly belongings. Amid all the excitement that she had felt at the prospect of going abroad, it was a sobering reminder that the war continued to bring misery to people up and down the land.

At the dispersal camp, Margery was given a draft number, which she dutifully painted onto her kitbag – there were no brushes available but she managed to improvise with a twig – and lined up with about thirty other girls to be issued with a khaki shirt, skirt and ankle socks. 'We must be going somewhere hot then,' one of the others commented gleefully.

Then it was time for their injections – tetanus, typhoid and yellow fever – all of which Margery endured bravely. She had come a long way since her basic training at Innsworth, when she had fainted at the mere sight of a needle.

The WAAF girls continued to play a guessing game as to what their destination might be. Surely the yellow fever vaccine meant they were headed for India, one girl reasoned. Another was convinced that the wide-brimmed topee hats they had been issued with indicated a trip to the Far East. But as if to frustrate those desperate to decipher the clues, the topees were collected up again an hour or so after they'd been handed out. Did that mean the girls' destination had been changed, or had someone in the stores simply made a mistake?

That evening the girls were taken by lorry to a railway station, where they boarded a train waiting in a siding. They were each issued with some bread and corned beef for dinner, as well as a cotton 'ditty bag' paid for by the *Daily Mail*, which provided each girl with a notebook, pencils and playing cards to help pass the time on the journey.

A little after midnight the train finally began to move, and the girls woke at 7 a.m. the next morning to find they had arrived in Greenock, Scotland. There they were ushered on board the *Capetown Castle*, a beautiful white ocean liner with a large red-and-black funnel. 'You can leave your kitbags in the cabins and head straight to breakfast,' one of the crewmen told them.

In the dining room, the WAAFs found themselves waited on by men in white jackets, seated at little tables which were covered in crisp tablecloths and vases of flowers. The refined atmosphere made it feel almost as if they were heading off on the grand tour, not being shipped to a military base overseas. 'There's no need to make your beds in the mornings,' another crewman informed Margery. 'The stewards will take care of that for you.'

The WAAFs spent the next few days on board waiting to depart, but despite their impatience to get going the time passed pleasantly enough. Mostly, they were free to do as they wished, but once a day everyone would be summoned on deck to rehearse the 'abandon ship' procedure, to be used if they were hit by an enemy torpedo. In the event of such an attack, Margery's orders were to rush down to the lower decks and collect a box containing flashlights that could be attached to the girls' lifejackets so that they could find each other bobbing around in the sea.

No one really wanted to think about the possibility of a U-boat attack – least of all Margery, who literally couldn't swim to save her life. The girls were haunted by stories they had heard of the sinking of the *Laconia* in September 1942, when more than 1,500 people had perished. But the daily rehearsals of what to do in the event of catastrophe helped to take the edge off their fears.

After a couple of days waiting in harbour, Margery had grown used to the constant gentle rocking of the boat under her feet, and when somebody shouted, 'We're moving!' the news caught her off guard. She rushed up on deck to join the other girls as they slowly pulled away from the quayside.

When the *Capetown Castle* emerged into the Firth of Clyde it was joined by a couple of battleships, which would be escorting the WAAFs across the ocean. Together, the three vessels made their way down the West coast of Scotland and through the Irish Sea, until they found themselves not far from Penzance, at the southernmost tip of the British Isles.

As the ship continued its voyage south, the girls on board turned to watch their country recede into the distance. Before long everything that Margery had ever known was little more than a dot on the horizon. She could only guess what land might lie ahead of her.

9

Kathleen

After many months in the Land Army, Kathleen's body had gradually grown stronger and more resilient as she adapted to the rigours of 12-hour days working the land. Now she was determined to try again with the Navy, so she said her goodbyes to Minnie and the rest of the staff in the strange old house at Bury St Edmunds, and took a train down to London. There she made her way to the national headquarters of the WRNS, which was housed above Drummond's Bank in Trafalgar Square.

But despite her best efforts to convince the women there that she was just what the service needed, they insisted that there still wasn't a place for her. 'I'm sorry,' one of them told her, 'but we've just got too many people volunteering at the moment. Maybe you could try again in another six months.'

Kathleen was disappointed at being turned down by the WRNS for a second time, and it was especially galling to think that while she had been waiting to reapply, other girls had taken the available places. But she couldn't bear the thought of heading back to the house in Bury with her tail between her legs, so instead she began looking for war work in London.

Before long, Kathleen had swapped the jumper and breeches of a land girl for the blue overalls of an ambulance auxiliary. It was far from the high couture of the tailored Wren uniform that she had long coveted, but at least, she reasoned, the new job would bring with it different challenges – and, hopefully, less back-breaking work.

Since she didn't drive, Kathleen was paired up with a girl who did – a young woman called Hilde with whom she was soon sharing a small flat in Chiswick. The two girls hit it off instantly, and when Kathleen learned Hilde's sad story it only cemented the bond. 'My husband walked out as soon as he found out I was pregnant,' Hilde confided one evening, explaining that her daughter Joy was now living with a family in the countryside while she worked on the ambulances to support her.

Hilde and Kathleen's ambulance – in reality a converted van – was based at the offices of United Dairies in Chiswick, a location they came to know extremely well as they spent night after night there sitting around waiting for the phone to ring. The other volunteers included several members of the same family, who had all volunteered together and were all actors. Kathleen and Hilde soon grew used to being hugged and kissed effusively whenever they came into the office, and to being addressed exclusively as 'darling'. More of a trial were the histrionic rows between the father and his eldest daughter, which seemed to erupt on a daily basis and frequently descended into furious swearing matches.

On the whole, though, it was a quiet time for the men and women working on the ambulances. Since the London Blitz had come to an end in May 1941, German attacks on the capital had grown increasingly infrequent, limited to the occasional 'nuisance raids' on targets of no military significance. But while they might be little more than a nuisance as far as winning the war was concerned, these small, sporadic attacks could be deadly for the poor souls caught up in them.

The first time Hilde and Kathleen were called out, it was to a pub in Hammersmith which had suffered a direct hit. They hopped in their little van and sped over as quickly as possible, reaching the bombsite within ten minutes.

By the time the girls arrived, there were plenty of other people already on the scene. 'No point going in there,' a Special Constable told Kathleen, as she gazed in horror at the pile of rubble where only minutes before the pub had stood. 'There were a load of troops in the cellar when it hit. The pipes down there burst and the lot of them drowned before we could get them out.'

As the policeman turned and walked off into the darkness, Kathleen became aware of a dog barking somewhere nearby. She followed the sound to a house adjacent to the pub, which had also been badly damaged. Most of the front wall had come down, and Kathleen walked through a space where the door had once stood into what was left of the living room.

Inside she found a black-and-white sheepdog, which by now was howling plaintively, a few feet away from the body of an old man who was evidently its master. 'It's all right,' she told the distraught animal, in as calm a voice as she could manage. She didn't dare reach out a hand to stroke it, in case it lashed out and bit her in fear.

Kathleen continued to make cooing noises at the dog while she knelt down to examine the old man. He was alive, but only just. A large part of his face had been blown off by the explosion, and his breathing was shallow. She could tell at once that he had no chance of surviving his injuries.

Kathleen took a towel and wrapped it around the man's head. Then she sat on the floor, gently cradling him, all the while whispering to the frantic dog, 'It's all right, don't worry, it's all right.'

Within a couple of minutes the last spark of life had departed and Kathleen set the man's lifeless body down on the floor. Then she went to summon Hilde, and between them they heaved him onto a stretcher and carried him out to their ambulance.

As they drove away, she could still hear the poor dog howling, rooted to the spot in the room where its master had died.

The bomb had left no survivors for the girls to transport to the local hospital, so instead they drove straight to Hammersmith Cemetery, where a man on the gate directed them towards the mortuary. There were so many bodies coming in that night that the building was already full, and as the corpses arrived they were being laid out on the pavement outside. Kathleen tried not to look at the faces, but she couldn't help noticing that many of them had been terribly disfigured and some bodies were missing arms or legs.

By the time Kathleen and Hilde had got the old man out of the ambulance and laid him out alongside the other victims of the night's raid, their shift was coming to an end. They returned the ambulance to the United Dairies offices, and trudged back to their little flat. It was only once they were on their way home that the horror of the evening overcame them, and they both had to stop and vomit by the side of the road.

As the weeks and months went on, Kathleen and Hilde grew accustomed to the horrors of the air raids. Collecting severed arms and legs in an old tarpaulin and matching them up with dead bodies they had found became routine, as did braking suddenly when huge craters appeared in the middle of the road in front of them. They got used to sleepless nights and uneaten meals, and to frequent stops to throw up in the gutter.

Some of the girls' call-outs were almost surreal. One night they arrived at a house that had been ripped open by the blast from a bomb, only to find a woman sitting naked in a bath on the first floor, fully exposed to the street below. She was covered in blood from head to foot, and was screaming hysterically as a fireman climbed up a ladder to bring her down.

Although the work Kathleen was doing was emotionally draining, living in the capital did have its advantages, as it meant that she was able to meet up with Arnold from time to time. His parents lived in Clapham and he came down to London to visit them whenever he had leave.

Kathleen's dashing fiancé certainly knew how to show a girl a good time, and would wine and dine her in the smartest establishments he could find. One night they went to see a Polish orchestra perform at the Royal Albert Hall; another they took in a play on Shaftesbury Avenue. Arnold even took Kathleen to the famous Windmill Theatre in Soho, where they gawped at the tableaus of naked women.

As time went on, however, the horrors of working on the ambulances took their toll on Kathleen, and when an opportunity arose to take on some slightly less distressing employment, she decided that the time had come for her to leave. Her mother had heard that the hospital she worked at in Cambridge was looking for nursing auxiliaries, and suggested that Kathleen should join her there. 'You could live at home and save money on the rent,' she pointed out.

It was too good an opportunity to pass up, and before long Kathleen had handed in her notice at the ambulance depot. When she told Hilde of her plan, the other girl was sympathetic. 'I can't blame you for leaving, Kath,' she told her. 'I just wish you the best of luck.'

*

A few days later, Kathleen found herself seated in front of a couple of senior nurses in an office at Addenbrooke's Hospital. 'So, you're Mrs Skin's daughter?' asked a grey-haired matron with a no-nonsense manner, as she scribbled something on a piece of paper in front of her.

'That's right,' Kathleen replied.

'Mrs Skin is a natural,' said the other woman, a ward sister of around 40. '*Very* sympathetic with the patients.'

'Do you have any nursing experience yourself?' asked the Matron.

'Not exactly,' Kathleen replied, 'but I've worked as an ambulance auxiliary, and before that I was a nanny, so I'm used to looking after sick children.'

'Well, I'm sure we can find something for you to do here,' the Matron said briskly.

Soon Kathleen was kitted out in yet another new uniform – this time a white apron and nurse's hat – and learning how to make a bed, alongside around 20 other new auxiliaries. Under the watchful eye of the Matron, the girls worked their way around an empty ward, practising their hospital corners on all the beds, and then learning to lift a life-size dummy in and out of them. For Kathleen, who had mastered the procedure after about two or three goes, the endless repetition felt unbearable, but the girls weren't allowed to move on to the next lesson until every one of them had changed 50 beds in a row.

Next came crash courses in blanket-bathing their life-size dummies, and the correct procedure for emptying and cleaning out bedpans. 'Well done, everyone,' the Matron told them at the end of the day. 'Tomorrow you'll be putting what you've learned into practice.'

The next morning, Kathleen reported for duty bright and early. She had been sent not to Addenbrooke's Hospital itself, but to an overspill annexe that had been set up two miles away in the Ley's School – the same site, in fact, where Arnold and his friends had been billeted when she met him at the King's carol concert. It was a grand old red-brick building, with its own chapel and a beautiful lawn at the back – if anything it looked less like a school and more like one of the old colleges.

But the salubrious environment was certainly not matched by the work she was expected to do. After a brief stint putting her bed-making skills to use as assistant to the duty nurse, Kathleen was placed on toilet duty. As well as emptying the bedpans, this meant escorting those patients who were less steady on their feet to the loos, and helping them do their business. It was not the most pleasant of tasks, especially with the older men, who seemed to have no control over where their emissions ended up, but Kathleen always managed it with good humour.

As the days went on, the patients on the ward got to know and like Kathleen, and she began to grow fond of them too. One day, she came in to find that one of the men, an old fellow called Mr Smith who was suffering from bowel cancer, had gone missing. 'Have you seen him?' one of the other nurses asked her anxiously. 'He's been gone from his bed for a good hour now.'

'I'll go and look for him,' Kathleen replied, setting off down the long school corridor in search of the elusive patient.

She stopped at the nearest toilet to check if Mr Smith was in there, and as she opened the door she was hit by a smell that almost knocked her off her feet. Covering her nose with her hand, she cautiously went inside.

Mr Smith was sitting on the toilet, sobbing miserably. The floor all around him was covered in diarrhoea, and it had soaked through his pyjamas as well. The poor man had struggled to get to the toilet by himself, but he hadn't quite made it in time. 'I'm sorry,' he said feebly, when he saw Kathleen standing in the doorway. 'I don't think I can get up yet.'

As he sat there, red-faced and covered in his own excrement, Mr Smith looked like a broken man, and despite the disgusting smell – which left Kathleen struggling not to retch – she felt desperately sorry for him. 'It's all right, Mr S,' she said, trying to sound as cheerful as possible. 'I'll get you cleaned up in no time. You just wait here while I go and fetch a bucket.'

It took a good half-hour's cleaning before both Mr Smith and the toilet were fit for public view. But as Kathleen scrubbed away she made sure not to let her own discomfort show, keeping up a string of jokes and upbeat conversation in an attempt to raise her patient's spirits. By the time they left the little cubicle together – he leaning on her arm as she led him back to his bed – the old boy was almost back to his normal self.

'You know, you should think about nursing full time,' one of the older nurses told her, when she got back to the ward. 'You're a natural, just like your mum.'

'Thank you,' Kathleen replied. 'But I can't. I'm going into the Navy.' Despite her two rejections, she hadn't given up on her dream just yet.

Kathleen knew that getting too attached to the patients could make things difficult, especially since deaths on the ward were not uncommon. When one of their charges passed away, the nurses responded with a minimum of fuss, drawing the curtains around the bed and telling the other patients, 'He needs to get some rest.' Then, in the middle of the night, a couple of men would come and take the body away – and by the next morning, when the rest of the ward awoke, someone new would be lying in the bed.

But, inevitably, she became closer to some patients than others. When a young British soldier, Private Glover, was admitted to the ward suffering from cancer of the throat, Kathleen couldn't help feeling sorry for him. He was a Northerner and didn't know a soul in Cambridge, so when he was discharged after a short spell of treatment, she was determined to make sure he didn't feel lonely. Kathleen invited him round for tea at her mother's house, and even arranged a trip with some other young soldiers for her next day off from the hospital. The plan was to walk up the River Cam to Grantchester and spend the day there, watching the water go by.

But as Kathleen and the others gathered to begin the expedition, there was no sign of Private Glover. When she arrived at the Ley's School the next day, she asked one of the other nurses if the hospital had received any news of him.

'Oh, didn't you know?' the other girl replied. 'He was brought back in here yesterday, and he died.'

'He died?' Kathleen repeated, dumbstruck. 'But I thought he was almost ready to go home.'

For many days afterwards, she struggled to hold back tears whenever she thought of the poor young man, and she wished she had been with him at the end.

For Kathleen, it was a great relief that at the end of every shift she had her mother's little house on Pembroke Street to come home to. Mrs Skin was delighted at having her youngest daughter back with her, especially since her youngest son, Lance, had recently joined the Army. Much to Kathleen's chagrin, she was now the only one of her siblings who wasn't in the forces.

Before long, however, the Skins found themselves preparing for a major family reunion. Kathleen's oldest sister Maevis had got engaged to a man she'd met in the Army, and she wanted the wedding to be held in Cambridge. Her intended, a Sergeant Davies from Wales, didn't exactly sound like the ideal son-in-law – as he confessed in a letter to Mrs Skin, he had got another girl 'in trouble' when he was 18, and ten years later was still paying maintenance to keep her and the child.

But despite this blot against his character, it was clear that he was devoted to Maevis, and when Mrs Skin saw how happy he made her daughter, she felt she had no choice but to offer her blessing. After all, her family in South Africa had done their best to dissuade her from her own marriage, and despite everything that had happened to her husband later, she had never regretted that decision.

The wedding was set to take place at a beautiful medieval church called St Botolph's, and with the date fixed, the siblings all put in for leave from their various forces so that they could attend. Mrs Skin set about preparing for the big day, visiting all her friends to cadge a cup of flour here and a pound of sugar there until she had enough ingredients to make a decent wedding cake. She managed to borrow a lovely white gown, altering it herself to fit Maevis, and even booked a band to play at the reception. By the standards of wartime weddings it was set to be a splendid affair. All that was missing was the father of the bride to walk his daughter down the aisle, since poor Mr Skin was languishing in the asylum.

On the day of the wedding, the family set out for the church together. Maevis was looking immaculate in her beautiful white gown, while her sisters had their best dresses on as bridesmaids. The neighbours all stood on their doorsteps to watch them go. 'Fancy spending all that money at a time like this,'

Kathleen heard one of them mutter. She only hoped that her mother hadn't heard it.

But there was little that could have dented Mrs Skin's good mood that morning. Getting her three daughters married off had always been a concern to her, so she was over the moon that her eldest was finally tying the knot.

When they arrived at the church, the vicar was waiting outside. 'The congregation are all seated,' he told Maevis. 'We're just waiting for the bridegroom.'

'Oh,' Maevis replied, with an awkward little laugh. 'It's not like him to be late.'

'Well, not to worry,' the vicar said, smiling reassuringly. 'I'm sure he'll be here before long.'

But as the minutes ticked by, still there was no sign of Maevis's fiancé. Mrs Skin was doing her best to keep her daughter from becoming upset, reassuring her that she had heard from him the day before and he was definitely coming – perhaps his train had just been held up.

After three quarters of an hour, though, the vicar emerged from the church again, and this time the smile was gone from his face. 'I'm very sorry,' he said, 'but I have another wedding party arriving in ten minutes. I'm going to have to tell the congregation to leave now.'

Maevis nodded silently, the tears already beginning to stream down her face. 'All right, thank you, vicar,' Mrs Skin said quietly, as she led her distraught daughter home.

Back at the house on Pembroke Street, the family changed out of their best clothes, and gathered round in the little living room. There was nothing anyone could say to make Maevis feel any better.

On Monday morning, Maevis went back to her ATS camp, and the other brothers and sisters all departed for their wartime postings as well. Once again it was just Kathleen and her mum left at the little house. But news of the failed wedding had spread, and the neighbours were muttering once more. 'You know he got a girl into trouble before,' Kathleen heard one of them tell another.

Being stood up at the altar was every girl's worst nightmare, and Kathleen wished to God it could have happened to anyone other than her favourite sister. She didn't say anything, but privately she couldn't help wondering what on earth had caused Sergeant Davies's change of heart. Maevis tried contacting the War Office to see if they had any information on his whereabouts, but they told her they could do nothing to help her – and she never heard from her fiancé again.

It was many months since Kathleen had clapped eyes on her own intended, Arnold. They wrote to each other regularly, but since his work with the Army seemed to take him all over the country, it was only rarely that they could snatch any time together. One day, though, Kathleen was coming to the end of a long shift at the hospital when a girl rushed up to her and announced breathlessly, 'There's an Army officer outside who wants to see you.' Kathleen knew at once that it must be him.

Unfortunately, she had spent all day in the small operating theatre which was housed in the school's basement, assisting one of the surgeons on a string of tonsillectomies. As the news came of Arnold's arrival she was wearing an apron covered with blood, and holding a metal bucket full of all the tonsils that had been removed. But the girl's urgent tone made it clear that there was no time to go and get changed.

Kathleen ran up the stairs two at a time until she reached the school entrance. Looking out across the perfectly manicured lawn she could see Arnold, standing in his Army greatcoat while the rain lashed down upon him.

But the weather was the last thing on Kathleen's mind. She rushed over to her fiancé, dropping the bucket of tonsils as she ran, and pulling the bloody apron over her head. As she reached him she threw her arms around his neck and he swept her into a passionate embrace.

'I'm afraid I can't stay more than a few moments, darling,' Arnold said, gazing earnestly into Kathleen's eyes. There was a pained look on his face that she had never seen before. 'I've come to say goodbye,' he told her sadly.

'Goodbye?' she repeated. 'But you've only just arrived.'

'We're being shipped out,' Arnold explained. 'I can't tell you any more about it, but I could be gone for some time.'

He squeezed her so tight that for a moment Kathleen could barely breathe. 'You know I love you, don't you?' he asked her.

'Yes, of course,' Kathleen replied. 'And I love you too – so much.' She clung to him, wishing with all her heart that somehow she could make him stay longer.

But there was nothing either of them could do to delay Arnold's departure. 'My men are waiting for me,' he said quietly. 'I'm sorry, darling, but I must go now.'

There was just time for one final kiss, and then he turned and walked away from her.

Kathleen watched, helpless, as he disappeared into the rain.

10

Jessie

When Jessie returned to 518 mixed battery at the end of her compassionate leave, she found a bundle of letters there waiting for her, tied up with a piece of string. She teased the package open and out fell the last two weeks' worth of messages she had written to Jim.

There was also a letter from her late husband's commanding officer, informing her that Jim had been buried at a cemetery 40 miles west of Tunis, and offering Jessie his condolences. From it she learned that, far from being killed instantly as she had hoped, Jim had in fact been badly wounded in a German attack. 'I saw him taken away in an ambulance, and later heard that he had died,' the CO told her, doing his best to reassure Jessie that he was sure Jim had not suffered.

But Jessie found it hard to take much comfort from the officer's words. After all, wasn't that what people always said? She would never know for sure what Jim's last moments had been like, but in her heart she felt that he had probably suffered greatly.

The fact that Jim was really gone was beginning to sink in, but the dazed feeling that Jessie had experienced before had been replaced by a terrible hollowness. Knowing that her husband would never be with her again, she could no longer imagine a future for herself, and her life in the present seemed utterly pointless too. She stopped playing the piano and barely even ate, only forcing down just enough food to keep going. She continued to apply herself to her work, knowing that if she made a mistake she would be letting other people down, but as she stood working the height-and-range finder throughout the long nights on the gun-site, she felt strangely detached from what was happening, as if someone else was in control of her body.

Determined to keep the pain of Jim's death at bay, Jessie proceeded to destroy what relics remained of their love, burning the photos she had kept of him, as well as the letters they had written each other. The only memento she kept was her wedding ring, which she continued to wear.

Although she knew her friends wanted to help her, Jessie couldn't bring herself to burden them with the misfortune she had suffered. She didn't even feel she could talk about Jim's death to Elsie Acres, in case it brought back difficult memories of her fiancé dying at Dunkirk.

But the camp offered few opportunities to grieve privately either. In fact the first time Jessie found herself alone for any length of time was when she was put on guard duty. Previously she had passed the nights in the sentry-box humming songs to herself or reciting old poems she had learned, but now she found that one sonnet in particular was playing over and over in her mind.

Remember me when I am gone away,
Gone far away into the silent land;
When you can no more hold me by the hand,
Nor I half turn to go yet turning stay.
Remember me when no more day by day
You tell me of our future that you plann'd:
Only remember me; you understand

It will be late to counsel then or pray.
Yet if you should forget me for a while
And afterwards remember, do not grieve:
For if the darkness and corruption leave
A vestige of the thoughts that once I had,
Better by far you should forget and smile
Than that you should remember and be sad.

Jessie had learned Christina Rossetti's poem at school, and had always thought it was rather beautiful. But now, as she sat alone in the dark and the words tumbled around in her head, she was beginning to feel she truly understood it.

One of the battery's officers, Second Subaltern Torla Tidman, was more sensitive than most and, aware that a recently bereaved woman might appreciate a bit of extra privacy, she began sending Jessie off on her bicycle to perform various errands away from the camp. 'There's no need to hurry back,' she told her kindly.

One day while Jessie was out on one of Lieutenant Tidman's chores, she got talking to a local shipyard worker called Jim, who lived with his family in a little bungalow a couple of fields away from the gun park. When he heard that the ack-ack girls were running out of Silvo to polish their buttons with, he offered to get some for Jessie.

A few days later, she received a note at the camp, telling her to come and collect the package. When she arrived at the little house, Jim and his wife Hetty insisted she come in for a cup of tea. Their two boys gazed in fascination at the young woman in her smart khaki uniform, while Jim went off to fetch the tin of polish.

'It's very kind of you to get this for us,' Jessie told him when he returned.

'Oh well, we've got to do our bit for you girls on the guns, haven't we?' Jim replied. 'But there is one thing you can do for us in return. Next time you're about to fire one of them things, give us a bit of wárning, will you?'

Despite herself, Jessie couldn't help laughing. 'You want to listen out for the word "Engage!"' she told Jim. 'Once you hear that, the next thing's going to be "Fire!"'

Jessie spent the rest of the evening in Jim and Hetty's little kitchen, answering all their questions about life in the ATS. Somehow their cosy bungalow seemed cocooned from the harsh world outside. She felt safe there, and soon she was visiting the couple whenever she had an afternoon off.

Back at the camp, the other girls had been begging Jessie to come and play the piano like she used to, and after a few weeks she finally relented. Perhaps, she thought, it would help everyone else forget their worries, even if she couldn't forget hers. She didn't want to carry on being the grief-stricken widow, bringing down everyone around her. She would just have to learn to put on a mask, she told herself – the face of someone who was coping, who could talk and sing and laugh along with her old friends, even if inside she felt nothing.

Before long, Jessie was back at the piano every night, taking requests from the noisy crowd in the NAAFI. She learned to fake the enjoyment she had once felt at the sound of music, and nobody seemed to be any the wiser. But try as she might to convince the other girls that she was back to her old self, there was one tune she just couldn't play any more – 'We'll Meet Again'.

*

By now, 518 mixed battery had started using radar, and a group of girls had been brought in who knew all about the strange equipment that had been set up around the camp. The new arrivals kept to themselves and never spoke about their work to anyone else, something which lent them quite an air of mystery. Jessie got the feeling that they saw themselves as a cut above the ordinary ack-ack girls, and the impression was reinforced by the fact that they were exempted from fatigues such as guard duty and peeling potatoes in the cookhouse.

The new radar equipment required regular maintenance, and groups of male technicians from the REME – Royal Electrical and Mechanical Engineers – were soon seen around the camp as well, helping to calibrate the machines. One day, Jessie had been put to work raking some cut grass, when a lorry carrying half a dozen radar specialists drove past. A young man with curly dark hair shouted out in a thick Scottish accent, 'Yer making a right mess of that, yer know.'

'Mind your own business!' Jessie retorted.

But to her surprise, when she went into the NAAFI for a cup of tea a few hours later, the dark-haired young man came and sat down opposite her, cradling a pint of beer. 'Did ye get yer raking done, then?' he asked, taking a swig of his drink.

'Yes, thank you,' Jessie replied.

'I'm relieved to hear it,' he told her. 'Must have taken you a while, I imagine.' He was soon chattering away in his melodic Scottish brogue, telling Jessie all about his work in the REME and asking her questions about the camp. His group were to be stationed there for the next few weeks, he told her, and although they would be sleeping in their lorry, they were going to have to share most of the camp's facilities, including the canteen. 'Wherever we go, I always make sure to get friendly with the cooks as soon as possible,' he told Jessie. 'That way, if there's anything left over, I'll be the one to get it.'

Jessie looked at the young man, with his handsome face and sparkling greenish-brown eyes. She could imagine that his job travelling from camp to camp suited him very well, and his confident, easy manner probably won over the ack-ack girls wherever he went.

But his charms were wasted on Jessie – her heart was soldered shut. 'I've got to go,' she said, finishing her cup of tea. 'Nice meeting you.'

'Aye, maybe see you again,' he said. Then he was off to find someone else to chat to.

A few days later, when 'C' Section had the evening off, Elsie Acres suggested to Jessie that they should go to a dance in Barton upon Humber together. Instinctively, she wanted to decline – the pleasure she used to get from dancing had all but disappeared. But her friend was insistent. 'Oh go on, Jessie,' she said. 'It'll do you good. And if you don't come, who will I go with?'

'All right then,' Jessie replied, remembering the decision she had taken not to bring other people down.

It was a good three-mile walk to Barton, and the girls took a route along a railway track. When they arrived at the little hall, Jessie saw a crowd made up of equal parts uniforms and civilian clothes.

As she entered the room, one of the uniformed men turned around and she recognised the cheeky Scottish lad she had talked to in the NAAFI. As soon as he saw her, he made his way over and asked her to dance.

The number was a foxtrot, and the young man, whose name turned out to be Donald Macbeth – 'Mac' to his friends – was an excellent dancer. But as she let herself be guided around the room by him Jessie felt totally detached from the experience, as if she was looking down on herself from above. It was a feeling that she had grown used to ever since Jim had died.

'You know, I heard you were widowed,' Mac said softly. 'That must have been terrible.'

'It could happen to anyone, and it happened to me,' Jessie replied simply.

Although Mac was no older than she was, he too had already suffered his share of bereavement. When he was just 18, his mother had gone to bed with a headache and never woken up, having died of a massive brain haemorrhage in the night. Not long afterwards, Mac had volunteered for the Army.

But neither he nor Jessie had any desire to talk about their losses, and for the rest of the dance, and several more afterwards, he kept up a steady stream of light-hearted banter. Jessie just let it wash over her, smiling now and then when it seemed like an appropriate moment, but still feeling nothing inside.

After that night, whenever Mac saw Jessie in the NAAFI he would always stop and have a beer with her while she drank her tea. They soon discovered a shared interest in music – Mac was a violin player, and specialised in traditional Scottish reels. When he heard that Jessie was part of the camp band, he begged her to let him come and play with them.

For the next few weeks, while Mac and his team were stationed at Humberside, his fiddle became a key part of the musical ensemble in the NAAFI, alongside Jessie's piano and Stan's trumpet. The band played the same popular tunes that they always had, but now the evenings always seemed to end with everyone dancing the Gay Gordons.

When they weren't performing, Jessie and Mac often danced together. As he laughed and joked she did her best to play along, never letting her carefully cultivated mask slip. But underneath it all she still felt she was living a lie.

After almost a year on Humberside, orders finally came for 518 mixed battery to move on. Jessie packed up her kitbag and boarded a lorry, filled with relief. After the horrors of the air raids and the pain of losing Jim, the camp had too many sad memories for her to regret leaving it.

To begin with, instead of being sent to a new gun-site, the battery was ordered to a practice camp in Whitby, on the Yorkshire coast, where they would be able to hone their skills again without the threat of actual bombing raids. As in Sheringham, they were billeted in the town's empty hotels, and Jessie couldn't help recalling the time that Jim had arrived in the lobby of the Grand Hotel to meet her, and been shocked at the sight of his fiancée in her ATS uniform. He had always worried about her job in ack-ack being dangerous, and yet it was him they should have been worrying about all along.

The gun-site in Whitby was on top of the cliffs, facing directly out to sea, and every day the girls had to walk up 199 steps in order to reach it. The climb was exhausting, and often they would stop and rest on an old, flat stone to catch their breath.

One day, Jessie lingered a little longer than the others to admire the view. She had always loved the sea, and if the circumstances had been different she knew she would have enjoyed the posting in Whitby. It was the height of summer and the little town was bustling with holidaymakers. Down below she could see happy couples strolling hand-in-hand along the sea front, some of them with small children excitedly running ahead of them. Looking out to sea, Jessie was struck by the beauty of the place. Jim would have liked it here, she thought to herself.

But Jim was never going to be here, she realised a moment later. He was never going to see any of this. The two of them would not be walking along the beach together, they would have no children running ahead of them. He was gone – really, and truly, and for ever.

The realisation hit her with a physical force, making her gasp and then choke, as sobs rose up in her throat and the tears she had been holding in for so long finally came gushing out of her.

Alone on the cliff, staring out across the beautiful sea, Jessie cried and cried and cried, until at last she was left with nothing but a strange sense of calm.

11

Margery

Margery sat cross-legged on the deck of the *Capetown Castle* as it sailed on through the Mediterranean. The sun was beating down, but the fresh sea breeze meant that it never felt too overpowering. The only problem the WAAFs on the boat had encountered was that their new Airtex khaki shirts were easily penetrated by the rays, leaving little pin-pricks of sunburn dotted across their backs.

Other than that, the three-week voyage had been a dream. Margery was sharing a cabin with a sweet Scottish girl with curly brown hair called Elspeth, who for some reason seemed to rather look up to her. Since there was nothing much to see on the journey except endless, still waters, they passed their time on deck playing cards or dice from the ship's games cupboard. Often they were joined by a stocky, middle-aged ex-RAF man called Bob, who was on his way to join the British Overseas Airways Company as a storeman. Clearly a little lonely, he was happy to find a couple of girls willing to listen to tales about his beloved wife back home.

Suddenly there was a shout of 'We're coming into port!' and Margery leapt up from her chair, dropping the cards she was holding. Squinting into the sunlight, she could indeed see land in the far distance. A steward was passing and she ran over to him. 'Excuse me – where are we?' she asked.

'Port Said,' the man replied.

'Oh,' said Margery, baffled. 'Where's that?'

'Egypt!' he told her, with a chuckle, before carrying on along the deck.

Margery watched him go in disbelief. She had read about Egypt during her bible studies at Sunday school, but had always assumed that, like the Garden of Eden, it was just a made-up place. The thought that she was about to set foot in it was hard to grapple with.

Yet her first glimpse of this fabled land, as the boat came into harbour, was even more confusing. Looming over Port Said from the top of a hotel was a very familiar figure – even to a non-whisky-drinker: an enormous cut-out of the Johnnie Walker man, looking resplendent in his top hat and tails. Margery could only blink in astonishment.

The Allied victory in Egypt in November 1942, when General Montgomery's forces finally overpowered those of the German commander Rommel, had proved a major turning point in the war, and all over England church bells had rung in celebration. Victory in the Middle East meant a supply route from Europe to Asia via the Suez Canal, as well as access to oil from Iran and Iraq. 'This is not the end,' Churchill had declared at a banquet in the City of London. 'It is not even the beginning of the end. But it is, perhaps, the end of the beginning.'

But in Egypt itself, not everyone was so thrilled at the recent victory. Some Egyptians had been taken in by rumours spread by Axis agents, who claimed that Hitler was actually a Muslim whose intention was to liberate the country. For decades they had yearned for full independence from Britain, and the influx of over 100,000 Allied troops had not exactly changed their minds. Aside from the occasional bouts of loutish behaviour, carjacking and vandalism, even the well-behaved British soldiers had contributed to the suffering of the local people. Spending up to £3 million per month, the foreigners had pushed prices up by two-thirds – well beyond the means of the Egyptian working classes, who had seen no corresponding rise in their wages.

By the time Margery and her cohort of WAAFs arrived in Egypt, many of the British soldiers had already begun to leave the country. But there was still plenty of work to be done, especially when it came to maintenance and administration. Margery's draft of girls was part of a 2,000-strong WAAF contingent arriving in the Middle East, most of them to take up clerical jobs. The Air Force had originally hoped to employ locals for this kind of work, and 700 girls, mostly Palestinians, had donned the 'khaki drill' overseas uniform. But still more womanpower was needed, and since conscription outside Britain was out of the question they had summoned the WAAFs from home to fill the gap.

When Margery and the other airwomen disembarked from their ship, they were marched to a nearby railway station and onto a white wooden train bound for Cairo. As it left the station, they were given their rations for the day – a hard-boiled egg and a bar of chocolate, which the girls were advised to break open and check for maggots. Purified water was distributed from what looked like a large petrol can. All in all, it was a stark contrast to the weeks of silver service on board the *Capetown Castle*.

The train journey took six hours, and once they had left Port Said, there seemed to be nothing on either side except sand, stretching as far as the eye could see. To Margery, it was hard to comprehend that so much of the stuff could exist in one place, and the more she stared, the more surreal she found it.

At one point the train slowed at a level crossing and three Arab women, dressed from head to toe in long, black robes, peered in at the WAAFs. Their faces were almost completely covered by their traditional veiled clothing, but their wide eyes revealed an undisguised fascination at the sight of the red-faced British girls with their bare arms and legs sticking out of their khaki uniforms. 'Now we know what the animals in the zoo feel like,' Margery whispered to Elspeth. She felt quite relieved when the train sped up and continued on its way.

At Cairo the girls were transferred onto the back of some Air Force lorries – known locally as 'gharries', after the horse-drawn carts popular in the area – and set off on the half-hour drive to Almaza transit camp, where thousands of troops arriving in the Middle East were processed. Before dinner, they were taken to their billets to drop off their bags, and were shocked to discover that they would be sleeping in nothing more than large holes in the ground, two to a pitch, with a piece of canvas on top of them. Sleeping below ground level might make sense in the blazing Egyptian summer, but the primitive conditions came as quite a shock, especially after such a long journey.

While the girls waited at Almaza to find out where in Egypt they would be sent, their days were filled with lectures, medical checks and vaccinations. When Margery enquired what one of the many needles going into her arm was for, the medic replied, 'Bubonic plague'. At first she thought he must be joking, but the look on his face was deadly serious.

In one lecture, the WAAFs were warned to be careful how they behaved around the locals. Their exposed flesh meant they could be mistaken for loose women, they were told, so to avoid any unwanted attention they were instructed to walk in a dignified manner at all times. Egyptian restaurants, meanwhile, were strictly off limits, since eating fruit and vegetables that had been washed in Nile water was a sure way to contract dysentery. So far, Margery thought, the fabled land of Egypt was sounding like a rather grim place.

Just when Margery and Elspeth were beginning to wonder what on earth they'd let themselves in for, their day was brightened by the arrival of Bob, the former RAF man they had met on the boat. He turned up at the camp gates in a staff car, along with another older chap, who was tall, thin and very bronzed.

'This is Teddy Deason,' Bob told the girls excitedly as his friend shook their hands. 'I couldn't believe it when I bumped into him at breakfast at the Helio Hotel – my wife used to be his secretary back home!'

Teddy was handsome, in an older-man sort of way, and distinctly debonair. 'I hear you two have just arrived in Egypt,' he told the girls with a smile. 'Bob thought you might appreciate a tour of Cairo.'

'You'll be in safe hands with Teddy,' Mac chipped in, having clocked the nervous look on Margery's face. 'He's been here for years. Knows the place like the back of his hand.'

Margery and Elspeth glanced at each other, before taking in the miserable sight of the camp all around them. 'We'd love to come,' Margery told Teddy.

As the staff car sped towards Cairo, they passed through the city's smartest suburb, Heliopolis, where Teddy and Bob were both staying in one of the many European-style hotels. As they drove, Teddy told the girls a little more about himself. He was married, a squadron leader in the RAF, and worked in security in Cairo. He had the air of a man of the world, and Margery felt at ease in his company.

When they reached downtown Cairo, Teddy began offering a running commentary on the city and its history. 'As you can see, the centre of town was inspired by Haussmann's Paris,' he told the girls, as they peered out at tall, elegant brick buildings that stood along wide streets lined with palm trees.

They turned a corner and Teddy pointed out of the window at an enormous building with a grand, pillared façade. 'And that,' he told them, 'is the opera house built by Ismail the Magnificent to celebrate the opening of the Suez Canal.'

As they drove closer to the town centre, the traffic was becoming heavier. Margery could see a mixture of military vehicles, European cars such as Fiats and Austin Sevens, battered local buses and trams, and tired-looking donkeys pulling wooden carts piled high with vegetables. With the windows down, the assault on the senses was overpowering – a heady mix of exhaust fumes, animal manure and incense.

In among the European-style buildings, the minarets of various mosques provided a reminder of Cairo's Muslim population, and in the distance Margery could see a huge Islamic citadel towering over the city. The Cairene people, meanwhile, were as cosmopolitan a mix as the architecture suggested, and heads wrapped in turbans bobbed alongside khaki caps, bowler hats and red fezes. Next to the city's rich European class and large military population, the ordinary Egyptians looked ragged and impoverished. Many of them were begging in the street, and outside the grand hotels native guides in long coats crowded around, in the hope of being summoned by a wealthy visitor.

'First things first – we *must* take you to Groppi's,' Teddy announced. 'It's the most famous tea-room in Egypt, and the ice-cream is to die for.'

The car dropped them off outside a building that reminded Margery of a Lyon's Corner House back home in England. As they passed through the doors into the glitzy interior she breathed in the sweet scent of patisserie and coffee. After years of rationing, the smell of so much sugar and butter was intense.

Teddy ordered the girls a couple of 'Marilyn' ice-creams, a dessert which he assured them was one of the finest in the world. It turned out to be shockingly rich and packed with little pieces of fruit, and as Margery tasted it, she closed her eyes in pure bliss. Perhaps Egypt wasn't such a rough place after all, she thought.

But if Cairo in the daytime was a pleasant surprise, by night it was something else again. When the sun went down, the city lit up like a fairyland, and for girls who had grown used to black-out Britain, the effect was spectacular.

That evening, over dinner at the Lyset Hotel, the little party debated what to do next. 'I think it's time these ladies sampled Cairo's nightlife,' Teddy announced, with a twinkle in his eye. Mac huffed and puffed, protesting that he didn't think it was quite right to take the girls to a nightclub, but it was obvious that Teddy was going to get his way.

The club was a luxurious establishment, with tables and chairs laid out in cabaret style and a raised platform for dancing. Looking around her, Margery could see that the other patrons were the *crème de la crème* of Cairene society – European men and women in smart suits and glamorous ball gowns, mingling with important-looking Egyptians in traditional Arab dress. 'Those are our friends the sheiks,' Teddy told her, following her gaze.

He ordered a round of gin and lemons for the table. 'This place is where you come to see and be seen,' he told Margery. 'In fact, I think you've been noticed already – someone just offered me two sheep and a goat for you!'

Margery stared at Teddy, horrified. Then she saw from the broad smile spreading across his face that he was only joking.

Suddenly, the lights in the room were dimmed and the first of the night's floor acts came on – a belly dancer dressed in a skimpy red costume, embellished with glittering gold sequins. As the woman began to writhe suggestively, moving closer and closer to the tables as she undulated around the room, Margery didn't quite know where to look. It was a mesmerising sight – although the spell was rather broken when the girl paused to scratch herself midway through the routine.

'Well, I think we've seen enough here,' Bob said, as the act came to a close, reminding Teddy that the girls had a 10.30 p.m. curfew.

Teddy acquiesced, but not before reminding Margery and Elspeth that, as squadron leader, he had authority to sign their late passes if they ever wanted a proper night out.

By the time Teddy's staff car dropped them back at the gates of Almaza camp, the two WAAFs were utterly exhausted. They felt as if they had experienced enough new sensations for a lifetime, and as they lay in their little hole in the ground that night, their heads were swimming with the bright lights of Cairo.

The next morning, however, the reality of Almaza seemed grimmer than ever. The heat felt more oppressive than before – unlike anything Margery had ever experienced. It was like a physical weight, dragging you down and making every small action twice as hard as it should be.

Margery found that she had lost her appetite completely, and to begin with she put it down to the high temperature. But soon she also began to suffer from a horrible churning sensation in her stomach, and then she felt a sudden urgency to rush to the loo. She had succumbed to one of the nasty bugs that afflicted most foreign visitors to Egypt – known to the girls in the camp as 'Gyppo tummy'.

Elspeth helped her to the sick bay, where a nurse gave her a large white pill. 'It'll make you feel worse for a while, but it'll clear your system out,' she told Margery.

The woman hadn't lied, and the next few hours felt like pure hell. After her umpteenth visit to the ablutions Margery came back to her hole in the ground and passed out. Elspeth ran to fetch help, and a few minutes later, Margery regained consciousness just long enough to hear the words 'We'd better get a stretcher.' The next time she awoke, she was back in the sick bay.

The evil tablets did their job eventually, and slowly Margery began to feel better. But her enthusiasm for Egypt had been sorely shaken.

After more than a week, the recruits were finally assigned to their new camps, and Margery and Elspeth set off together for a place called 107 Maintenance Unit, otherwise known as RAF Kasfareet, which was situated on the Great Bitter Lake, in the Suez Canal Zone. After a hot and dusty 100-mile drive, the girls' gharry finally drew up at the camp gates, and they got their first glimpse of the sprawling three-kilometre stretch of brick and corrugated-iron huts, aircraft hangars and storage facilities. Outside the perimeter fence at one end, a large control tower loomed over an airfield where planes were being brought in for repair.

As they entered the camp, Margery could see the troops' billets on her left, and opposite them a little church and outdoor cinema, while straight ahead was the YMCA bar. The camp was well equipped, with a NAAFI canteen, its own football and hockey fields, and even some tennis courts in the distance. The idea was to create an entirely self-contained world, providing everything the troops could possibly need – a little bubble of civilisation in the middle of an alien landscape. Outside the camp perimeter, the desert stretched for mile upon mile, with nothing but flat, gritty sand and a few low hills off to the west. Margery felt like she had come to the end of the earth.

As the two girls jumped down from the lorry, they were struck by another unsettling realisation: the ratio of men to women in the camp was pretty extreme, with just 100 British and 300 Palestinian WAAFs working alongside over 4,000 airmen. For the lads there, English girls were a rare and special phenomenon, and as Margery and Elspeth made their way towards the women's compound, which was hidden away behind a high screen, the men gathered around them on all sides, eager to get a good look at them.

Margery was taken to a large brick hut, where she was met by a Scottish corporal called Collie. After living in a hole in the ground at Almaza, having an actual roof over her head seemed positively luxurious, although she noticed that despite the building's sturdy construction, the desert sand had found a way inside, and a light dusting of it lay all over the floor and beds. 'We wash the hut down every morning,' Collie told her, 'but it gets in all the same.'

Once Margery had dropped off her kitbag, she was taken to the mess next door, where she was surprised to find that all the benches and tables were made of stone. 'It's because of the bugs,' Collie explained. 'They're rife out here, and they'll eat up anything made of wood.' Margery, who as a child had always avoided her sister Peggy's camping trips for fear of insects, did her best to repress a shudder.

Since Kasfareet was out in the middle of the desert, the heat there was truly unbearable. Margery hoped that by night-time her hut would cool down a little, but as hour after hour went by it never seemed to. As she tossed and turned, unable to sleep, she felt suffocated by the dry, parching air. Some of the other girls had dragged their little camp beds out onto the veranda, and she decided to follow their example. At least outside there was a slight breeze, but as she lay there all night long beneath her mosquito net she still felt stifled.

The next morning Margery reported to Equipment Accounts. It was a large office near the main entrance to the camp, and was run by an Irish warrant officer who had evidently been out in the desert rather too long. His skin was so weather-worn and darkened from the sun that it looked like ancient leather, and he arrived for work most mornings already well on his way to being drunk. Perhaps, Margery thought, a constant supply of alcohol was the only thing enabling him to face another day at Kasfareet.

Unsurprisingly, the warrant officer did not exactly run a tight ship. In the office most Air Force rules and formalities seemed to have gone by the wayside. The WAAFs and airmen were encouraged to bring their breakfast to their desks if they felt like it, and often the warrant officer himself would come dancing in with a large pile of toast to share around.

It was scarcely a quiet working environment either. To keep themselves awake in the stultifying heat, Margery's colleagues spent many hours composing elaborate symphonies with the aid of pencils and pens, tapping away on mugs, desks, whatever they could find. A man called Jimmy, meanwhile, who had worked as a dancer in Civvy Street, would occasionally leap up onto his desk and perform a tap number.

Even with the constant entertainment, the heat left everyone in a perpetual state of drowsiness, and the ceiling fans whirring away overhead only seemed to stir the hot air around – as well as agitating the swarms of flies that perpetually buzzed around the room. 'Now we have a rule here, Margery,' the warrant officer informed her tipsily when she first arrived. 'No one is to begin work for the day until they can produce a dozen dead flies.' Margery found it hard to tell whether or not he was joking, but she noticed that everyone in the room had a fly-swatter close at hand, and they were absent-mindedly slapping away as they worked.

As in any office, the afternoon slump was the hardest part of the day – and the long, hot afternoons at Kasfareet often felt like torture. To keep them going on the final slog to the day's end, the men and women in Equipment Accounts were visited by a tall, elegant Sudanese boy, who brought them large cups of chai tea. Margery and her colleagues guzzled the stuff down, not just for a burst of caffeine to help them stay awake, but in the hope there was some truth to the idea that a hot drink would actually cool you down.

But the heat wasn't the only problem posed by the inhospitable environment. Outside the office, the desert periodically asserted its power by blasting the camp with a sudden, violent sandstorm that sent everyone running for cover. Oil drums had to be placed along the sides of the asphalt roads to mark them out, so that no one got lost in a storm.

One day, Margery was caught out on her way across the camp, and suddenly found herself being pelted by heavy, gritty granules of sand. Instinctively, she dropped to the ground and covered her head with her arms so that she could breathe.

The storm whirled around her for about five minutes, and then as rapidly as it had appeared, it was gone. Margery was covered in sand from head to foot, but she was just relieved that no vehicles had come by. She blushed to think that anyone might have seen her adopting such a ridiculous pose, like an ostrich with its head in the sand.

For their first few days at Kasfareet, Margery and Elspeth had been too scared of the large numbers of men there to venture out of their compound in the evenings, but the other WAAFs who had recently arrived had been rather more adventurous. Such was the gender ratio in the camp that by now most girls had an entourage of four or five male admirers following them around at all times.

Margery had no desire to acquire her own gaggle of young men, especially since – after her experience with James Preston – she was convinced that they would probably turn out to be married. But it seemed a shame to spend every evening holed up in her hut, so eventually she and Elspeth decided to brave the NAAFI for a cup of tea.

Sure enough, as soon as they sat down, a small group of lads made a bee-line for them. The girls were apprehensive at first, but as they sat and chatted to the young men, they realised that they were pretty decent chaps. What they were most desperate for was simply news of England, having been away from home for so long. Their war had been a strange one, stuck in limbo at a maintenance depot in the middle of nowhere, far away from any kind of action.

There was one topic that the men were particularly keen to learn about – the American GIs who had arrived in Britain since they left for Egypt, and were now stationed up and down the country. 'Is it true that they're over there stealing our girlfriends with chocolate and silk stockings?' one of them asked Margery.

Margery was well aware that many girls found the Americans irresistible, with their smart, figure-hugging uniforms and aura of Hollywood glamour. But she couldn't bring herself to tell the men the truth. 'Oh no, that's just German propaganda,' she said, wondering whether any of them would believe her.

One of the lads, a blond chap called Geordie, was swaying slightly on his stool while Margery spoke, and she had a feeling that, like the warrant officer in Equipment Accounts, this was probably his regular state. He had the look of someone who just didn't care what happened tomorrow, and she realised it was a look she had seen on the faces of many young men at Kasfareet. Despite having been at the camp for several years now, most of them had never ventured beyond the perimeter fence, aside from an occasional swim in the Bitter Salt Lake, and by now they had almost lost the will to live.

But one man in the group seemed different – a tall, sporty chap with brown hair who was called Doug. He had a boyish, happy-go-lucky air about him that seemed to have endured despite the circumstances. When he discovered that Margery came from near Portsmouth, he was thrilled. 'I'm from Bishop's Sutton,' he told her. 'It's only 20 miles away.'

Out in the desert, it felt like a miracle finding someone who had even heard of her neck of the woods, and Margery was soon chatting away to Doug, reminiscing about life back home. Before they left the NAAFI at the end of the evening, they had made a plan to visit the camp's outdoor cinema together later in the week, along with Elspeth and a friend of Doug's called Norman. The films on offer were generally rather crummy, he warned her, and the projector was always breaking down – but to Margery it certainly sounded better than hiding away in the compound.

Margery and Doug soon developed an easy friendship, and when Elspeth was transferred to 111 Maintenance Unit, a camp 100 miles away in Turah, they began spending more and more time together. Before long, Margery found herself going about with Doug, Norman and their buddies almost all the time, just like the other girls at the camp with their collections of young men. She had never received much attention from boys when she was younger, and to her surprise she found she quite enjoyed all the male companionship.

The boys had organised a camp football league, with a different team for every department, generally named after whoever they supported at home – Spurs, Aston Villa or, in Doug's case, Queen's Park Rangers. Out in the desert with little else to do, these team loyalties had become as tribal as those of the actual clubs. Thanks to his height Doug generally played in goal, for a team he had formed with Norman and Geordie, along with a few of their mates. Whenever they had a fixture against another side, Margery went along to cheer them on, and celebrated or commiserated with them afterwards over egg and chips.

As winter approached, the evenings at Kasfareet became colder and the WAAFs swapped their khaki drill uniforms for standard Air Force blue. The daytimes were now pleasantly balmy, not unlike a mild English summer, and Margery found it strange to think that they would soon be celebrating Christmas with the sun shining in a perfect blue sky.

The boys had decided to embrace the hot weather by giving the festive season a Wild West theme. They spent all their spare time remodelling the YMCA bar into the 'Red Gulch Saloon' and putting their cowboy costumes together. But Margery yearned for something more traditional, so she and a few other girls arranged for a Christmas tree to be put up in the camp chapel, which they decorated with oranges and sugared almonds.

As Margery was helping to festoon the tree, a thought came to her – maybe if she made stockings for the boys, it would remind them of Christmases at home and cheer them up a bit. She ran back to her hut and found a spare mosquito net, which she cut into stocking-shaped pieces. Then she sewed them up and filled them with fruits, nuts and sweets. On Christmas morning she woke early and nipped out of the women's compound and over to the men's billets, leaving the stockings outside their door.

A few hours later, when Margery ran into the lads in the NAAFI, she was surprised to see that they were looking glum. 'What's wrong?' she asked Doug. 'Didn't you like what Father Christmas brought you?'

'Oh, Margery, it was a very kind gesture,' he replied, 'but I wish you hadn't done it. The boys are more homesick now than ever!'

Margery felt terrible that her actions had only made the situation worse, but she soon had a chance to make amends. To cheer the boys up, Doug was planning a little party on their veranda that evening, and he asked her to bring some of the girls from her hut along, promising that he would get hold of a bottle of cherry brandy for them.

Margery's hut-mates willingly accepted the invitation, but when evening came she found them dolling themselves up as if they were heading out somewhere fancy. She couldn't believe they would make so much effort just for the boys at Kasfareet. 'What's going on?' she asked one of them.

'We got an invite from the Americans at Deversoir Air Base,' the girl replied excitedly. 'They're bound to throw a better party than our lot, and they're sending a truck to pick us up!'

Margery was sad that the other girls would be going elsewhere for the evening, although in a way she couldn't blame them. The American party was bound to be more exciting than the little get-together Doug had planned. She just hoped he wouldn't be too disappointed when she turned up on her own.

'Sorry, but you'll have to make do with just me,' Margery told the boys when she arrived at their hut. 'Everyone else has gone to see the Americans!'

Her friends groaned, but they seemed to take the news with good humour. 'Those bleeding Yanks, stealing our women again!' laughed Doug. 'Well, it looks like this is all yours, Margery.' He pulled out an enormous bottle of cherry brandy and began filling up an enamel mug for her.

'Merry Christmas!' she said, as she clinked his mug of imported Stella Artois.

It was certainly the most unusual Christmas Margery had ever spent, and not one she could ever have imagined back home in North Wallington. Here she was, drinking hard liquor as she watched the African sun go down – surrounded by men! Yet as she looked around at the sun-kissed faces of her new friends, she couldn't have been happier.

Gradually, the alcohol began to take effect on the little group. One by one the boys more or less collapsed onto the floor and had to be carried inside the hut and put to bed. Margery, who had the brandy bottle all to herself, soon began to feel herself swaying. 'Quick, catch her before she goes!' someone shouted, and Doug grabbed her just in time to stop her keeling over.

He helped her back to the entrance to her compound, and she went straight to bed, giddy with the excitement of her first, glorious Egyptian Christmas.

12

Kathleen

As an auxiliary nurse at Addenbrooke's Hospital in Cambridge, Kathleen had found a role that suited her talents, but she still hadn't quite given up on her dreams of joining the Navy. So when a letter arrived at her mother's little house in Pembroke Road one morning bearing the stamp of the WRNS, she could barely contain her excitement. She hastily ripped open the envelope, scanning down the page until she had confirmed that it really did say what she hoped it did: finally, after many long months of waiting, they had found a place for her.

There was just one snag. Having failed the medical when she first applied to join the service, Kathleen would have to get her GP to assess her and confirm that she was in peak physical condition – as the service with the longest waiting list, the WRNS insisted that all new recruits were passed Grade I.

But when Kathleen stepped onto the scales at the doctor's office, he shook his head sadly. 'I'm afraid you're still underweight,' he told her. 'I'll have to put that down on the form.'

Kathleen looked crestfallen. 'No, please don't,' she begged the doctor. 'I really want to get in, and I think this is my last chance.'

The doctor thought for a moment. He was a good friend of Kathleen's mother and didn't want to disappoint her. Finally he said quietly, 'Why don't you put your shoes back on?'

Hastily, Kathleen slipped her feet into her shoes and stepped back onto the scales. She waited anxiously while the old man scrutinised the needle.

'And your coat,' he said after a few seconds.

Fully dressed, Kathleen weighed just enough to tip the needle over to a healthy weight. 'Well, I suppose that means you're in,' the doctor said with a smile.

Kathleen soon received a railway warrant to travel to Mill Hill in North London. There she and several hundred other new recruits were rounded up and taken to a large modern building, shaped like an elongated 'X' and topped with a bright green copper roof. It had been designed for the Medical Research Council by the architect Maxwell Ayrton, best known for the nearby Wembley Stadium, but now it was the WRNS basic training depot. Like all shore establishments in the Navy, the facility was named after a ship, HMS *Pembroke*.

In fact, as she settled into her fortnight's training in Mill Hill, Kathleen found that almost everything about life in the WRNS was built around the naval template. New recruits slept not in dormitories but in 'cabins', and their food was prepared in the 'galley'. They learned to use 'port' and 'starboard' instead of left and right – and to say they were 'going aloft' rather than simply heading upstairs. Everything about the experience was distinctly nautical, even down to the particular method of saluting which the girls were taught – with the palm of the hand tilted slightly towards the face, a relic of the days when sailors on board ship didn't want their superiors to see the tar on their hands.

In British military tradition, the Navy was known as 'the Senior Service', and the WRNS, whose history went back as far as the First World War, proudly saw itself as senior to the other women's forces as well. Everyone knew that their numbers were much lower than the ATS and the WAAF, and this lent the girls an aura of exclusivity.

Certainly, the WRNS demanded a high standard of recruit. Sitting up in her bunk bed one evening, with a cup of thick Navy cocoa in her hand, Kathleen pored over the five-page booklet of regulations that she had been given on arrival. 'Every member will on all occasions endeavour to uphold the honour of the WRNS,' it told her, 'and by the good order and regularity of her conduct prove herself worthy of the Service to which she belongs.' There were special admonitions against engaging in 'noisy or rowdy behaviour' and 'loitering' in public, especially if there were men around.

Clearly, Wrens – whether officers or ordinary 'ratings', as the Navy referred to the lower ranks – were supposed to see themselves as a cut above other servicewomen. And judging from the clipped accents of many of the young women Kathleen trained alongside, there was certainly a fair proportion of upper-crust girls among their number. Many of them, in fact, seemed to already have connections in the Navy, and it wasn't unusual to hear a shrill voice ring out, 'Oh, you must be Cynthia! I think Daddy knows your uncle from the Admiralty.'

But despite the number of top-drawer recruits and the Navy's air of self-importance, for much of the training period Kathleen and her fellows were treated as little better than deckhands. In between bouts of 'square bashing' on the parade ground, lectures on the history of the Navy, and demonstrations of how to tie a dozen different seaman's knots, the girls spent hours every day on their hands and knees, scrubbing and polishing floors that had looked pretty much perfect to begin with. Paving stones would be swabbed with water and carbolic soap, wooden floors buffed with shoe polish, and windows scrubbed until they gleamed. Since the girls were still in a probationary period, they wore not the smart navy blue uniform that so many of them had long admired, but a pair of faded denim overalls – and despite their pride at being chosen for the WRNS, they couldn't help acknowledging that they looked more like skivvies than anything else.

By the end of a fortnight at Mill Hill, a number of girls had dropped out of the training. Kathleen, however, was enjoying herself. Having worked as a nursing auxiliary she was used to putting in long hours, and she still couldn't quite believe her luck that she had finally made it into the service. When the time came to don her smart blue serge uniform for the first time, she did so filled with pride.

The next stage was the allocation of the girls to different trades, and again Kathleen found she was in luck. After a brief interview and some fairly straightforward aptitude tests, she was assigned not to the drudgery of the kitchens or the tedium of office work, but to train as an armourer in the Fleet Air Arm.

The FAA was the part of the Navy responsible for aircraft carriers, as well as the planes that were launched from them. This relatively new technology had already proved itself vital to the Allied forces, helping to defend shipping convoys and enabling them to attack targets out of range of the RAF.

As an armourer, Kathleen would be responsible for ensuring that the Fleet Air Arm's complement of Seafire, Swordfish and Barracuda aircraft were equipped for combat. For training, she was sent to HMS *Excellent*, a gunnery school on Whale Island in Portsmouth Harbour, where she spent a fortnight learning about different types of ammunition – tracers, armour-piercing bullets and more – and practising stripping, cleaning and reassembling machine-guns until she could do it wearing a blindfold. When she was fully trained, it was time for her to be sent to her first posting – an FAA base known as HMS *Hornbill*.

Kathleen had no idea where HMS *Hornbill* was, beyond the fact that it was somewhere west of London, but when she arrived at Paddington Station, laden down with her kitbag and satchel, plus a large tin box of armourer's tools, a Railway Transport Officer directed her to the correct train. 'You'll have to run,' he told her. 'It's about to depart, and the next one isn't until this time tomorrow.'

The man took a couple of Kathleen's bags and rushed her along the platform, just as the guard was raising a green flag in the air to signal the train to leave. Behind them a lanky, ginger-haired young sailor was running for the train too. ''Ere, wait for us, mate!' he shouted, in a strong Cockney accent.

As Kathleen and the sailor reached the nearest carriage, a door was flung open, and several hands reached out to grab their bags and yank them up into the train. Kathleen fell onto the floor of the carriage and found herself surrounded by legs clad in naval officers' trousers. Scrambling to her feet she was even more embarrassed to see that, judging by the amount of gold braid on the men's uniforms, she and the young sailor had stumbled into a first-class carriage.

But there was no chance of them moving to a different carriage now since the train was packed to bursting. Two officers squeezed up and made a little room for Kathleen to sit down, but the poor ginger-haired sailor was squashed right up against the window, with his face pressed into the glass.

It was just as well that Kathleen was able to sit down, since she had no idea whether HMS *Hornbill* was half an hour or half a day's journey away. When she finally plucked up the courage to ask the officers sitting next to her whether they knew where it was, they simply shook their heads.

'I'm heading to Hornbill too,' the red-headed sailor piped up when he heard Kathleen's question. 'But blow me if I know where it is!'

Kathleen and the young man, who introduced himself as Ginger, resorted to pulling down the window every time the train stopped, much to the annoyance of their fellow passengers, and shouting out, 'Is this the right stop for Hornbill?' But time after time they were met with blank stares from the people on the platform.

As the sun set and a bright moon slowly rose in the night sky, Kathleen began to wonder if they would ever arrive at their destination. When, some time after midnight, the train stopped at a little station called Culham and she posed her usual question to a guard holding a lantern, she was astonished to be answered in the affirmative. 'This is it,' he told her. 'Get out, quick!'

Kathleen and Ginger were hurled off the train just as unceremoniously as they had boarded it, their bags and boxes clattering down onto the platform after them.

'You'll have to walk to the camp from here,' the guard told them. 'Left out of the gate, up that road, over the bridge and then it's only about a quarter of a mile.'

'We can't walk that far carrying all this stuff!' Kathleen protested.

'Not my problem,' the man retorted. 'I'm off home now.'

'Oh well,' said Ginger cheerfully, swinging his kitbag onto his shoulder, 'I reckon we'd better make a start.'

The two new arrivals set off into the night. Ginger was even more heavily laden than Kathleen, and they staggered slowly along the dark country roads like a pair of worn-out donkeys. By the time they reached the entrance to the base they were both exhausted from the physical effort.

'Oh, you aren't half going to cop it,' a guard remarked with evident pleasure, when they finally made it to the gate. 'You were meant to be here hours ago.'

'Well, the train only just arrived!' Kathleen said.

The guard called a lorry to take Ginger to the men's camp, which was known as Argos, and Kathleen to the women's camp, Pegasus. Soon they were trundling along through the darkness on a little dirt road.

A few minutes later, the vehicle stopped and Ginger jumped down to the ground. 'Blimey, that were an adventure!' he remarked cheerily.

Kathleen smiled.

'Maybe I'll see you again if there's a dance on camp,' he told her. 'Save one for me, won't yer?'

'All right!' she replied. 'But I warn you, I'm not a very good dancer.'

'That's all right – I am!' he said with a grin, as he disappeared into the night.

By the time Kathleen finally arrived at Pegasus Camp, everyone there had gone to bed. A Wren officer gave her a cup of tea and showed her to a bunk in one of the Nissen huts, and after the arduous journey she collapsed gratefully onto her pillow.

The next morning, Kathleen was woken bright and early by the call of the bugle, relayed over the base's Tannoy system. Bleary eyed, she rose, dressed in her uniform and made her way back to the mess for breakfast. She had just finished a bowl of porridge when the Wren officer she had met the night before walked up to her. 'Come with me, Wren Skin,' the woman told her. 'You're under arrest.'

Kathleen was astounded. She had only just woken up! How could she have done something wrong already?

'Come on,' the Wren officer said, leading her back outside, where a lorry was waiting for them.

As they drove through the camp, Kathleen recognised the route she had taken the night before, only now – in the daylight – she could see where she was going. Heading back in the direction of Argos Camp, she passed by an area of thick woodland, and off to the left she could make out a large airfield, with three runways in a triangular formation. That must be where she would be working, she thought – assuming she was allowed to work after all.

At Argos, Kathleen was taken into a building where the captain of HMS *Hornbill* had his office. As she sat outside waiting to see him, she was met by a familiar face. 'Ginger! You're here as well,' she exclaimed, as the red-haired young man was led in. Someone had obviously decided he was a flight risk since his feet had been shackled together.

'The captain will see you now,' a stern-looking sergeant told Kathleen. Nervously she stood and made her way into the office.

Seated behind a large wooden desk was a smart, middle-aged man, clean shaven and with neatly parted grey hair. In his youth, Kathleen imagined, the captain might have been rather dashing, but now he had a distinctly fatherly air.

Kathleen approached the desk, and the captain looked up from the papers in front of him. 'Wren Skin?' he asked her wearily.

'Yes, sir,' Kathleen replied, giving an enthusiastic salute.

The man smiled. 'I see you're a newcomer,' he remarked. 'So tell me, how is it you have managed to arrive more than three hours late for your very first assignment?'

Kathleen met the captain's gaze. 'I'm very sorry, sir, but it wasn't my fault,' she began, launching into a blow-by-blow account of her journey the previous day. 'I'd never even heard of HMS *Hornbill*,' she told him, 'and nor had anyone else on the train.'

By the time she had got to the man with the lantern at Culham station and the arduous trek she and Ginger had made from there to the front gate, Kathleen thought she saw a slight twinkle in the captain's eye. 'Well,' he said, 'I suppose I'll let you off this time. But I want you to remember one thing.' He leaned forward a little. 'Naval time is always one minute before.'

'Yes, sir,' Kathleen replied, gratefully.

'All right then, dismissed,' he said, waving his hand for her to go.

Kathleen left the office and returned to the lobby outside, where Ginger was still waiting in chains. From inside she heard the captain shout, 'You can send in Seaman Ferguson now.'

'Wish me luck,' Ginger whispered with a wink, as he hobbled in for his own dressing down.

With the disciplinary rigmarole concluded, Kathleen was free to report for duty at the Armoury. She was met there by a cheerful, red-faced master gunner with a strong Devonshire accent, who soon began showing her the ropes. The camp largely dealt with Seafire aircraft – the Navy's equivalent to the RAF Spitfire – and every time one came in to land, Kathleen's job was to rush over to it on the runway and, once the pilot had gone off for a cup of tea in the ward room, get inside the cockpit and begin stripping out the ammunition. Alongside her were the girls who checked and repacked the parachutes – an arduous job since every one of the 72 pieces of silk they were made up of had to be inspected in turn – the radio mechanics, who confirmed that the plane's communications systems were still working correctly, and the air mechanics, who checked it over for more serious problems. When things ran smoothly, it was like a perfectly choreographed dance, each girl playing her part efficiently and keeping out of the others' way.

The more Kathleen practised, the more swiftly she was able to carry out the procedure. After a couple of days, she found she could leap into the cockpit, strip the ammunition and get it back to the Armoury hut while the other girls had barely begun their work. Once inside the hut, her job was to count and weigh the .303 machine-gun bullets and 20mm-calibre shells to make sure that all were accounted for. She had heard tales of unscrupulous pilots selling ammunition on the black market, and the Navy were keen to make sure that no ordnance was lost without a pilot actually engaging the enemy.

Over her first few days at HMS *Hornbill*, while Kathleen was settling into her job at the Armoury, she began getting to know her cabin-mates as well. As at Mill Hill, many of the other Wrens at Pegasus were from distinctly well-to-do backgrounds. A young woman called Imogen had a father who was a shipping magnate, with a fleet of vessels currently sailing the seven seas. Another's owned several aeroplanes, while a very tall girl called Penelope was the daughter of a highly successful banker. With her clipped, precise vowels she could almost have been a member of the royal family, and Kathleen couldn't get over the fact that she always called her fellow Wrens 'gels'.

The more upper-class girls in the cabin also seemed to be the least worldly. They were shocked when a dark-haired Wren called Ethel described her time working in a factory before she joined up, explaining that her job had involved putting 'male' engine parts into 'female' ones.

'What on earth do you mean?' asked Imogen with a grimace.

'Well, you know, like a bolt going into a nut,' Ethel told her, forming a hole with her left hand and poking her right finger into it.

'Good God!' said Penelope, as they all stared at Ethel in horror.

Penelope in particular had led a very sheltered existence. Aside from boarding school, she had never been away from home on her own before, and had never had to deal with washing her own clothes, let alone scrubbing floors. 'Whatever would Daddy think if he could see me now!' she laughed.

But despite their different backgrounds, Kathleen found she got on well with her new cabin-mates. At night, they would all sit around together in the hut for a singalong, or share the latest bit of news they had heard around the camp. For all their refinement, the posh girls loved nothing better than a good bit of gossip, or a risqué joke, and Kathleen was happy to oblige them. One night she told them about a sign she had seen up in the clothing stores, where a delay on new material coming in had meant that men's uniforms were being prioritised over women's. The prankster who had written the sign had put it this way: 'Wrens skirts will be held up until the men's needs are satisfied.' The young ladies in Kathleen's cabin thought the joke was the most outrageous thing they had ever heard, and they laughed like drains for hours.

Another time, the talk of the cabin was how a female petty officer had been caught inviting girls back to her private room in the evenings. Whether or not anything untoward was actually going on, the Navy had acted swiftly and removed the woman from *Hornbill* altogether. In the women's forces there was a clearly defined procedure to be followed in the event of suspected lesbian affairs, and on raising the alarm, a base commander would be sent a copy of a memo euphemistically entitled, 'A Special Problem'. Nearly always, the offending servicewoman was quietly posted elsewhere and the matter swept under the carpet as quickly as possible.

One topic the girls in the cabin never tired of hearing about was Kathleen's dashing fiancé Arnold, and the romantic dates he had taken her on in London. Since he had been posted abroad, Kathleen had written to him regularly, but his own letters had become a little less frequent, and often took several weeks to arrive. Sometimes all Kathleen received was a standard-issue Field Service Post Card on which Arnold had scratched out the various multiple-choice entries, leaving only, 'I am quite well', along with his signature and the date. He still wasn't able to tell her exactly where he was or what he was doing, but Kathleen was just relieved to know that he was alive and in good health. In the absence of any actual words from her beloved, the little cards were enough to keep her going.

Although the women at Pegasus Camp were half a mile away from the men stationed at Argos, they spent plenty of time socialising together in the evenings. *Hornbill*'s roster of events and entertainment always took place in a large wooden building at the men's camp, and Kathleen and her friends soon grew used to trudging along the road after work, on their way to the latest concert or film screening.

It was the dances, though, that really brought *Hornbill* to life, and Kathleen had not been working there long before she and her new friends were setting off to one. Since they weren't allowed to wear anything more glamorous than their uniforms, the Wrens put extra effort into their make-up, sharing around one girl's lipstick and another's mascara until everyone was done up to the nines.

When they arrived at the dance hall, which had been decked out with balloons and a mirror ball, Kathleen kept her eyes peeled for Ginger Ferguson. She hadn't forgotten her promise to dance with him if they should run into each other again.

Sure enough, the cheerful young man was soon at her side, and offering to lead her in a tango. 'I don't know how to do this one,' Kathleen protested. 'Can't we wait for a waltz?'

But Ginger was not to be dissuaded. 'Ah, it's easy,' he told her. 'You just follow me.' Soon the two of them were whizzing around the room together, and Kathleen was having a whale of a time.

Ginger was a wonderful dancer, and as the night went on he found himself very much in demand, but every so often he made sure to return to Kathleen and lead her back onto the dance floor.

At the end of the evening, after one final dance, Ginger brought Kathleen back to the table where the girls from her cabin were sitting. But when she tried to introduce him to her cabin-mates, she found they weren't exactly keen to get acquainted. 'Don't you think we'd better be going?' Penelope asked pointedly, just as Ginger was about to draw up a chair.

'All right then,' Kathleen replied, a little disappointed. 'I'll see you next time, Ginger.'

'Cheerio, Kath,' Ginger replied as he went on his way. 'Nice to meet you, ladies.'

On the walk back home to Pegasus, the other girls made their feelings about Kathleen's friend clear. 'He's rather a funny boy, isn't he?' remarked Imogen, and Penelope asked, 'How did you come to pick *him* up?'

Kathleen was a little surprised at her friends' attitude. 'What do you mean?' she asked innocently.

'Well, he's so ...' Penelope faltered, wrinkling her nose. 'I'm afraid I don't know quite how to describe it.'

'Oh, don't mind Ginger,' Kathleen replied with a laugh. 'He's just a Cockney. He's a nice bloke, you know.'

'What's a Cockney?' Penelope asked with genuine confusion.

'A Londoner,' Kathleen replied, a little incredulous. 'You know, from the East End. Haven't you ever met one before?'

'Certainly not,' Penelope replied with a frown. 'When my family goes to London we always stay at Claridge's.'

Kathleen found her friends' incomprehension hard to get her head around, but she was determined to give them an education in all things Cockney. They listened, fascinated, as she told them all about the rhyming slang, and sang them a few of the Cockney songs she knew, including 'Knees Up Mother Brown' and 'Knocked 'em in the Old Kent Road'. By the time the little group arrived back at Pegasus Camp, they were all merrily doing the Lambeth Walk together.

One day, the girls had been granted what the Navy called a 'make-and-mend' – an afternoon off, which, as the term suggested, they were supposed to use for tending to their kit and uniform. In practice, though, most Wrens simply treated the time as holiday, and Kathleen and her friends decided to make the most of it, catching a lift on a Navy lorry that was heading into the local town of Abingdon. As it passed Argos Camp, the vehicle picked up a handful of men who'd had exactly the same idea, and among them was Kathleen's friend Ginger.

The mixed group of Wrens and sailors spent a pleasant afternoon looking around the ancient, picturesque town, and afterwards they lazed on the riverbank, watching the water roll by. Kathleen and Ginger sat next to each other, and fell into a relaxed conversation. She found it so easy talking to him – although he was a man, there was never any hint of romance between them. He had heard plenty of stories about her fiancé Arnold, and had told Kathleen all about the girlfriend who was waiting for him back in London.

'Ain't this beautiful?' Ginger said thoughtfully, after they'd been sitting there for an hour or more. At first Kathleen thought he meant the river, but as she turned to look at him, she saw he was holding out a flower to her.

'What, this daisy?' she replied as she took it from his hand.

'Is that what it is?' he asked. 'I ain't never seen one before.'

'You've never seen a daisy?' Kathleen asked, astonished.

'Well, I don't know much about flowers,' Ginger admitted. Kathleen couldn't help noticing that he pronounced the word with one syllable – 'flars'.

Kathleen looked around her to see what else she could show him. 'Well, here's a buttercup,' she said, offering up a perfect yellow flower. 'If you put it under your chin it'll make it glow. And this one with all the little seeds is a dandelion.'

Ginger listened, fascinated, as Kathleen talked him through the various common flowers that were growing all around them. She knew he had grown up in London, in the heart of the East End, but the idea of being so cut off from nature seemed very sad to her. Ginger, meanwhile, was clearly determined to make up for lost time, and he pestered her with dozens of questions about the anatomy of the little plants, and what all the different bits were for.

'Ginger, what made you want to join the Navy?' Kathleen asked after a while.

'Well,' he said, 'it all started one day when I was a kid. Me dad came home with half a crown he'd been given for lookin' after some bloke's horse. He told us we could either 'ave a slap-up meal at home, or go to Sarfend for the day.'

'Sarfend?' Kathleen repeated, confused.

'You know, by the sea,' Ginger told her.

'Oh, Southend, you mean,' she replied.

'Yeah,' he continued. 'Well anyway, we decided to go to the seaside, so we took a bag of broken biscuits to eat for the day, and we got in this charabanc. And as soon as I saw the sea coming in on the beach, I said to my dad, "I'm going to join the Navy."'

'That's lovely, Ginger,' Kathleen told him. She felt touched by her friend's story, but it wasn't so much his first glimpse of sea that affected her, as the realisation that, for Ginger's family, a bag of broken biscuits might be all they ate in a day. She looked around at her well-to-do cabin-mates from Pegasus – their childhoods couldn't have been more different from his. They had grown up with everything they could wish for, while for Ginger the three square meals he was given in the Navy must seem like a luxury.

Kathleen had never felt closer to Ginger than she did at that moment, and a few months later, when he was sent away to sea, she felt very sad to see him go. Of everyone she had got to know since joining the WRNS, he was the best friend she had made.

13

Jessie

It was a bright sunny day, and as Jessie and Elsie Acres walked along the little country lane to the bus stop, a couple of rabbits hopped across their path. 'I can see why they call this place Bunny!' Elsie joked.

They were camped in the grounds of a stately home called Bunny Hall, ten miles outside Nottingham, and it was their most rural posting yet. Surrounded by gentle hills, beautiful countryside and the sound of birds singing, Jessie was starting to feel human again, and so far there had been no raids at all.

The girls caught the bus into the city together and spent a relaxed day drinking tea, walking around the shops and going to the pictures. When they got back to camp that evening there was a note waiting for Jessie. It was from Mac, the Scottish radar engineer who had visited them on Humberside. He'd heard she was in Bunny, and said that he hoped to be able to come and see her some time soon.

Jessie read the letter with mixed feelings. It was one thing letting Mac join the band in the NAAFI and dancing with him now and then while he was staying at her camp, but the idea of him coming specially to visit her was different. Her heart was finally starting to heal after Jim's death, but she certainly wasn't ready to get involved with another man yet. If Mac did turn up, Jessie told herself, she would just have to explain that to him, but she doubted he would get round to it anyway – his job meant he was constantly on the move from one camp to another, and she was sure that wherever he went there was no shortage of girls eager to spend time with him.

Several weeks passed, and Jessie had forgotten all about the little note, when one day, as she was sitting in her hut doing some embroidery, a girl came running in and announced, 'Mac's waiting for you in the guardroom!'

'What?' Jessie replied, taken aback.

'He came on a motorbike!' the girl said, excitedly.

Jessie put away her embroidery and walked over to the guardroom. There was Mac all right, with his dark curly hair looking a little more windswept than she remembered it.

'What are you doing here?' Jessie asked.

'I've come to see you, of course!' he replied. She couldn't help feeling rather flattered.

'Can ye get the evening off, then?' Mac asked her.

'I'm afraid not,' Jessie told him. 'I don't have a free night until Friday.'

'Ach, come on!' Mac protested. 'I'll bet yer can swap with someone.'

'Well, I'll try,' Jessie said weakly. Since he had made the effort to come out to the middle of nowhere to see her, it hardly seemed right to send him away again.

As it turned out, one of the other girls was happy to swap shifts for the evening, so Jessie found herself spending it with Mac at a cinema in Nottingham. He was as cheeky and talkative as she remembered, doing his best to entertain her with funny stories, and telling jokes about other people in the battery.

At the end of the evening, he asked if he could come and see her again. 'I get moved around a lot, but I can always borrow the dispatch rider's motorbike,' he told her. 'As long as I move the mileage back afterwards no one'll ever find out!'

Jessie laughed. Mac was incorrigible. 'Listen,' she told him, 'I do like spending time with you, but I don't want anything more at the moment.'

'Of course,' he replied kindly, giving her a peck on the cheek before zooming off on his motorbike.

After that, Mac became a regular visitor at Bunny. The girls in Jessie's dormitory grew used to spotting him waiting for her in the guard hut, and would rush back excitedly to let her know he was there. 'He's just a friend,' she always insisted, as she gathered her things and ran out to meet him.

Mostly, they spent their time together just walking and talking. Neither of them had much money, and, having grown up in the Highlands, Mac was happiest out of doors. He told Jessie all about the beautiful countryside in Morayshire, and how he loved to go climbing when he was back home. 'You'll have to come and try it for yourself one day,' he said.

Jessie ignored the comment. Her friendship with Mac was a pleasant distraction – as long as it remained on the surface. That was how she liked to keep things these days.

Mac, however, evidently had other ideas. When he wasn't visiting Bunny, he was sending Jessie cards, or calling her from whatever ack-ack camp he had been sent to. One day a poem arrived in the mail, carefully cut out of the latest issue of *Punch*. Entitled 'Gunfight Goodnight', it was an ode to an ack-ack girl, in which the author waxed lyrical about the alluring smell of cordite in his loved one's hair.

That evening, when Jessie showed the poem to Elsie Acres, the two of them fell about laughing. How could the wretched stench from the guns ever be considered attractive, they wondered. The girls always did their best to eliminate it, scrubbing their scalps furiously with antiseptic soap – yet it seemed to linger regardless.

The next time Jessie saw Mac he arrived bearing news. 'We're going to be neighbours!' he announced. 'I've just signed up for a course in Derby.'

'Why?' Jessie asked him, astonished.

'Because it's closer to you!'

She laughed. 'Well, I hope you're interested in the course as well.'

'Oh no,' he said, grinning. 'I can't stand it!'

The next time Mac was granted a week's leave he asked Jessie if she would like to come and spend it with him in Scotland. 'You have to save me,' he implored her. 'I get so bored hanging around with my sisters!'

Heaving heard him wax lyrical on the wonders of the Highlands, Jessie had to admit she was tempted. Although her job in ack-ack was taking her all over the country, she had never been to Scotland before.

The following week they travelled up together by train. It was late by the time they reached the small picturesque town of Grantown-on-Spey, but the Macbeth family were all still awake, and were thrilled at the prospect of meeting Jessie. The door to the house flew open and Mac's father Willie pulled her into a hug, declaring, 'So here's our Mac's bonny wee girl!'

'Oh, Mac, she is bonny,' said his eldest daughter Isabel, hugging Jessie in turn and planting a big kiss on her cheek.

Next it was the turn of Mac's younger sister Betty, a pretty girl who couldn't have been more than 13. She threw herself on Jessie, smothering her with hugs and kisses as if she was her favourite person in the world.

Jessie felt quite overwhelmed by all the physical affection. Her own parents had never showed any, either to her or to each other.

'Well, I think this calls for a celebration!' Willie Macbeth declared. 'Let's crack open the whisky.'

Over a late dinner, he and Mac set about demolishing an entire bottle, while he regaled Jessie with tales of his time in the trenches during the First World War. 'I'll show yer my battle scars if ye like,' he said. 'Right on the shoulder blade!'

Meanwhile Mac's sisters showered Jessie with questions, wanting to know everything about her. They had clearly been filled in quite a bit already, she realised. Mac must have been writing home about her a lot, and from the way they talked it was clear they thought of her as his girlfriend.

After dinner, the neighbours piled in to meet Mac's 'new lass' too. Before long he had got his violin out and the whole clan were singing merrily. The warm, jovial atmosphere couldn't have been further from what Jessie was used to in her own family home, and she could feel herself relaxing into it.

In the morning, when Mac took her out for a stroll in the surrounding countryside, she realised how different the landscape was to what she had grown up with around Holbeach Bank. Jessie was used to flat fenland country, but Grantown was on the edge of the snow-topped Cairngorms, by the crystal clear waters of the River Spey. Mac hadn't been exaggerating when he told her the area was stunning.

As an only child, Jessie had always longed for siblings, and now she felt as if she had two new adoptive sisters in Isabel and Betty, who treated her like one of their own. The girls joined Jessie and Mac on a boat trip to the Hebridean Islands, showing her around Iona and Mull, and taking her to the strange rock formation on Staffa known as Fingal's Cave. It was a magical time, and in the bosom of Mac's family Jessie felt happier than she had for months.

Being treated like an established couple by everyone else had an undeniable effect on Jessie and Mac, too. Now he kissed her whenever he got the chance, and she kissed him back. The earth never moved like it had when Jim held her in his arms, but after months of keeping Mac at arm's length, Jessie finally had to admit that she had feelings for him.

While Jessie and Mac were getting closer, Elsie Acres' relationship with her young sailor was developing as well. It was the first time Elsie had allowed herself to get close to someone since her fiancé had been killed at Dunkirk and, back at Bunny, Jessie could see that the quiet sadness her friend had carried around with her for so long was finally lifting. 'We're going to get engaged the next time Charles has shore leave!' Elsie confided one evening.

'Oh, I'm so happy for you,' Jessie told her.

But while Elsie waited and waited for the expected shore leave to come up, it always seemed to be delayed for some reason. Then one day, Jessie came into the hut to find her friend clutching a letter. 'It's from Charles's mother,' Elsie said quietly. 'His ship went down, and there were no survivors.'

Jessie could scarcely believe it. How could fate be so cruel to one girl, she wondered, taking away a second boyfriend just when she had finally got over the loss of the first? 'Oh Elsie, I'm so sorry,' she said, squeezing her friend's hand. She knew from her own bitter experience that there was nothing anyone could say or do to stop the pain Elsie was feeling right now.

'Every man I love seems to die on me,' Elsie said, limply. 'I think I must be jinxed.'

'Please don't say that,' Jessie told her. 'You know it isn't true.'

'No, I think it is,' Elsie replied desperately. 'I'm cursed! How can I ever get involved with anyone again, if this is what always happens to them?' Miserably, she lay down on her bed.

Since Elsie and Charles weren't married, or even officially engaged, she wasn't entitled to compassionate leave, and she received no formal letter of condolence. Jessie could see her friend's heart was breaking, but she knew that Elsie wouldn't make a fuss, she wouldn't cry – she would just carry on, like they all had to.

Before long, the battery was on the move again, this time to Gorleston-on-Sea, a small town about three miles down the coast from Great Yarmouth. The popular seaside resort had endured its fair share of bombing from the Luftwaffe, with more than 50 air raids that had left 10,000 houses damaged, many of them beyond repair. During one attack, eight Wrens had been killed when their hostel sustained a direct hit.

By the time the men and women of 518 mixed battery arrived in the area, however, things had quietened down considerably. At most, Jessie found herself hauled out of bed a handful of times every week, and even when the alert did sound, it was only rarely that any targets could be engaged. Most enemy bombers seemed to veer off course just before they came in range of the guns, leaving the ack-ack team to stand down and return to their Nissen huts.

Nonetheless, Jessie and her friends remained in readiness, drilling every day, brushing up on their aircraft recognition, and making sure that their instruments were perfectly calibrated. The Regent cinema in Great Yarmouth was a handy local landmark by which Jessie could check that her height-and-range finder was reading distances correctly.

It might have been a quiet time on the actual gun park, but as ever Jessie and her friends were kept busy with fatigues around the camp. One day, instead of normal cookhouse duty, she was assigned to the officers' mess, to cover for an orderly who was on leave.

Jessie crawled out of bed before reveille had even been sounded, and sleepily reported for duty. She was met by the officers' cook, a thin, fastidious bombardier called Albert. He had been a butler in civilian life and had the smooth voice to match – although, rather incongruously, whenever the officers were out of earshot he swore like a navvy. 'Well, bugger me!' he announced when he saw how perfectly Jessie had laid the table, a skill her mother had drummed into her in childhood. 'You're the first ATS girl I haven't had to show how to do that.'

Once everything was ready for the officers, Albert asked Jessie if she would like to have some cornflakes for breakfast. At the camp, they were normally reserved for officers only, so she jumped at the chance, but when they got the box down from the shelf, she was shocked to see a mouse leap right out of it. She peered inside the packet and saw that mixed in with the cereal were a number of tiny dark droppings. 'We can't eat this, Albert,' she said.

'No, we can't,' the cook agreed. Then he added, 'But *they* can. The light's not very good in here so I doubt they'll notice a few black bits.'

Albert began distributing the pooey cornflakes among the bowls on the table, and then opened a fresh packet for him and Jessie to tuck into. When they had finished, it was time for the officers to be called in to eat. 'All right, go and let those bloody swine know their swill's ready,' Albert told Jessie.

Jessie stifled her laughter and went off in search of Captain

Rait and the other officers. 'Breakfast is served, sir,' she told the captain in her most polite voice.

As the officers sat down, Jessie watched from the doorway, feeling a secret thrill at the fact that for once she was one up on her superiors. For the rest of the day she kept a close eye on Captain Rait to see if the breakfast had left him with any adverse effects, but as far as she could tell he seemed to be in perfect health – and blissfully ignorant of what he had eaten.

Despite the lack of action on the gun park, the war continued to rumble on – and it soon became clear to Jessie and her friends that something significant was brewing. The local beaches had been placed off-limits to all but infantry men, but in her time off Jessie enjoyed walking along the cliff-tops around Yarmouth. Looking down at the sand below, she could see the men of the Hallamshire Battalion practising wading ashore from landing craft.

Jessie knew well enough not to ask questions about military manoeuvres, but it was obvious what was going on: at last, the long-awaited 'D-Day', when the Allies would finally take the war back to Europe, was on its way. What she was witnessing was a rehearsal.

As Jessie gazed down at the men on the beaches, scurrying up to the foot of the cliffs like a thousand little ants, she couldn't help wondering how many of them would survive the real thing.

It wasn't long before 518 mixed battery sustained a nasty casualty of its own, when one of the radar girls, Corporal Pottle, fell from the top of an aerial she had been cleaning and suffered a blow to the head. As she lay on the ground, with blood seeping out of one ear, a crowd gathered round her unconscious body. 'I reckon she's a goner,' remarked one of the men, shaking his head.

Corporal Pottle was rushed to hospital in a military ambulance, and was diagnosed with a serious brain injury. Gradually, she recovered well enough to be able to walk and talk again, but those who knew her said she was never quite the same.

After the accident, a sergeant announced at parade one morning that some of the girls were to be sent on a first-aid course. Jessie was one of those singled out, and soon found herself billeted at a grand house in South Walsham, learning to make splints and bandages. She didn't mind the practical side of the course, but the girls were also taught to diagnose various battlefield injuries, with the instructor talking them through a series of grisly colour photographs that made Jessie feel sick to her stomach. Many of them showed dead soldiers with their heads half blown away, or their guts spilling out from abdominal wounds.

This was the reality of warfare, Jessie realised – the horror that Jim must have experienced in Tunisia. In a way, despite doing one of the most dangerous jobs in the ATS, she had been sheltered from the most awful side of the conflict. The sight of the bombed-out houses in Hull had moved her profoundly, but she had seen them after the event, when the blood had been wiped away and the screams of the injured had fallen silent. Now she was getting a glimpse of war in all its gory detail.

Back in Gorleston, Jessie found that things were busier than ever. The roads were packed with jeeps and lorries from dawn until dusk, and among them she saw several American units passing through the town on their way south. Everything was gearing up for the big event.

Jessie couldn't help having mixed feelings about all the preparation for the invasion. Like everyone in the country, she had been waiting for this moment for years now, but she knew too that the forthcoming battles would exact a heavy cost. How many more women would soon be getting letters like the ones she and Elsie had received, telling them that the men they loved were never coming home?

Since Jessie had arrived in Gorleston, she and Mac had written to each other regularly. While they were with his family in Scotland she had allowed herself to grow closer to him, but now she began to worry that she was setting herself up for another heartbreak. Until the war was over, no one was truly safe, she realised. How could she risk falling in love again, with all the pain she knew it could bring?

Despite her fondness for Mac, and all the kindness he and his family had shown her, Jessie felt determined to end things between them before she got hurt. 'It's the wrong time in my life to get involved with someone,' she explained in a letter, 'and anyway, who knows what might happen to either of us.'

But the young Scot wouldn't take no for an answer. He wrote back straight away, telling her that there was no need to call a halt to what had developed between them, and if needs be he was willing to wait until she was ready for a more serious relationship. Clearly, shaking him off was not going to be easy, now that they had got closer in Scotland.

That night, Jessie put on her service dress and went down to the Floral Hall in Gorleston, along with a couple of sisters who worked with her at the camp. The Navy had a fleet of motor torpedo boats moored in the River Yare, and the ballroom was full of young sailors eager to twirl the ack-ack girls around the room. Before long, Jessie and her friends had found themselves a trio of petty officers – she danced with a lad from

Gloucestershire called Bernard, while the two sisters paired up with his friends George and Chris. The boys were all too pleased to find some Army girls to partner with, since apparently the Wrens they worked with wouldn't look at anyone lower than an officer. By the end of the night they had made plans to meet the girls again the next time they were on shore leave.

The following morning, Jessie sat down to write a reply to Mac's letter. 'I'm involved with the Navy now,' she told him, 'and I'm having fun.'

His shocked response arrived a few days later. Mac told her he was hurt and amazed by her letter, and that he hadn't seen it coming at all. 'I knew this happened to other people,' he wrote, 'but I never thought it would happen to me.'

This time, Jessie simply didn't reply.

On 5 June 1944, the group of young men Jessie had gazed down on as they crawled along the beaches on their bellies left Great Yarmouth on a train bound for the south coast. That night, no air-raid alarm sounded, but the girls in her hut were kept awake nonetheless by the drone of aircraft passing overhead. By the time they rose from their beds in the morning, the sky was thick with planes, and all of them were heading in the same direction: France.

It was a glorious summer's day, and the girls spent the morning outside, listening to a lecture on aircraft recognition. On the roads beyond the camp they could see a steady stream of vehicles trundling by. Just before noon Jessie and her friends were ordered to report to the NAAFI, where a wireless had been set up so that they could listen to a 'special announcement'. Men and women from all around the camp gathered as the midday bulletin from the BBC Home Service began, and the newsreader John Snagge declared, 'D-Day has come.'

Everyone held their breath as further details of the invasion were announced. A combined air and sea assault was in progress, involving more than 150,000 men. Six thousand ships were crossing the Channel, along with many smaller vessels. The night before, British gliders had landed in France, and their crews had successfully captured the bridges that would allow the Allied forces to advance. American paratroopers, meanwhile, were already behind enemy lines, ready to link up with the main invasion force.

The newsreader went on to quote General Eisenhower's Order of the Day, which he had addressed to every member of the Allied Expeditionary Force. 'The free men of the world are marching together to victory,' he read. 'Good luck, and let us all beseech the Blessing of Almighty God upon this great and noble undertaking.'

As soon as the broadcast came to an end, Jessie and her friends were ordered straight back to work. As they filed out of the NAAFI, a girl who did Jessie's job on the height-and-range finder in 'D' Section commented thoughtfully, 'There'll be a lot of sore hearts by the end of the day.'

The girls did their best to concentrate on the jobs they had to do, but the wait for further news of the invasion was agonising. Jessie couldn't help wondering – what happened if the great gamble didn't pay off? She had always been a natural optimist, but losing Jim had affected her profoundly, and right now she wished she had a little more of her old buoyant confidence.

By the following morning, however, it was clear that D-Day had gone well, and by 9 p.m. that night the BBC was broadcasting that a solid foothold had been secured in Europe. But in the first 24 hours of the invasion more than 3,000 Allied soldiers had been killed. Among their number was the husband of Jessie's counterpart in 'D' Section – the girl's prediction had proved more true than she could have imagined.

14

Margery

The more time Margery spent around the lads at RAF Kasfareet, the more she began to see in them the innocent teenagers they had been when the war first interrupted their youth. She was taking a shortcut through the men's billets one evening, when she spotted them inside their hut, clumsily trying to teach themselves ballroom dancing using Victor Sylvester's handbook. They had missed out on the dances and parties that they should have been attending in their teens, and had no idea how to foxtrot or tango.

One of the lads spotted Margery watching through the window. 'Are we doing it right?' he asked her uncertainly.

Margery did her best to make a few helpful suggestions, but she could see that the room they were in just wasn't big enough to practise properly. 'Why don't we go out on one of the football pitches?' she suggested.

They headed over to the pitch, where Margery found herself in the unfamiliar role of dance teacher to a class of eager students. There was no doubting the lads' enthusiasm, but the nimble footwork she had witnessed when they played sports together was sorely absent now.

A few days later, a dance was being held at the Warrant Officers' Club, and Margery and the lads decided to go along. With a gramophone playing familiar numbers, the men did their best to remember the steps she had taught them. They had made some progress, but they lacked confidence, and whenever Margery danced with one of them, she found herself having to virtually shove him around the room.

As usual at Kasfareet, the women were ridiculously outnumbered by men, and Margery found herself much in demand as a dancing partner. But as the evening drew to a close, she found Doug suddenly by her side, insisting that they dance the last waltz together.

A little uncertainly, Margery agreed. Although she liked Doug very much, so far she had always been careful to keep him at arm's length. When they went on long walks around the camp together, strolling between the mountains of cases piled up in the storage area and talking for hours on end, she allowed him to escort her back to the entrance of the women's compound afterwards and give her a quick peck on the cheek, but no more. Despite her best efforts, though, she was aware that the other lads were beginning to see her as Doug's girlfriend.

One day, Margery was excited to receive a letter from her sister Peggy, who was now based only a couple of hundred miles away in Palestine. With some leave coming up, she had decided to visit her little sister and see how she was getting on in Egypt.

Not long afterwards, Margery was nearing the end of her day in the Equipment Accounts office when Peggy appeared at the door. Instinctively, she leapt up from her seat and ran over to embrace her, but then, remembering that, as a Queen Alexandra Nursing Sister, Peggy was technically an officer, she quickly saluted instead.

Peggy returned the salute a little awkwardly. 'Oh God, I wish you wouldn't do that,' she told Margery, as soon as they were out of the office. 'I can barely tell my right arm from my left!'

Margery took her sister over to the NAAFI, where they sat and chatted over a cup of tea. It felt strange seeing her all the way out in the desert, and as she looked into Peggy's eyes she noticed that something about her was different. She seemed far from her normal robust self – a bout of illness she had picked up at work had left her thin and frail – and Margery found the change in her rather alarming. After all, Peggy had always been the tough one in the family.

As the two girls talked, Margery realised that life in the Middle East had been a struggle for her sister. One of the hospitals she had worked in had been little more than a collection of tents, and when it rained the nurses would get covered in mud from head to toe. At another, she had been responsible for picking away the infected skin of men suffering from impetigo.

Clearly the work was beginning to take its toll on Peggy. 'I'm so homesick, Margery,' she said wearily. 'Aren't you? What I wouldn't give to be back in North Wallington right now!'

Margery nodded, smiling sympathetically. But the truth was that she hadn't felt homesick for months and she was enjoying her life at Kasfareet.

When Margery learned that she was being transferred to another maintenance unit, she was disappointed – and once the whole story came out, her disappointment turned to anger. One of her fellow corporals had recently been sent to Turah, the camp 100 miles away where her old friend Elspeth now worked. But apparently the new posting hadn't agreed with her, and with tears in her eyes she had begged the wing commander to be allowed to return. Now Margery was being sent in the girl's place.

'But I don't want to go either!' she replied desperately, when she was informed of the news by a WAAF officer. She knew that the wing commander was fond of the other corporal and wouldn't have made the switch for anyone else.

But Margery's complaints fell on deaf ears. 'I'm afraid this is over my head,' the officer told her. 'The wing commander's made his decision.'

After work, Margery went to watch a football match with Doug and the other lads. She didn't want to spoil their evening, so she waited until the game was over before she delivered the bad news. When she told them about the wing commander's soft spot for the other corporal, they were furious. 'That just isn't right!' Doug exclaimed, uncharacteristically vehement. Beneath his anger, Margery could see he felt utterly despondent.

'Is there anything we can do?' asked Norman helpfully.

Doug's face brightened a little. 'Well,' he said, turning to Margery, 'you could tell them we're getting married.'

'What?' Margery exclaimed, unsure if she had heard him correctly.

'Let's get married,' he said. 'I'll do it, Margery. If it'll help.'

She looked at his boyish, handsome face, staring at her earnestly. Everyone at Kasfareet loved Doug – he was good-natured, funny and caring, the kind of man any girl would want to marry. But Margery had deliberately never let him get too close to her. What if there was another side to his personality, she asked herself, one that only came out at home? In the desert, the lads were in a state of suspended boyhood, with their food, clothing, housing and entertainment all taken care of by the Air Force. There was no way of knowing for sure whether, back in England, Doug would be the same man he was here.

Margery returned Doug's gaze for a moment, before turning away with a laugh.

A few days later, on Valentine's Day, an orderly sergeant came and told her that it was time to go. Doug and the others were at work, so she didn't even get a chance to say goodbye to them.

The sergeant packed Margery's bag for her, and helped her up into the cab of an air-freight gharry. As it trundled off into the desert, she watched her life at Kasfareet fade into the distance.

111 Maintenance Unit, otherwise known as RAF Turah, was a smaller camp than Kasfareet and was nestled at the foot of a range of large rocky hills to the south-east of Cairo. When she arrived, Margery was greeted by the beaming smile of her old friend Elspeth. 'Oh, I'm so pleased you're here!' the Scottish girl told her cheerfully. 'Come on, I'll show you to the tents.'

Following Elspeth across the camp, Margery was surprised to discover that the canvas sleeping quarters seemed to have brickwork incorporated into them. 'The walls are so we can open the flaps in the summer, without getting caught up in a sandstorm,' her friend explained as they went inside. 'The storms around here are a nightmare, and the sand gets into everything at the best of times.'

Looking around the tent, Margery could see that Elspeth wasn't exaggerating. The sand was everywhere, and when she scooped up a handful she realised it was different to the kind she was used to – finer and paler. 'It's the limestone,' Elspeth explained. 'There's a quarry just the other side of the hills.'

Now that Margery looked more closely, she could see that even Elspeth's hair was lightly dusted with the white powder.

'You'll get used to it,' her friend reassured her. 'It's the bugs you want to look out for here.' She gestured around the tent, and as Margery's eyes adjusted to the dark she saw that the legs of the beds were standing in little tins of paraffin, designed to keep the insects, which were hopping around all over the floor, from crawling up into them.

Margery left her kitbag in the rather unappealing sleeping quarters and set off in search of her office. She had been told that it was in a cavern somewhere up in the hills, but fortunately a gharry was on hand to drive her there. She wasn't sure what she thought about going to work in a cave, but when she got there she realised that the choice of location was very wise. Compared to the camp down below it was blissfully cool, and there were no bugs to be seen.

Margery was in charge of the Equipment Accounts office for the entire maintenance unit, and she even had some staff at her disposal – two WAAFs and an Egyptian boy, who soon began showing her the ropes. 'What are these?' she asked one of the girls, pointing at some strips of sticky tape attached to the walls, with dates written on them by hand.

'We have to inspect the caves for cracks every few days,' the girl replied. 'Each time we find a new one, we stick a bit of tape across it, so we can see if the rock keeps on moving. That way we've got a bit of warning before the cave collapses completely.'

'I see,' Margery replied, not exactly reassured by the explanation. She tried to push the idea of being crushed to death at her desk to the back of her mind, and got on with some work instead.

*

That night over dinner in the mess, Margery got to know some of her new colleagues at RAF Turah. One among them stood out in particular – a tall, manly looking girl with cropped blonde hair who spoke with a heavy German accent. Margery learned that her name was Anne Schilling, and that she had come from Germany to Palestine before the war because her husband was a Jew.

The other girls from Anne's tent all seemed to be giving her a wide berth, and several of the men at the camp regarded her with outright contempt, pulling a variety of unpleasant faces as they walked past her. To Margery it didn't seem fair – even if she was German, she was clearly no fan of Hitler.

Suddenly, Margery heard a scream from a nearby tent, and a few seconds later a young WAAF rushed in, trembling. 'Are you the new corporal?' she asked desperately.

'That's right,' Margery replied. 'What's the matter?'

'There's a scorpion in our tent!' the other girl squealed.

Margery looked at her. 'Well, what do you want me to do?' she asked.

'Come and kill it for us,' the young woman begged her. 'Please!'

Since childhood, Margery had always hated bugs and creepy-crawlies, and the idea of getting up close to a scorpion filled her with dread. But as the only NCO present, she couldn't really dodge the responsibility. 'Does anyone know how I should do it?' she asked the other girls.

'It is not so hard,' Anne Schilling replied confidently. 'You must take one of your shoes, hold it by the toe and bring the heel down on the creature's head.'

Margery nodded slightly, before reluctantly following the young WAAF back to her tent. Once they were inside, the girl led her to where the scorpion had been spotted, lurking underneath a kitbag in the corner.

As she carefully lifted up the bag, Margery steeled herself for a scary encounter. But up close the scorpion turned out to be far from terrifying. Margery had envisaged a great black thing the size of a crab, whereas what she found was a small, pale specimen, only an inch or so from pincers to tail.

In a matter of moments, she had whipped off her shoe and brought it down on the unsuspecting bug. 'There you go,' she told the young WAAF triumphantly. 'Nothing to worry about!'

After that, whenever one of the creatures needed dispatching, it was Margery who was summoned to do it. Somehow the girl who had once been terrified of creepy-crawlies had become the camp's resident scorpion slayer.

Compared to Kasfareet, which had its own bars and sporting facilities, as well as plenty of opportunities to make friends, Margery found life at Turah rather dreary and confined. She enjoyed the chance to catch up with Elspeth, but the other girls at the camp were no substitute for Doug and his mates.

It didn't help that the girls at Turah seemed to spend a lot of their time in a state of high anxiety. A little way from the main entrance, along the road that ran down to the local railway station, was a small encampment of East Africans, who were employed by the RAF to guard against opportunistic thieves. They had a large searchlight which they kept pointed at the camp after dark, and if a girl went to the loo in the middle of the night the bright beam would follow her there and back.

'I can't bear it,' one of the other girls told Margery, after suffering this indignity late one evening. 'It's like they're stalking you wherever you go.'

'Don't be silly,' Margery replied. 'They're protecting you. If anything, you should feel grateful.'

But Margery's confidence in the East Africans' good intentions didn't last long. One day, a WAAF staggered into camp in a terrible state. Her hair was matted with blood and there were heavy gashes all over her head. When she was questioned, the girl said that she'd been attacked by one of the men camped out by the road. By the time Margery saw her in the sick bay, the medics had shaved her hair off completely so that they could stitch her head back together.

From then on, the WAAFs were warned to avoid the road that ran past the encampment after dark, and even Margery felt a chill when the beam of the searchlight caught her on the way to the loos late at night.

After a week at Turah, Margery was desperate to see Doug and the rest of the gang, so on Saturday morning she got up early and headed over to see the warrant officer responsible for granting leave. In her hand was a 48-hour pass that she had brought with her from Kasfareet, but when she showed it to the man, he was unimpressed. 'There's no leave until you've been here a month,' he told her brusquely. 'Pass or no pass.'

Margery was still stinging with indignation at having been sent to Turah in the first place, and the man's refusal to let her visit her old friends felt like another slap in the face. So, believing that she had every right to take the leave she had earned, she decided to break camp for the first time since she had arrived in Egypt.

She waited patiently outside her hut for one of the gharries that made regular tours of the base, picking up and dropping off WAAFs and airmen at their various posts. When it arrived, she got in quietly and sat up right against the front, where she hoped that nobody would notice her. She knew that when the vehicle reached the end of its loop, it would have to turn around in the road outside the camp entrance, and that would be her moment to escape.

Sure enough, after the gharry had completed a circuit of the camp, it went right out past the guardhouse and then began to turn around in the road outside. Margery seized her chance to make a discreet exit, silently slipping out of the back of the vehicle as the driver was completing the manoeuvre. Then she ran down the main road as fast as she could, hoping that she hadn't been spotted.

It was a busy road, and Margery had no trouble hitching a lift to Kasfareet. She arrived there just in time for a late breakfast – Doug, Norman and the boys were still asleep on the veranda outside their hut, and when Margery turned up with steaming plates of bacon, eggs and toast, they could not have been more delighted to see her.

Margery spent the whole weekend hanging out with the boys, just like old times, and by the time she'd hitched back to Turah on Sunday evening and sneaked back into camp, she was feeling much better about her new posting. It was near enough to her friends that she could see them regularly, and – as several of the boys had pointed out – it also had the benefit of being much closer to Cairo.

In fact, as the weeks went on, Margery found herself spending more and more time in the capital city. From Turah, Cairo was only a short train ride away, and there were regular gharries back to the camp from the local station, so the girls didn't have to risk encountering the East Africans on the road late at night. Margery began making the journey several times a week, and soon she was a regular at some of the city's most popular hotspots for British expats and service personnel – among them Lady Kilearn's yacht, which cruised up and down the Nile every day serving delicious tea and cakes, the Tedder Club, where the Air Force's lower ranks could relax over a plate of egg and chips, and Café Groppi, home to the famous 'Marilyn' ice-cream.

When Doug wrote to tell Margery that he was due a 48-hour pass of his own, she was determined that he should make the most of it and let her show him around Cairo. He had never been to the city before and was a little apprehensive about venturing so far away from Kasfareet, but she promised to take good care of him and after a bit of arm-twisting he agreed to give it a go.

They met at the YWCA, where Margery had booked herself a room for the night. Although officially she wasn't supposed to be seen in anything other than her khaki drill uniform, she had changed into a dress she had made herself, having purchased some cotton material with a pretty palm-tree print from a local market trader. She had also bought a packet of henna and, with the help of the other girls in her hut, had managed to dye her hair a brilliant red. When Doug saw it he was evidently impressed. 'All the boys love a redhead,' he joked.

The YWCA was housed in an old marble palace with magnificent gardens, and was one of Margery's favourite spots in Cairo. As she and Doug sat outside eating together, waited on by elegant Sudanese men, they could almost have been a couple sharing an exotic holiday, rather than just two off-duty Air Force personnel.

For dessert, they feasted on delicious sweet cakes with coffee. 'Make sure you keep an eye on your food,' Margery warned Doug. There were sky hawks circling overhead, and she had seen plenty of customers lose their meals to a sudden swooping raid.

That weekend, Margery and Doug spent hours walking around Cairo, snacking on sugared almonds as they traipsed through the busy streets. On Saturday night, they headed to a palatial, air-conditioned picture house to catch a movie starring Gene Kelly and Deanna Durbin. It was a far cry from the grotty camp cinema at Kasfareet.

When they parted the following evening, Doug thanked Margery for showing him such a wonderful time, and back at his camp he obviously raved about the experience to all his friends, because she soon found herself giving tours of the city to several of them as well. First up was Geordie, who she took to see an orchestral performance at the NAAFI lounge and a film called *Broadway Rhythm* at the picture house, but before long Doug was sending a whole string of young men her way. Somehow, Margery realised, she had become the Air Force's unofficial holiday rep in Cairo.

Certainly, there was no one else who could have shown the men around with more enthusiasm. Margery had truly fallen in love with Cairo, and every weekend she would happily while away hours there on her own, sipping chai tea in the YWCA gardens or wandering around the giant marketplace and soaking up the atmosphere.

Rather than waste money on train fares, she had increasingly taken to hitch-hiking to and from the city. One time she persuaded Elspeth to come with her, although her friend proved to be a rather anxious traveller. It didn't take long for them to catch a ride, but it turned out the driver wasn't going all the way, and when he dropped them at a crossroads in the middle of the desert, Elspeth began to panic. 'What if no one comes along?' she asked Margery anxiously.

'Don't worry,' she replied. 'They always do.'

But Elspeth was not reassured by Margery's words, and after

an hour had passed with no sign of a vehicle in either direction, she was growing increasingly distressed. 'Someone's going to find our skeletons out here,' she moaned. It was approaching the hottest part of the day, and the girls hadn't brought any water with them.

Eventually, a car pulled up and the two WAAFs bundled in. 'I told you someone would come,' Margery told Elspeth cheerily. But her friend had been shaken by the long wait in the desert, and struggled to enjoy the rest of the day.

Although hitch-hiking through the desert necessarily brought with it certain dangers, taking the train wasn't completely free of hazards either. Margery hated the walk between downtown Cairo and Babalouk station, through a large marketplace filled with meat carcasses and buzzing with flies. There was a short cut, but that involved cutting through dingy back alleys, and one shop in particular always sent a shiver down her spine. Outside was a statue of a giant black cat, with glassy eyes that seemed to follow her as she walked past.

One night, Margery stayed out in Cairo on a late pass, before catching the last train back to Turah. But, exhausted from a long day in the city, she fell asleep on the way home, missed her stop and didn't wake up until it had reached its final destination. By now it was well after midnight, but there were still trains going back in the other direction, so she hopped on the next one that came along.

By the time she arrived back at Turah station, the gharry shuttle service to the camp had long since ceased, and as she looked around, Margery couldn't see another soul.

She knew better than to risk walking along the main road in the dark on her own, which would take her right past the East

African encampment. But that meant there was only one option – to cut across the desert.

The distance could only have been about a mile, but for Margery, striking out alone across the sand, it felt like the longest walk of her life. Far ahead she could see the faint light of the guardroom at the camp, but every so often, as the sand dunes dipped up and down, it would disappear from view, leaving her in perfect darkness.

For the first time since she had arrived in Egypt, Margery felt genuinely terrified. Since childhood she had always had a horror of the dark, and although joining the WAAF had helped her get over many of her fears, now – all alone, in the pitch blackness of the desert – she could feel them gradually creeping back again.

Margery's eyes began to water, and the tears started streaming down her cheeks. But she wasn't about to crumble now. Corporal Pott had come this far by facing her fears, not giving into them. She forced herself to keep putting one foot in front of the other, telling herself that if she only kept going long enough, she would eventually be home.

At last, Margery came over the final rise in the sand, and saw the guardroom clearly lit up in front of her. She dashed the final hundred yards up to the gates, a great wave of relief washing over her as she passed through them.

That night, despite the ordeal, Margery slept soundly in her bed. Walking home across the desert wasn't an experience she would ever care to repeat, but it had proved one thing – when push came to shove, she had faced her greatest fear and overcome it.

*

After a few months in her new posting, Margery had got to know Cairo like the back of her hand, but she was aware that there was more to Egypt than the capital city. Other girls at Turah had been raving about the trips they'd taken to see the tourist sites further down the Nile – the grand temples of Luxor and Hatshepsut, and the Valley of the Kings.

The sites were several hundred miles away, but it was possible to see them in a weekend. Margery and Elspeth both had 48-hour passes coming up, so they went to Lady Tedder's travel agency in Cairo and booked themselves onto a tour. That Friday after work they hitched into town and caught the sleeper train to Luxor, arriving on Saturday morning just in time to meet up with the rest of the tour group at their hotel.

In the lobby, they found the others were already waiting for them. Aside from the two girls, there was a Polish officer called Sam, who was based at a camp not far from Turah, and two British Army men, Ted Abel and Charles Luck, both of whom worked in Pay Accounts. Ted had been with the Army Pay Corps in Cairo for some time, while 'Lucky' – as he insisted the girls call him – had only recently arrived in Egypt from Cyprus.

The tour was led by an Egyptian man called Abdul Abudi, who informed the small group that they were exceptionally lucky themselves – normally he would take tours of around 20 people at a time, but as it was off-season theirs would be a much more intimate gathering. 'Ordinarily, we travel by donkey,' he told them, 'but as there are just five of you, we can take a gharry instead.'

For Margery, though, travelling around the ancient ruins in a lorry didn't sound very exotic. 'That doesn't seem right,' she objected. 'I think we should do it properly, donkeys and all.'

'If that is what madame wishes, then of course the donkeys it must be,' Abdul Abudi said, with a little bow.

Lucky laughed heartily, and caught Margery's eye. 'You know, something tells me you're going to regret that decision,' he told her.

The tour began with a visit to the temple complex at Karnak, where Margery gazed in wonder at the rows of ram-headed sphinxes and the giant sandstone pillars of the Great Hypostyle Hall. This, she realised, was all that was left of the ancient civilisation that she had read about in her bible studies – a world that until recently she had believed was no more than a myth. It was strange to think that thousands of years before the Romans had even landed in Britain, the Egyptian people had been hard at work constructing such incredible monuments.

After Karnak, the little group moved on to the Temple of Luxor, marvelling at the vast statue of the Egyptian Empire's greatest pharaoh, Ramses II. Abdul Abudi did his best to talk them through the beautiful hieroglyphics on the walls of the temple, but Lucky seemed more interested in offering his own comical interpretations of the ancient carvings, and despite Abudi's frequent attempts to check that the group was listening carefully, Margery went away having learned very little about the site. She was beginning to find the cheeky Englishman rather annoying.

On the second day, the group took a felucca across the Nile to visit the Valley of the Kings, where they travelled from one tomb to another by donkey. It was baking hot, and as the bright sun beat down on them everyone was becoming exhausted. 'Are you beginning to regret insisting we travel like this yet?' Lucky asked Margery, as he wiped a bead of sweat from his forehead.

'No,' she replied. 'I'm glad we're seeing things the traditional way. It's much more fun than travelling around in a lorry.'

'Yes, much more fun,' Lucky echoed thoughtfully, drawing a little closer to her. Then he reached out and slapped her donkey hard on the behind.

Before Margery knew it, the animal was racing forward, shooting ahead of the rest of the group. 'Stop!' she yelled, but the poor beast took no notice. Behind her, she could hear Lucky shouting something at it in Arabic, evidently egging it on.

Margery held on for dear life, until the donkey finally ran out of energy and came to a stop, panting heavily under the shade of a palm tree. She clambered off the wretched animal and stood by its side as she tried to catch her own breath as well.

It took a few minutes for the others to catch up with her, and when they did Lucky was at the head of the group. He dismounted and strode over towards Margery, laughing heartily. 'That was quite a ride you had!' he told her.

'It certainly was,' Margery replied, in as calm and composed a voice as she could manage. She had no intention of giving Lucky the satisfaction of knowing that he had riled her.

But despite her best efforts her irritation must have been plain to see, because a frown began to work its way across Lucky's normally cheerful face. 'Oh, I am sorry, Margery,' he said. 'I was just having a bit of fun. I do hope I haven't upset you.'

Something about Lucky's tone told Margery that the sentiment was genuine. 'Don't worry about it,' she told him, giving a little smile to show that there were no hard feelings.

He smiled back, and reached out to touch her on the shoulder, but as his hand approached, Margery instinctively flinched.

Lucky looked at her, and his flippant persona seemed totally absent for a moment. 'You've had a bad experience with men, haven't you?' he asked.

Margery was stunned by the question. 'I don't think so,' she muttered awkwardly.

But Lucky just shook his head and said, 'You must have been hurt very badly.'

To Margery's relief, the rest of the group was approaching. She hopped back on her donkey, taking care not to meet Lucky's eyes, and they all set off together to see the Tomb of Tutankhamun.

15

Kathleen

Since she had started as an armourer at HMS *Hornbill*, Kathleen had lost track of the number of aircraft she had worked on. As well as the common Seafires, which stopped at the camp daily on their way to bases further afield, she had grown used to a whole roster of Fleet Air Arm planes. There were biplane bombers like the Swordfish and Albacore, as well as the more modern Barracuda, fighters including the Firefly and the American Hellcat, and even amphibious craft such as the Walrus and Sea Otter.

But although Kathleen had seen inside the cockpits of all of them, she had never been up in the air – until one day in the Armoury hut a young pilot offered to take her for a spin.

Kathleen couldn't believe her luck. 'I'd love to,' she told him, 'only I mustn't be found out.'

'Well, as long as you stay down low and keep quiet, no one will know,' he replied with a wink.

Kathleen accompanied the pilot back to his plane, checking to see that no one was looking, and quickly scrambled up into the cockpit after him.

'All right, keep your head down,' he told her, as he pulled the glass roof of the Seafire closed over them. She crouched as low as she could, hoping that the top of her hat wasn't visible to anyone on the ground. She could feel the plane slowly begin to move as the pilot manoeuvred it to one end of the runway. He turned to her and asked, 'Are you ready?'

Kathleen nodded enthusiastically, and they began to pick up speed. She felt the plane storming along the tarmac, every tiny bump on the ground shuddering through her bones. It got faster and faster, and the juddering felt more and more alarming until, suddenly, there was a feeling of lightness, and she realised the nose of the plane was beginning to tilt upwards. A few seconds later, they were soaring into the sky.

'All right, you can sit up now,' the pilot told her. 'No one can see you.'

Gingerly, Kathleen straightened herself up and looked out of the little glass bubble. All around her was the brilliant blue of the sky, and down below she could make out the huts of the camp. Dozens of little navy-blue ants seemed to be scurrying this way and that, and it took her a moment to realise that they were her colleagues.

'Well, what do you think?' the pilot shouted to Kathleen, as the plane began to level out.

'It's beautiful,' she replied.

There wasn't much time to enjoy the scenery, however. The pilot knew that it could only be a brief flight, just long enough to check that all the equipment was in working order – anything longer might look suspicious to the people on the ground. So after a few minutes he began banking to the left, heading back in the direction of the runway. 'You'd better get down again,' he told Kathleen, as they began their descent.

Once again, she squeezed herself as low down in the cockpit as she could. After a little while, she felt the sudden impact as the plane's wheels made contact with the runway, and then it bumpily ground to a halt. 'All right, out you get,' the pilot told her, 'before someone finds you in here.' He slid open the lid of the cockpit and popped down the hatch, and Kathleen hastily clambered out onto the runway.

'Thank you,' she told him, as she turned to head back to the hut. 'That was marvellous.'

'My pleasure,' the pilot replied, with another little wink. Kathleen watched as he readied the plane for take-off once again. A few minutes later, he was soaring through the skies, on his way to who-knew-where.

As it happened, Kathleen herself had begun longing to fly the nest of HMS *Hornbill*. She had joined the WRNS hoping for foreign adventure, and while working on an airfield had its glamorous moments, in reality she was still spending most of her time in a field eight miles south of Oxford. By now Wrens were serving all over the globe, everywhere from New York to San Francisco, from Aden to Alexandria, and from Colombo to the Rock of Gibraltar. Fleet Air Arm bases had sprung up in plenty of exotic locations, including Mombasa, Nairobi, Bermuda and Sierra Leone.

When Kathleen saw a notice calling for Wrens who were willing to accept a transfer to HMS *Golden Hind*, a naval base in Sydney, Australia, she put her name down immediately. The lucky 12 girls who were chosen would be embarking on a month-long voyage, with stopovers in New York, San Francisco and Cape Town. She crossed her fingers, hoping that the posting would come through, but when the names of the dozen successful applicants went up on the board, sadly Kathleen's was not among them.

Arnold's battery, meanwhile, had been serving on the Continent since just after D-Day, and Kathleen worried constantly about his safety. Many of the men who served under him had been killed in the great Allied advance, among them his good friend 'Ding Dong', who was shot by a sniper in

Holland. His friend John, the lad who had played the oboe on Christmas Day, had been wounded and was recovering in hospital. To Kathleen, the fact that Arnold himself had survived so long seemed nothing short of a miracle, and every hastily scribbled postcard she received to say he was still alive and well was a blessed relief.

At least Kathleen had plenty of work to keep her busy at *Hornbill.* In addition to going through the ammunition of each plane that came in, she had been given another important responsibility. In the Armoury shed were the camp's pyrotechnics, green and red flares which were used to signal planes coming in – the former to reassure the pilot that all was well on the ground, and the latter to abort an unsafe landing. 'It's very important that the pyros are kept at precisely the right temperature,' the master gunner informed Kathleen. 'Too low and they'll stop working, but if they get too hot there's a danger they'll go off unexpectedly.'

The temperature had to be checked every couple of hours, which was all right in the daytime when Kathleen was working in the Armoury hut anyway, but during the nights it meant a half-mile journey from her cabin at Pegasus. At two-hour intervals, Kathleen's alarm clock would go off and she would stagger from her bed to the little bike she kept propped up outside the hut, then pedal along in the darkness with only a torch strapped to her handle bars to show the way in front of her. To make matters worse, the torch had been blackout-proofed with two strips of packing tape, so that only a tiny sliver of light shone out of it.

Every time Kathleen set out she was convinced she would end up in a ditch by the side of the road, but somehow she always got to the pyros in time, and then back to her bed in one piece. Two hours later, the ritual would begin again, but she grew used to snatching what sleep she could in the intervals between her nocturnal excursions. With practice, she found she could make the trip there and back within 15 minutes – meaning that as long as she fell asleep the moment her head hit the pillow, she could still get a pretty good night's sleep.

Since Kathleen's friend Ginger had left *Hornbill* for service overseas, she had been spending more and more time with the girls in her cabin. She had even managed to persuade Penelope, the tall girl whose father was a banker, to try her hand at gardening, and between them they had dug out a little flower-bed by the side of the hut. Penelope had always struck Kathleen as too refined to be much use when it came to manual work, so she was surprised to find that her friend really threw herself into it, and once they had 'borrowed' a few cuttings from a nearby country estate, they had a pretty respectable flower-bed.

In fact it turned out that gardening was the least of Penelope's talents. Although she had grown up in a house full of servants, and had never had to wash her own clothes before, she proved to be a dab hand when it came to washing and ironing the girls' blouses. Soon she and Kathleen had set up their own little laundry business, scrubbing the seamen's smelly shirts for sixpence a pop – until the captain found out about their scheme and had it shut down.

Even when they weren't coming up with activities to keep themselves busy, the girls at *Hornbill* were well provided for when it came to entertainment. In addition to the roster of dances and concerts, there were regular film screenings at the little cinema in the men's camp, Argus. Most of the movies shown there were hand-me-downs from a nearby American camp, and some of them were rather risqué by British standards. One film included a scene in which girls in

French knickers danced on a grand piano, which caused such a commotion among the Wrens and seamen present that the captain began personally screening all movies in advance to check they were suitable.

Unfortunately, the films' previous owners weren't very conscientious about keeping the reels in the right boxes, so the story often played out in a random order. Every so often a great groan would go up from the audience as they realised they had jumped back to an earlier part of the movie, and the cowboy they had just seen shot dead was suddenly alive again. The walk back home afterwards was generally spent deep in conversation as the cinema-goers tried to piece the plot together.

One night, Kathleen and her friends were watching a particularly ropey Western, which concerned a young cowboy who had got his boss's daughter pregnant. At a pivotal moment in the plot, the girl's father stepped out into the street with his pistols drawn and demanded angrily, 'Now, which one of you sorry bastards is the father?' It was a moment of high tension and the audience were on the edge of their seats, when suddenly the camp Tannoy blared out, 'Seaman McKinley, please report to the main gate.' The room erupted with hysterical hoots of laughter, and the red-faced sailor shuffled out of the room, doing his best to avoid making eye contact with any of his peers.

On their make-and-mend afternoons, Kathleen and her friends generally headed into the nearby town of Abingdon, but one day she, Penelope and Ethel decided to set off on foot and explore the area beyond the far end of the camp instead. When they reached the gate, they were stopped by an unfamiliar guard. 'Do you know where you're going, girls?' he asked them.

'We just thought we'd have a wander down this way,' Kathleen replied.

'Well, make sure you're back by five,' the man warned her.

The girls went on their way, following a winding path away from the camp until they reached the Thames. It was a glorious late summer's day and as the river flowed gently alongside the beautiful green fields, Kathleen could almost forget there was a war on.

The walk had left the girls feeling parched, and when they spotted a quaint old thatched pub nestled in a crook of the river, they felt irresistibly drawn towards it. 'Ooh, let's go and get a lemonade,' said Kathleen, leading the way across a little bridge over the river. Outside the pub they found a couple of men sat at a table, their cheeks flushed red from the cider they were drinking. Above the entrance hung a large sign that read simply, 'Come in!'

Kathleen and her friends knew a thing or two about following orders, and right now they needed no further encouragement. 'Come on, then,' said Kathleen, leading the others inside. She walked straight up to the bar and ordered a lemonade for each of them.

'Sorry, luv, no can do,' the barmaid replied. 'We're all out of lemonade today.'

'Well, what other soft drinks do you have?' Kathleen asked her.

'We're running a bit short,' the woman told her, 'what with the good weather and all. Right now, it's cider or nothing.'

'Three ciders it is, then,' Kathleen replied. The girls hadn't come out in search of alcohol, but at least it would help quench their thirst. A few minutes later, the three of them were sitting at a table in the garden outside, sipping from their glasses as they watched the river go by.

It was a blissful scene, and when the three glasses were drained, no one was in any mood to head home again. 'Shall I get us another drink, then?' Penelope asked, giving a little hiccup.

Once the glasses had been emptied for a second time, it seemed only right that Ethel should buy a third round. The girls continued to guzzle the warm fruity nectar, and Kathleen felt like she was in heaven. 'This is the life, eh?' she said to Penelope and Ethel, as the three of them clinked their glasses together.

It was only when the girls were finishing up their third round of drinks that Kathleen suddenly noticed the time. 'It's nearly five o'clock!' she exclaimed.

Hastily, they swigged what was left in the bottom of their glasses and stood up from the little wooden table. But the moment they did, they were suddenly hit by a wave of dizziness. 'Do you know what?' Penelope declared, as she swayed from side to side. 'I think I might be ever so slightly blotto.'

'Never mind,' Kathleen replied, striding away from the table. 'We've got to get back to camp. Follow me!' She made for the little bridge, but found she had to hold on to the side to steady herself as she crossed it.

The other girls were equally the worse for wear, and it took an enormous effort for the three of them to stagger back to camp. By the time they reached the back entrance, they were exhausted from the march, and they bent over for a moment to catch their breath.

Suddenly, Kathleen became aware of the guard on the gate, staring at them with his arms crossed. Through bleary eyes she could make out a distinct smirk on his face. 'Oh, you won't half be for it now, girls,' he told them, doing his best to suppress a chuckle. 'They'll have you up for drunk and disorderly.'

'We're not drunk!' Kathleen protested, as she heaved herself back up to a standing posture and did her best to stare the guard down, a task that was rendered rather difficult by the fact that he seemed to be sporting two heads.

'Ab-so-lutely not!' Penelope agreed, slurring a little. 'And we certainly aren't … dis-ord-erly.' She nodded her head primly in what she thought must be the guard's general direction.

'All right, whatever you say, girls,' he replied. 'In you come!'

The guard pulled aside the gate so that the girls could get back into the camp, but now, try as she might, Kathleen couldn't find her way to the opening. She willed her feet to go in a straight line, but it seemed much harder than it had on the way out.

Evidently her two friends were suffering the same problem. 'I can't get through!' Ethel protested, with evident frustration, as she pushed and shoved at what she thought must be the gate.

'That's a hedge, darlin',' the guard said, laughing heartily. 'You want to try over here.'

Finally, Kathleen found her way to the entrance. 'Now just stand still, would you!' she implored the gatepost, as she carefully stepped past it and began the trek back to the cabin.

'I hate to think what your CO will say when she sees the state of you lot!' the guard shouted, as the three girls made their way up the path.

Luckily, they got back to their cabin without being spotted by a senior officer, and that night they slept more soundly than they ever had before.

16

Jessie

Almost half a year had passed since Jessie and her colleagues huddled around the radio in the NAAFI, listening anxiously for the latest news of the D-Day landings – and during that time the invasion had continued to go well. Paris had been liberated, followed shortly afterwards by Brussels and Antwerp, and the Allied forces were continuing their inexorable march towards Germany.

Jessie and her friends, meanwhile, had remained at their camp outside Great Yarmouth, with even less to do than before. Eventually, they had received an order that their battery was to be disbanded. There was a silver lining to the sad news, however. The other three batteries in their regiment were about to ship out for Belgium, and anyone from 518 who wanted to join them was invited to apply for a transfer.

Jessie didn't hesitate to put her name down, and she was delighted when Elsie Acres volunteered as well. Elsie Windsor, however, would be staying at home, having accepted a transfer to an Army Ordnance Corps depot in Shrewsbury, where she was responsible for greasing tanks. Jessie was sorry to say goodbye to her old friend, but at least she knew that Stan would keep her up to date on his wife's news. He had willingly volunteered for the Belgian posting, and would be bringing his trumpet along with him.

Before they set sail, the girls were given a week's embarkation leave so that they could say goodbye to their families. On her way back to Holbeach Bank, Jessie found herself sharing a train carriage with Molly Norris, the cuddly orderly sergeant who had reluctantly disciplined her for impersonating the PT instructor during her training.

Since then, Jessie had never really spoken to 'Aunt Molly', but on that long train journey she was able to make up for lost time. She learned that the sergeant had been wrestling with a dilemma about how to spend her leave. 'I'm in a bit of a funny situation,' she confided. 'You see, when I was 14 I ran away from home and I've never been back since.'

Jessie nodded sympathetically. She had always thought her own family situation was difficult, but here was someone whose childhood must have been much harder than hers.

'The thing is,' Molly continued, 'I just feel I ought to see my parents before we ship out.' She hesitated for a moment before adding, 'In case something happens to us out there.'

Before long the train was arriving at Peterborough station and Molly stood up to leave. 'Good luck, Sarge,' Jessie said, with a smile.

Back in Holbeach Bank, Jessie was relieved to find that her own mother seemed less stern and controlling than usual. Since Jim's death Mrs Ward had begun writing to her again, and she seemed to have decided to go a bit easier on her around the house as well.

In fact, if anything it was Jessie's father who was less than happy about her heading off to Belgium. 'I must say I'm surprised they're sending girls overseas already,' he told her, furrowing his brow with anxiety.

'Well, it's a man's job we do, Dad,' Jessie replied gently. 'And remember, we've had plenty of practice.'

*

Before Jessie and her friends were allowed to set sail for the Continent, there were a few matters that had to be dealt with. They were each given a supply of Belgian francs, their pay books were blacked out in case they were captured by the enemy, and everyone was handed a pen and paper to write a will.

Jessie didn't have much in savings, beyond some money she had received from the Army when Jim was killed, but she decided to leave what she did have to her parents. It felt strange setting down her assets in black and white, although she had always known that the Army considered death a routine matter, for men and women alike. In the back of every pay book were two sections to be competed if its owner was killed, euphemistically labelled Diagnosis and Disposal. 'In other words,' as one of the girls had remarked, 'what killed you and what they did with your body.'

With the paperwork completed, the mixed batteries were ready to depart, and soon Jessie and her colleagues were marching three abreast up the gangplank of the *Lady of Man*. As its name suggested, in civilian life the little vessel had been an Isle of Man ferry, and it had certainly seen better days. Some of the planks of wood that made up the deck were so rotten that the girls' feet went right through them.

The channel crossing was a pretty grim experience. The boat was buffeted by a nasty squall and the girls inside were thrown this way and that. Jessie found a railing that seemed to have been bolted down fairly securely, and clung on to it with both hands.

Before long, many of the girls were suffering from seasickness, and a whiff of vomit began to suffuse the boat. Jessie fared better than most, suffering only a mild bout of queasiness, but one girl was so badly affected that when they finally docked in Ostend she had to be taken ashore on a stretcher.

As the girls marched off the vessel, and through the ancient Belgian city, men and women in the streets began to applaud them. *I suppose they've never seen a girl in uniform before*, Jessie thought, looking out at the faces in the crowd. Despite their smiles, many of them were pale and drawn, and their children looked worryingly thin.

When the girls arrived at their temporary billet – an old hotel that had evidently been abandoned for some time – they were given strict instructions not to offer any food to the locals. Normally, Jessie had no problem doing as she was told, but some orders were harder to follow than others. 'You can't see children starving and do nothing,' she told one of the other girls. Many of them still had sandwiches they had been too ill to eat on the boat, and they wasted no time in sharing them out among the local children.

After a couple of days in Ostend, Jessie and her friends were loaded onto a fleet of Army trucks for transport to their various gun-sites. That night the girls stayed in an old German barracks on the outskirts of Malines. The wooden buildings were in reasonably good shape, but the billet was far from popular with the English girls. The walls were plastered with posters proclaiming '*Achtung!*' and '*Rauchen Verboten!*' and, Jessie couldn't help feeling uncomfortable sleeping in what had until recently been a Nazi soldier's bed.

But most unsettling of all were the silhouettes of British Spitfires and Hurricanes pinned up on the walls, just like the cut-outs of Dorniers and Messerschmitts Jessie was used to seeing at Army bases back home. 'I don't like this place,' she told Elsie. 'It gives me the jim-jams.' For some reason, she couldn't shake the feeling that the camp was haunted, as if the Germans had never really left.

The German barracks might have been creepy but at least it was warm, which was more than could be said for the girls' final destination, an anti-aircraft camp near the tiny town of Winksele-Delle, on the road between Louvain and Malines.

In fact, to call the site a camp at all was being generous. In reality, it was little more than a load of gun equipment dumped in the middle of a field, with a handful of wooden huts knocked together nearby. There was no running water, no gas and no electricity – the Germans had cut off the local supply when they left the area. Fortunately someone had brought a generator to provide power to the command post, but the rest of the camp would rely entirely on paraffin lanterns outside daylight hours.

Then there was the mud. Peering out of the back of their lorry, Jessie and her friends gazed upon field after field of what looked like molten chocolate. In between the duckboard paths that led from the wooden huts to the gun-site, the ground was little better than a quagmire. In fact, rumour had it that a gunner at one of the other nearby camps had drowned when he lost his footing and fell off the path in the middle of the night.

'You'll need some of these,' called the driver, coming round the side of the vehicle and hurling several pairs of wellies into the back. The girls put them on and reluctantly lowered themselves to the ground. 'Welcome to Paradise!' one of them quipped.

As it turned out, the problem with the mud proved to be temporary. A couple of days after Jessie and her friends arrived at the camp, the temperature plunged dramatically, and in place of knee-deep gloop there was now hard ice underfoot. It wasn't pleasant, but at least there was no danger of drowning in the night.

On the gun-site, the girls were issued with leather jerkins to keep them warm, but in their huts at night they struggled to protect themselves from the cold. Each girl slept under three or four blankets, with a greatcoat draped on top for good measure, and when their supply of firewood ran out, they resorted to burning slats from the bunks.

Jessie's battery was one of several defending Brussels and Antwerp from German bombardment. The latter city, in particular, was critical to the Allied effort in Europe, since its docks allowed supplies from Britain to reach the front lines without a long journey through France and Belgium. Hitler had wasted no time in attempting to obliterate the city, and had recently given the order for his V1s – flying bombs launched from sites behind enemy lines, which had been pounding London since a week after D-Day – to target Antwerp instead, along with other sites in Belgium.

Compared to piloted planes, the V1s – or 'Doodlebugs', as they were popularly known – were even tougher to hit. They flew at up to 400 mph, and generally below the ack-ack guns' optimum range. But at least the men and women on the gun-sites got plenty of opportunities to practise. Every couple of hours they would hear the characteristic chugging of the V1 engine and look up to see a new wave of the weapons approaching, one after the other. 'They're like London buses,' one of the girls commented wryly. 'You wait for one, and then three come along at once.'

Before long, Jessie and her friends were becoming more proficient at downing the flying bombs. They came over so frequently that there was little point even attempting to sleep at night, so whichever section was on duty would wait up in a little hut by the gun park, playing cards, reading books or just chatting while they waited for the next wave to come over.

Never before – not even on Humberside – had Jessie found herself in action so often.

If the cold was the most immediate hardship for the girls at Winksele-Delle, the lack of clean water soon began to trouble them even more. The closest available source was a well in the grounds of a nearby château, and every day a company of men and women from the camp would head over there with some empty buckets to fill.

But before long, Jessie and her colleagues began to feel unwell, and soon they were coming down with dysentery. 'I reckon there must've been a dead Jerry in that well,' gasped one of the girls, as she abandoned the morning parade and rushed off to the ablutions.

The toilet facilities at the camp were far from luxurious – just a hut containing a long row of buckets, without even any screens between them for modesty. One day, after Jessie had succumbed to the dreaded illness herself, she raced to the nearest bucket, only to find that the girl squatting next to her was in a similarly miserable state.

'How many times have you been today?' Jessie asked her, trying to take her mind off the corkscrewing pain in her guts.

The other girl replied miserably, 'I got as far as nine and then I stopped counting.'

Unsurprisingly, the area commander soon declared the well at the château off-limits, arranging instead for a local brewery to bring around a tank of water every morning. There wasn't enough for the girls to wash themselves properly, but Jessie grew increasingly resourceful, finding that if she melted a bucket of snow she could get about a mugful of liquid out of it, enough to rinse her whole body.

While her skin was clean, though, Jessie's uniform was growing dirty. Fortunately she and Elsie soon met a Belgian couple in the local village who were able to help. They ran a café-cum-bar where the two girls often went to write letters, and when the woman heard that their clothes needed washing she insisted on doing it for them. She refused to accept payment for her work, insisting that there was nothing to buy with it anyway. What she really wanted, she told them, was soap – something she hadn't seen for many years.

Jessie managed to get hold of a slab of Pear's finest, and when the girls presented it to the Belgian woman she was ecstatic. '*Zeep! Zeep!*' she cried, holding it aloft as if it were a bar of gold bullion. Before long she had invited Jessie and Elsie back to her house to say thank you, where she served them coffee made from ground acorns – the closest approximation to the real thing that the struggling Belgians could manage.

While Jessie and Elsie were making friends with the locals, some of the girls in the battery were getting to know the other Allied forces stationed nearby. The whole area around Brussels was swarming with American troops, and with their smart uniforms and even smarter wise-cracks, they had made a strong impression on the English girls.

In fact several of Jessie's colleagues were now dating GIs. Marie Rose, a girl from a small town near Birmingham, was going out with an American soldier called Dave, who had apparently been seduced by her strong Brummie accent. 'He thinks moy voice is lov-lay,' she told the other girls in their hut one night. 'He says it sounds like sing-ging.'

Personally, Jessie had always found the American soldiers rather hard to get along with. To her, they seemed big-headed and boastful, and the success of the D-Day landings and the battles that followed had only made them worse. When one of the Yanks told her confidently that they were winning the war for the British, she countered sharply, 'But you only joined in once you knew we were going to win.'

It wasn't long before the Americans' swagger began to falter, however. On 16 December, only weeks after Jessie's battery had arrived in Belgium, Hitler launched his final offensive of the war, ordering his troops to punch through the Ardennes Forest and attempt to capture Antwerp. The protrusion they created in the front lines gave the ensuing fighting its nickname: the Battle of the Bulge. For the first time since D-Day, there seemed a real chance that the Allied invasion might crumble, and that the hopes and dreams of every free country in Europe could once again be crushed under the tread of Nazi tanks.

After just over a week of fighting, the advancing Germans had got as far as Dinant, only 60 miles away from Jessie's position. She and her colleagues suddenly found themselves in a terrifying situation. What if the Allied Expeditionary Force went the way of its predecessor, they wondered, and was forced into another Dunkirk?

As the battle continued to rage in the snow-covered forest, the ack-ack girls waited anxiously for news. Finally, two days before Christmas, the tide began to turn in the Allies' favour once again. A spirited counter-offensive by the Americans brought the German forces to a halt, and then gradually began to push them back.

On Christmas morning, Jessie was woken early by a voice outside her hut calling her name. She rushed to the door and opened it to find the Belgian lady she and Elsie had befriended, shivering in the snow outside. 'This is for you,' the woman said, pushing something into Jessie's hand. She looked down to see a large speckled hen's egg.

Jessie felt overwhelmed at the Belgian woman's kindness – traipsing across fields in the snow to deliver a gift that her own family surely needed more than an English girl. 'Thank you,' she said, folding the other woman into a hug. 'This is the best Christmas present I've ever had.'

That morning, Jessie took some snow from outside the hut and heated it up on the fire in her mess tin. Then she boiled the egg and shared it around between her friends in the battery.

The German advance had been halted, but they hadn't given up altogether, and on New Year's Day 1945 they launched a major aerial attack, Operation Baseplate. The ack-ack girls watched in horror as waves of bombers flew overhead, on their way to the nearby Allied airfields. They did their best to shoot the planes down, but the majority got through unscathed.

The bombers were flanked by fighter escorts, some of which swooped down on the gun park, firing their machine-guns at the crews there. Fortunately, Jessie and her friends escaped serious injury, but the already chilly wooden huts were now even frostier at night, thanks to the addition of several dozen bullet holes.

The German operation was a limited success, but in the long run it didn't make much difference. The Allies soon recovered from the damage done to their airfields, while the losses sustained by the Luftwaffe were enough to cripple the German fighter force for the rest of the war.

Meanwhile, the Battle of the Bulge was continuing to favour the Allies, and on 7 January, Hitler ordered his troops to withdraw. For the American soldiers the fight had been a costly one

– they had lost almost 20,000 men. But at last the battle for Europe was back on track, and Jessie and her friends were out of danger.

A week later, some of the ack-ack girls were celebrating at a dance on a local Army base. Among them were Marie Rose, the Brummie girl who was dating an American GI, and Molly Norris, the cuddly orderly sergeant. It was Friday the thirteenth, but nobody was feeling superstitious. Buoyed by the recent victory in the Ardennes, the girls partied hard, and it was not until the early hours of the morning that they finally piled into a lorry for the drive back to Winksele-Delle.

But the late hour brought with it a new obstacle for the driver, when he reached a railway crossing and found that the gate had been bolted shut. There was no way he and the 20 girls in the back were going to spend the night in the vehicle – it was one of the coldest Januaries on record and the roads were already thick with snow. Leaving the engine running, the driver took a pair of bolt cutters and snapped off the padlock on the gate. Then he pushed it out of the way of the lorry, got back into his seat and put the vehicle into gear.

Why the driver failed to see or hear the train speeding towards him through the dark night, no one could say. All they knew was that the lorry never made it to the other side of the level crossing. Instead it was hurled off the track and into a signal box, where it promptly burst into flames.

Several of the girls inside were killed instantly, among them Marie Rose, whose sing-song accent had so charmed her GI boyfriend. But Sergeant Molly Norris was less fortunate. She was thrown from the vehicle into a nearby field, breaking her back as she hit the ground. It wasn't until the following day that her body was finally found. She had frozen to death in the snow.

When news of the accident reached the rest of the battery, the men and women there were devastated. Jessie found one of the gunners, a tough, burly chap, who went by the incongruous nickname 'Tiny', crying his eyes out round the back of the cookhouse. 'I just can't believe Marie's gone,' he explained, looking up at her with bloodshot eyes.

Jessie, meanwhile, was haunted by the thought of poor Aunt Molly, dying alone in the cold dark night. She thought back to the conversation they had shared on the train down to Peterborough, and wondered how the sergeant's parents had greeted her in the end, after so many years of separation. She hoped that the family had been reconciled before it was too late. Soon, she knew, Mrs and Mrs Norris would be receiving their own life-changing letter from the Army Records Office.

The whole battery was invited to the funeral for the girls killed in the accident, which was held at a church in the nearby town of Louvain. Jessie told the others that she didn't want to go – she feared it would bring back too many difficult memories of when Jim had died. But as she waited back at the camp while her friends said goodbye to their lost comrades, she couldn't help feeling like a coward.

Before long the other girls returned, shell-shocked from the traumatic experience of burying their friends. 'It was awful,' one of them told Jessie. 'Marie's boyfriend Dave just cried and cried. He couldn't stop, and there was nothing anyone could say to help him.'

*

In February 1945, the ranks of the ATS were swelled by the arrival of a very important new recruit. The king's eldest daughter had chosen to join the service as a mechanic and driver, and soon newspapers and magazines were printing pictures of Second Subaltern Elizabeth Windsor in her khaki overalls, checking engine oil and changing tires. For Jessie and her fellow 'ATS tarts', it felt like a kind of vindication – no longer could snooty Wrens claim that being in the 'senior service' meant they were special. Of the three women's forces, it was the ATS that the future Queen of England had chosen.

Meanwhile, the conditions at Winksele-Delle were beginning to improve, bit by bit. The first notable development was in the ablutions, where a carpenter from the local village had been persuaded to carve toilet seats for the girls. They sat loose on top of the buckets, requiring significant agility to prevent the whole thing from topping over, but at least it was a start.

Next, a group of engineers arrived to wire the camp up for electricity, meaning the girls could have proper light bulbs in their huts instead of relying on paraffin lamps. A makeshift NAAFI counter was set up in the dining hut, and one day, to Jessie's delight, she arrived to find a piano in there too. She couldn't help wondering where the new instrument had come from, privately suspecting that it had been plundered from one of the local houses, but she knew better than to look a gift horse in the mouth. Soon she and Stan had started up their little band again and the battery were singing and dancing just like in the old days.

But even better than the improvements to the camp was the fact that the girls were now allowed into Brussels at the weekends. As a German leave city it had been spared by the Luftwaffe, and Jessie marvelled at all the magnificent old buildings. She made the most of her time there, visiting the stunning Gothic cathedral and the Museum of Fine Arts, while some of her colleagues put their energies into buying Belgian chocolates on the black market.

The girls generally ate in the Monty Club, an enormous canteen for forces personnel where the food was always plentiful and cheap, before dancing the night away with a cosmopolitan mix of soldiers – British, American, Free Dutch and others. By the time they got back to camp they always felt absolutely shattered, but finally life seemed to be worth living again.

One evening, while Jessie was sitting in her hut, a girl rushed in and announced, 'There's a man from Signals in the guardroom who wants to see you.'

'Really?' Jessie replied, surprised. 'I don't think I know anyone in Signals.'

'Well, he says he knows you,' the girl told her.

Jessie shrugged and headed over to the guardroom, wondering who the mysterious stranger could be. But when she got there she found herself looking at a very familiar face – just one she hadn't ever expected to see again.

'Mac!' she exclaimed, the final letter she had written to the young Scotsman flashing guiltily through her mind.

But if Mac had been crushed by Jessie's words a year earlier, he showed no sign of it now. His face lit up as if she was his favourite person in the world. 'Ach, it's so lovely to see you again!' he exclaimed.

'It's nice to see you too,' Jessie told him. Since she had the evening off, she agreed to accompany him into Louvain for a cup of tea.

As they sat in a little canteen, facing each other across the table, Mac filled Jessie in on what he had been doing since they had last seen each other. He had been transferred to a new unit, he explained, helping to repair signal wires that had been damaged in bombing raids. He had gone over to France shortly after D-Day, following closely behind the front-line troops. 'There were a couple of hairy moments,' he admitted. 'One time, we were trying to mend these great big cables and the Germans started shelling us. Every time a shell exploded the bloke with the soldering iron burned himself and jumped a foot up in the air. In the end I told him to bugger off and let me do it on my own!'

'So what brought you to this neck of the woods?' Jessie asked him.

'Why, you did, of course!' he laughed. 'I was in Brussels for the day and I noticed some ATS girls wearing white lanyards. I knew that meant ack-ack, and I figured if the guns had been brought over here, then you must be somewhere around too.' He shrugged his shoulders. 'This was the third battery I tried!'

Jessie couldn't help smiling. That was Mac, she thought, incorrigible as ever.

Now that he had tracked Jessie down, Mac began turning up at Winksele-Delle every couple of weeks. The two of them would head into Louvain or Mechelen together, or if she couldn't get an evening pass he would just sign in as a visitor and they would sit in the NAAFI. She asked him how his family back home in the Highlands were doing, and he asked after all the people from 518 he had got to know in Hull.

Jessie had forgotten how nice it was to talk to someone with whom she had things in common, who loved music as much as she did and shared her sense of humour. In the time since she had cut off their relationship in England she had rarely thought of Mac at all, but now, seeing him again, she realised how much she had missed him.

Mac never mentioned the letters that Jessie had sent ending their affair. In fact he acted almost as if the break-up had never really happened – as if the two of them had just been separated for a while by forces beyond their control. In a way, Jessie thought, perhaps they had. Pushing Mac away had been a means of protecting herself when she hadn't felt ready to get too close to him, fearful of setting herself up for another devastating loss. But now that the end of the war was in sight, maybe it was time to let that go.

On 7 May 1945, Jessie and Elsie hitch-hiked into Louvain for the evening to catch a film at the local cinema. When they emerged afterwards, they were confronted by a scene more dramatic than anything they had witnessed on the screen. The Belgians were running wildly up and down the streets, leaping in the air and shouting, '*La guerre est finie! La guerre est finie!*'

A man ran up to the girls and demanded to know why they weren't celebrating. 'I'm sorry, but we've got to be back by 10.30 p.m. or we'll be on a charge!' Elsie replied. The war might be over but Army rules still applied, and they dutifully hurried back to camp.

The following morning, however, the world awoke to the start of the biggest party in living memory. By 6 a.m., Mac was already waiting for Jessie at the camp gates, anxious that they should both be a part of it. 'Come on, the war's over!' he said excitedly. 'Let's go out.'

'I can't, I'm supposed to be on duty!' Jessie protested.

'Didn't you hear me?' Mac insisted. 'The war is *over*!'

Jessie stood staring at him for a moment, letting the words sink in. After all the years of loss, all the suffering and horror and fear, the great moment had finally come. The dark cloud that had been hovering overhead had lifted. Suddenly Jessie was hit by a palpable wave of relief, which left her so light-headed that she could barely stand.

After she had caught her breath, Jessie ran back to her hut, changed hastily into her service dress, and walked out of the camp before anyone could stop her. For the first time since she had joined the Army, she was going AWOL.

Out on the main road, she and Mac thumbed a lift to Mechelen, where he told her he knew a Belgian couple who would be delighted to see them. Pa Ribbens had worked for the resistance during the occupation and had escaped from a German prisoner-of-war camp, so Mac knew that on VE Day he would be throwing the party to end all parties.

When Jessie and Mac got into town, however, they found the streets were almost impassable. Enormous crowds had gathered everywhere, cheering, singing, laughing, crying, drinking and sounding paper hooters. The roads were so packed that there was barely any room to move, but Jessie did her best to follow Mac as he edged through the throng.

Suddenly, she realised that she couldn't see him any more. A large Belgian man had spotted her uniform and was shouting, '*Een soldaat! Een soldaat!*' A great cheer went up, and Jessie was promptly hoisted onto the man's shoulders, like a footballer who had just scored the winning goal.

'Let me down!' she laughed, but her words were drowned out by the whooping and clapping of the civilians, and soon she was carried away into the sea of people. In the distance she noticed a Belgian man proudly sporting what looked like an ATS cap – and when she reached up to her own head she realised it was bare. The reveller had evidently decided that the hat of an English *soldaat* was the perfect VE Day souvenir.

It was more than an hour before Jessie finally managed to find Mac again, and after her protracted lap of victory she was looking distinctly dishevelled.

'Where on earth have you been?' he asked. 'I was worried about you.'

'I've been trying to find you, but the Belgians had other ideas!' Jessie replied, as she followed him through the streets towards his friends' house. 'And somebody pinched my hat too!'

'Ach well, never mind about that,' he laughed, leading her inside. 'Come and have a drink, why don't you?'

Jessie found herself entering a little living room that was as busy as Waterloo Station, with friends and strangers alike coming and going – hugging, kissing, singing, dancing and raising toast after toast to victory and freedom. Mac's friend Pa Ribbens had already cracked open a bottle of cognac that he'd been hiding in the cellar throughout the war, and the party was well and truly underway.

When Pa and his wife found out that Jessie wasn't much of a drinker, they insisted on brewing up a pot of tea for her instead. Ma Ribbens explained that the British had left the stuff behind in 1940 when they began the retreat to Dunkirk, and she had kept it in the house ever since. 'I always knew you would come back one day,' she said, with evident emotion in her voice.

Jessie was touched by the gesture and did her best to gulp down the symbolic drink, but after five years in the Ribbens' damp larder the tea wasn't exactly at its best.

Not that she needed caffeine or alcohol to keep her going that day. The atmosphere of frenzied elation was infectious, and Jessie soon found herself singing and dancing, not to mention hugging and kissing perfect strangers, along with everyone else. The party went on all day long and then continued into the evening, and she was so caught up in the general hysteria that it was well after midnight by the time she finally remembered that she ought to be getting back to camp.

She and Mac hitch-hiked back to Winksele-Delle together, and after seeing her to the camp gates he left to make his own way home. But as she walked past the gun park on her way to her hut, she found a party was in progress there as well, and the revels were even more ecstatic than those she had witnessed on the streets of Mechelen. The local villagers had somehow got into the camp and had started an enormous bonfire, burning everything they could find, from tables and chairs to sentry boxes. Now they were dancing around the flames like whirling dervishes.

Their children, meanwhile, were running in and out of the command post – clambering all over the guns, looking through the eyepieces on the height-and-range finder and playing with the predictor's little knobs and levers, as if the state-of-the-art machine was just a toy. Jessie's first thought was to rush over and try to protect the equipment, but then she remembered – it didn't matter any more. The guns would never have to be fired again.

She made her way back to her hut and collapsed, exhausted and happy, onto her bed. Through the window she could see the light of the bonfire gently flickering outside.

17

Margery

One evening in the spring of 1945, Margery received an urgent call from Kasfareet. It was one of Doug's friends telling her that he was on his way to see her.

She dashed to the station and caught the next train into Cairo, before heading for their usual meeting place, the YWCA. She arrived just after 6 p.m. and settled down with a cup of chai tea, wondering what could have prompted Doug to rush into town so suddenly. Did he have something important to tell her?

But by the time Margery had finished her tea there was no sign of Doug. An hour and then two hours passed, and still he hadn't arrived. By 8.30 p.m. she had had enough, and returned to Turah utterly perplexed.

'Oh, Doug was here looking for you,' Elspeth told her, as soon as she got to their tent. 'He only left about half an hour ago.'

'I don't believe it!' Margery cried. She had waited all those hours in Cairo for nothing, and now it was too late to catch him.

The following morning Margery and Doug finally managed to meet at the YWCA for coffee, and exchanged their stories of crossed wires and missed connections. 'I was waiting two and a half hours for you here yesterday!' Margery told him.

'Well I was waiting longer than that for you,' Doug laughed. 'When you weren't at your camp I came looking for you here, and I didn't leave until 11.30 at night.'

Suddenly, he stopped laughing, and a serious look passed over his face. 'Margery, I wanted to tell you something,' he said. 'I'm being sent back home.'

'Oh,' said Margery, surprised. Although other people at her camp were gradually starting to return to England, and the so-called 'boat parties' held when they left were becoming more and more frequent, the idea that Doug might one day not be around any more had never really crossed her mind.

'Of course, we could still get married before I go,' he added quietly.

Margery looked at Doug, thinking for a moment. Everyone was always telling her what a nice chap he was, and they were right. He was gentle, kind, and good fun to be around. Her friends had all started asking what on earth she was waiting for.

But still the old wariness lurked at the back of her mind. A lot of people were fun, she told herself. That didn't necessarily make someone a good person. How could she know what Doug would be like in Civvy Street – living a normal life, in a normal house, back in England?

'I can't marry someone who's still in the service,' she replied. 'I'd have to see what you're like back home first.'

Doug didn't try to push the subject, although Margery could tell he was disappointed. They decided to make the most of the rest of the day, heading by taxi to the Alamein Club to watch Cairo play Alexandria at football. Then they paused by the river so that he could take a last look at the Nile.

When they parted that evening, Doug promised to write to Margery from England. And then, just like that, he was gone.

The following morning, Margery was woken by an unfamiliar noise on the canvas above her head: the pitter-pattering of a thousand tiny raindrops. When she peered out of the tent she could see that they were being deluged by a rare desert storm. For some reason the sand, unlike earth, seemed to resist the rain rather than absorbing it, and soon the entire camp was ankle-deep in water.

When she returned to her tent after work that evening, Margery discovered that the rain had found its way inside, and the area around her bed was completely flooded. As she did her best to mop up the soggy mess, she could hear the strains of singing coming from the NAAFI. Evidently someone else was leaving for England, and another boat party was underway.

7 May was a particularly hot day in Egypt, and the camp was also sizzling with the rumour that victory was about to be declared. A little before 6 p.m., a Scottish girl called Chris came rushing over to Margery's tent and shouted breathlessly, 'Come quick – I've got my wireless on!'

Margery, Elspeth and Ann followed Chris back to her tent, where a few other girls were already huddled around the radio to hear the official announcement of the end of war in Europe. 'That's it,' said Margery. 'It's all over then!'

She rushed to the NAAFI to share the monumental news. 'Did you know the war is over?' she called out to the girls who were sitting in there. But to her surprise they barely looked up. 'Apparently it's not VE Day until tomorrow,' one of them said, 'so there's no point doing anything now.'

Margery was astounded. How could the other girls be so nonchalant? But it seemed that even the desert didn't want anyone to celebrate. Before long a terrible sandstorm had begun – the worst, in fact, that Margery had ever seen. It was impossible to spend any time out of doors, and when the storm did finally abate, Margery and her friends discovered that the washing they had hung out on the guy ropes of their tent was not only covered in sand but scattered all over the camp. Instead of celebrating, they spent most of the rest of the evening hunting for stray pants and bras, and then washing them all over again.

When Margery finally settled down to bed that night she was startled by the sound of far-off explosions, and looking out of the tent she saw a series of beautiful starbursts in the night sky. 'Fireworks!' said Elspeth, joining her in the doorway. At least someone was celebrating the end of the war, Margery thought.

But the following morning a less cheerful sight met the girls' eyes. Looking up towards the hills where they worked, they saw that one of the caves was blackened, and smoke was pouring out of it. The 'fireworks' they had seen the previous night had in fact been explosions caused by canisters of poisonous gas being set alight by a raucous group of airmen, who had decided to celebrate victory with a little wanton vandalism.

The camp's commanding officer ordered everyone to carry their gas masks around for the rest of the day, in case the wind changed and blew the noxious fumes in their direction. The last thing he wanted was for his troops to be overcome by gas intended for the Germans, just when they had finally surrendered.

At RAF Turah, VE Day was formally marked with a drumhead service on the parade ground. The hymns were led by the camp choir, gathered around a little piano that had been dragged out from the NAAFI, while the chaplain stood on a wobbly wooden platform, his cassock flapping in the wind as he shouted out a few prayers to the rows of assembled airmen and WAAFs. When the brief ceremony was over, the CO announced that they all had the rest of the day off, and they were dismissed.

Margery felt more disappointed than ever. There was to be no party, no dance – in fact no celebration whatsoever laid on for the men and women who had stuck it out in Egypt for so many years. She could scarcely believe that it was true.

But there was something else on her mind that morning, and if anything it was bothering her even more. She had just received a letter from her mother, in which she mentioned that she had recently been visited by Doug. Once he'd got back to England, he and his father had apparently cycled over to the Pott residence in North Wallington to introduce themselves.

'I'm so pleased you've met someone,' Margery's mother wrote. 'Doug seems like a very nice young man, and he tells me you're going to get married.'

Margery was astounded that Doug should have taken it upon himself to turn up at her mother's door, without even asking her first – and even more so that he had spoken of marriage as if it was something already agreed between them. Hadn't she told him that she couldn't make a decision until they got to know each other at home? Yet now it seemed their families were meeting up behind her back, before she'd even got on the boat!

Margery dashed off an indignant reply, informing her mother that she had never made any promises to Doug, and she couldn't imagine what had possessed him to go round and visit. Then she sealed the envelope and dropped it off in the mail room to be posted, her irritation momentarily soothed.

With that out of the way, she headed over to the NAAFI, determined to find some friends she could head into Cairo with, to make up for the pitiful lack of celebrations at Turah. But as she looked round the room, Margery realised that pretty much everyone else had already left. Over recent months the girls at Turah had begun to couple up with the men there, and most of them were probably off celebrating in their little romantic pairs.

In fact, even the normally timid Elspeth had managed to get herself a boyfriend – a rather cheeky airman called Red. Margery wasn't exactly thrilled at her friend's choice. Red was a nice enough bloke, but he was the kind of man who, while he loved playing practical jokes on others, couldn't take it when the tables were turned on him. On one recent outing to the swimming pool at the Alamein Club he had jumped on Margery and held her under the water until she was struggling to hold her breath. It was a cruel trick to play on such a weak swimmer, and although Margery had laughed off the prank at the time, it had bothered her. Elspeth was so sweet natured that she always saw the good in everyone, but privately Margery thought she deserved better.

As it turned out, Margery wasn't quite the last person standing in the NAAFI that evening. A lad called Don, who was only 19 and looked about five years younger, had also found himself all alone. 'No one wants to celebrate with me,' he told Margery plaintively, his young face crumpling as if he was about to burst into tears.

Margery couldn't help feeling sorry for the poor lad – and as she looked around the otherwise empty room, she realised that she didn't have any other options. 'I'll go out with you, Don,' she sighed wearily.

The two of them caught the train into Cairo together, where Margery took Don to the Tedder Club for a slap-up meal. When they arrived, he insisted that they sit at a table in the corner so that no one could see him eating. The request struck Margery as rather odd, but as soon as Don began digging into his food she began to understand it. The poor boy had no idea how to handle a knife and fork, and his table manners left a lot to be desired. It was no wonder that he had struggled to find a date for the big day.

Margery was beginning to grow tired of life at Turah, and when a notice went up asking for girls to volunteer for a transfer to Aden, she quickly put in an application. She'd heard that Yemen was even hotter than Egypt, but right now she really didn't care. She'd had it with 111 Maintenance Unit and was ready to move on.

A few weeks later Margery was thrilled to learn that her application had been accepted, and soon a new blonde corporal called Dora arrived at Turah to take her place running Equipment Accounts. As Margery shook hands with her replacement she couldn't help wondering how long she would last out in the desert. The girl looked in quite a state already – she was coughing badly, and her voice was barely raised above a whisper – but perhaps, Margery reasoned, she was simply tired from the long journey.

Margery returned to her desk with more enthusiasm than she had felt in months, finishing off various little bits of paperwork so that Dora could make a fresh start when she took over. But, a couple of hours later, she was told that the new girl had been carted off to hospital in the camp ambulance – apparently she was now running a high fever and her lymph glands had swollen up like golf balls. Margery couldn't believe it – now her own departure would have to be delayed until Dora recovered from her illness.

A few days later, Margery went to visit Dora in hospital. She was hoping to see an improvement in the girl's condition that might indicate she would soon be back on her feet, but what she found did nothing to reassure her. Dora looked ghastly – her blonde hair was limp and greasy, her face deathly pale and her neck horribly swollen.

'I've brought you some things,' said Margery, emptying out a bag she had filled with Dora's clothes and belongings. As she leaned over the patient to arrange a few cosmetics on her bedside table, Dora let out a sigh, and a rancid gust of air met Margery's nostrils. It was the most disgusting thing that she had ever smelled, and she struggled not to vomit on the spot.

When she left the ward, Margery spoke to one of Dora's nurses, who informed her that the girl was suffering from a very bad throat infection, and would likely have to have her tonsils taken out. There was no way she would be returning to work any time soon.

Demoralised, Margery returned to camp – only to be greeted with even worse news. A decision had been taken to stop sending women out to Aden altogether, since it was no longer considered to be safe. Her ill-fated escape plan had failed completely.

With so many of the other girls at Turah now coupled up, Margery was increasingly spending her spare time with an older, married sergeant known as Brownie. He worked in the camp's metal-plating shop, which, like Equipment Accounts, was in one of the caves up in the hills, and since she was purposefully avoiding romantic attachments he proved to be the ideal companion. Brownie and his wife had always wanted a girl, he told her, and he treated Margery as if she was the daughter they'd never had.

Margery often took Brownie to the YWCA in Cairo, where they would sit and drink chai tea together, just like she used to with Doug. But one weekend he suggested a more exciting excursion. They hired a cab to take them to see the Great Pyramid at Giza, and scrambled up the enormous limestone blocks all the way to the top. From there, Margery could see the caves at Turah, including the burned-out hole that had been made when victory in Europe was declared.

With Germany defeated, everything was gradually slowing down at Turah. Soon Brownie got word that his plating shop was being closed, and he would be leaving the camp for a new posting at the Kasr-el-Nil barracks in downtown Cairo. Margery was sad to see him go, but it didn't make that much difference to their regular get-togethers – now, when they were both at a loose end, she joined him at the sergeants' mess in the barracks, where he could put their meals on expenses.

One evening as they were finishing their dinner, Margery asked if they could go back to Giza and see the Great Pyramid again.

'What, now?' Brownie asked her, confused.

'Yes,' she replied, feeling a little self-conscious. 'The thing is … I'd like to see it by moonlight.'

Margery explained that she had watched a glorious Technicolor movie called *The Garden of Allah*, in which her idol, Charles Boyer, wooed the impossibly glamorous Marlene Dietrich under the stars. By the light of the moon, the desert had looked incedibly romantic, and Margery longed to see the pyramids that way herself.

'Well, if that's what you want, then that's what we'll do,' Brownie told her indulgently. They hopped in a cab and set off over the English Bridge onto the west bank of the Nile. As they left the city behind them, the grand European buildings gave way to little villages of mud huts.

By the time they arrived at the Giza Plateau, the moon was shining brightly, and they strolled arm-in-arm looking up at the famous monuments. There was the Great Pyramid, Khufu, which they had climbed on their previous visit, along with its smaller siblings, Khafre and Menkaure.

Margery had expected the moonlight to add to the mysterious beauty of the pyramids, but if anything their looming shapes now seemed instead rather hulking and ugly. The Great Sphinx certainly wasn't looking its best, either, with a blast wall between its legs, and sandbags piled up under its chin.

'Can we just stop for a moment?' Margery asked Brownie. They stood perfectly still, and she breathed in the night air, trying as hard as she could to summon up the spirit of the movie. But the romantic atmosphere was sorely absent.

'It's no good,' she complained. 'It's nothing like it was in the film. The moonlight doesn't seem to be working.'

'Well,' he replied gently, 'maybe you're just not here with the right person.'

Before Margery could answer, a lorry came roaring into view, shattering the perfect silence of the night. As it pulled up, a noisy gaggle of British soldiers emerged, carrying a football. 'Perfect flat bit here,' one of them called, heading the ball to his mate.

Before long, a raucous kickabout was underway, while off to one side a couple of Egyptian men were busy setting up a little stall, where they began cooking eggs and chips for the soldiers. The greasy smell wafted through the still night air, and if Margery had been struggling to feel the atmosphere before, now her chances were slimmer than ever.

Defeated, Margery headed over to the stall, where she and Brownie bought some egg and chips of their own before heading back to Cairo.

While at Turah everything seemed to be winding down, with more airmen and women departing every few days, Cairo was also undergoing a period of change. Among the ordinary Egyptians there had always been a degree of hostility towards the British, and now that the prospect of a German invasion was off the table, the desire to see the back of them had only grown stronger.

Britain had recently found itself in the midst of heated disagreements over the thorny question of its plans for Palestine. The formation of a Jewish state in the area had been a long-term aspiration – ever since the Balfour Declaration of 1917, in which the British foreign secretary had called for a 'national home for the Jewish people'. But in the Arab world such proposals were generally met with resentment and hostility.

On 2 November 1945, Margery hitch-hiked into Cairo to get some photographs developed, along with another girl from Turah called Moxie. They had no idea of the significance of the date, but it was 'Balfour Day', the anniversary of the British declaration, and for the anti-Jewish forces in Cairo that meant a call to arms. The Muslim Brotherhood and the Young Egypt Party had joined forces to stage a major rally in the city, along with a similar protest in Alexandria.

The girls were dropped off next to Tahrir Square, where almost immediately they encountered the beginnings of the demonstration. Thousands of young men had gathered and were chanting loudly in Arabic.

Margery found the sight of the crowd mesmerising, but Moxie was horrified. 'They're going to kill us!' she exclaimed.

Margery did her best to reassure her companion that the Egyptians wouldn't do them any harm, but the girl could not be persuaded, so she put her on a metro train to El Gedida and headed off alone in the direction of the Kasr-el-Nil barracks, hoping that she might find Brownie there.

By the time she arrived, the barracks too was surrounded by a large crowd, and a man with a megaphone was whipping them up into a frenzy. Margery couldn't understand the Arabic words, but the sentiment was perfectly clear – the young men were angry, and they wanted to do something about it.

Suddenly, she felt a hand on her arm. 'I think you'd better come inside before this turns nasty,' a British soldier told her. 'Some of the men out there are carrying sulphuric acid.'

For the first time, Margery felt a chill run down her spine. Perhaps the soldier was right and this wasn't the best place to be standing. She followed him through the gate, casting an anxious glance over her shoulder.

As the soldier had predicted, the protest did indeed soon turn nasty, with injuries running into the hundreds. Jewish department stores were looted, homes were ransacked, and a synagogue was burned to the ground, with holy books thrown onto a bonfire. Meanwhile, in Alexandria, five Egyptian Jews were murdered by the crowds. A few days later, in nearby Libya, the situation was even worse, with 140 Jews killed in a series of copycat riots.

Margery remained in the Army barracks in Cairo until things had calmed down outside, and that night she took the train back to Turah rather than hitch-hiking. The city that had always seemed so welcoming had taken on a distinctly darker edge.

*

With Christmas approaching, Margery was, as ever, doing her bit to make sure the season was celebrated in style. Some of the airmen had managed to haul a tree into the NAAFI canteen, and she set to work decorating it with sweets and coloured paper, as well as helping to bake some mince pies.

On Christmas Eve, everyone gathered in the canteen to celebrate together. Brownie had travelled in from Cairo to spend the evening with his old friends, and the whole camp was getting into the festive spirit. Even Chico, an Egyptian boy of about 11 who made the tea, seemed caught up in the celebratory atmosphere. Margery watched in astonishment as he leapt up onto one of the tables and began performing a traditional dance, with a crowd of airmen cheering him on.

'That's not like Chico,' she remarked to one of the officers. 'He's normally such a shy little boy.'

'I know!' the man replied with a laugh. 'We had to spike his drink with rum. Poor chap hadn't the faintest idea what he was drinking.'

Just then, Margery was startled by the noise of a knife clinking against a wine glass. She turned to see Elspeth and Red standing at one end of the room, evidently planning to make some kind of announcement. A hush fell over the noisy rabble.

'It's so lovely to see all your smiling faces,' Elspeth began nervously. 'We've got something we want to share with you all.'

Red squeezed her hand as he stepped forward and announced loudly, 'We're only getting married!'

Right on cue, a cheer went up around the room.

Margery turned to Brownie, who was sitting next to her. 'Well, well,' he said wryly, 'I suppose we'd better get some drinks in.' Then he went off in the direction of the bar.

Margery sat alone for a moment, watching as a queue of people formed in front of the happy couple, lining up to offer their congratulations. The announcement shouldn't have come as too much of a surprise to her, but still it had somehow felt sudden.

Seated in the corner of the room, Margery was surprised to see Elspeth extricate herself from the throng and make a beeline for her. 'Congratulations!' she told her friend warmly, budging up a little on her bench so that Elspeth could sit down.

But the bride-to-be remained standing. 'Thanks, Margery,' she replied. 'Look, I was just wondering if you could do us a little favour.'

'Of course,' Margery told her. 'What is it?'

'Could you keep Brownie away from Red for the rest of the evening?' Elspeth asked awkwardly. 'It's just ... you know what he's like. He'll tease Red about getting married, and it'll put his hackles up.'

The request seemed extraordinary to Margery, since if anyone enjoyed winding other people up, it was Red. But then, she thought, it was true that he never liked having the tables turned on himself.

'Please, Margery?' Elspeth asked. 'I just don't want it to spoil Red's evening.'

'All right, then,' Margery replied, unsure what else she could say.

Elspeth shot off back to Red, leaving Margery alone again, and before long Brownie arrived with the drinks. 'Here you go,' he told her, placing a mug of Stella Artois down on the table. 'Why don't you make a start on that while I go and give my regards to Elspeth and Red?'

'Oh, stay and have a drink with me first, won't you?' Margery begged him awkwardly.

'All right, then,' Brownie replied. 'Whatever you say.'

Margery spent the rest of the evening trying to keep the two men apart – which, given that Elspeth and Red had become very much the centre of the evening, meant that she and Brownie were consigned to the periphery. They sat quietly in the corner, knocking back mugfuls of Stella and growing increasingly tipsy.

'Margery, I really think I ought to congratulate them,' Brownie told her, after she had put him off for the umpteenth time that night. 'Otherwise they'll think I'm being rude.'

'No, you honestly don't need to,' she told him. The frustration was beginning to show in her voice.

'Look, I don't know what your problem is,' Brownie snapped at her. 'If you're jealous of Elspeth getting married, then why do you spend all your time sitting around with me?'

'I'm not jealous!' Margery protested. But she couldn't tell him the real reason that the two of them had spent the evening hiding away in the corner, rather than enjoying the party.

At the end of the night, Brownie went to catch the train back to Cairo, still visibly annoyed with Margery. The whole experience had left her feeling lonelier than she had been at any time since she arrived in Egypt.

18

Kathleen

On the evening of Monday 7 May 1945, when official news of the German surrender reached HMS *Hornbill*, the timing couldn't have been better for Kathleen. She was just about to start a day's leave, and had been planning to spend it down in London anyway. Now she would be visiting the capital in time to join the big party.

Like everyone up and down the country, Kathleen greeted the news of Victory in Europe with enormous relief. But as she sat looking out of the window on the train to Paddington, there was one thought paramount in her mind – and in a way it was even sweeter than the knowledge that the war was almost over. Soon her beloved Arnold would be coming home to England, and at last they would be able to marry.

By the time Kathleen managed to find a YWCA hostel all the beds had already been taken, but she was allocated a small section of floor space. Next to her was another Wren called Sally, and as they bedded down for the night the two girls chatted about what they should do in the morning. Tuesday had been officially designated as VE Day and crowds would be gathering all over London to celebrate and watch the speeches.

'Why don't we just head to Hyde Park?' Sally suggested. 'It's not far, and there's bound to be lots going on there.'

That night, the city's streets were lashed with rain as a terrific thunderstorm opened up, illuminating the night sky with forks of brilliant white lightning. In the cramped dormitory of the YWCA, the girls struggled to get to sleep. Quite apart from the bright flashes of light and the occasional thunderclap, the day's momentous news was still swirling around in their heads.

But despite a fitful night on the hard wooden floor, Kathleen awoke the next morning full of energy. After breakfast, she and Sally set off together, through streets already thronging with people, many of them wearing paper hats or rosettes and carrying streamers and flags. There were servicemen and women of every possible denomination – and not just English ones either. In among the khaki and blues of the British forces were the uniforms of American GIs, Canadians, Free French and Poles as well.

Crowds of people were singing and dancing wildly in the streets, complete strangers embraced one another and couples kissed with abandon. Kathleen watched as two dozen people with their arms around each other's shoulders gave a spirited performance of 'Knees Up Mother Brown'.

By the time the girls reached Hyde Park, they had been swept up in a sea of bodies. They made their way along the tail end of the Serpentine until they spotted a magnificent bronze statue of a man on a horse. Some of the people around it were already clambering up onto the plinth. 'Let's go up there,' Sally said. 'We'll get a better view.'

The girls pushed through the crowds until they reached the base of the statue, where they begged a lift up onto the plinth from a couple of burly men standing below. Kathleen leaned back against one of the bronze horse's sinewy hind legs and gazed out at the scene in front of her. She had never seen so many people in her life before. Every inch of the park seemed to be filled with human beings, and the numbers were swelling by the minute. Looking around, she could see that the statue wasn't the only thing to have been climbed – in fact every post-box, every lamppost, and every monument in view appeared to have people draped over it.

It was a party the like of which Kathleen had never seen. Joyous men and women were joining hands to sing 'Roll out the Barrel', and strolling up and down together, dancing the Palais Glide. Many had brought their own musical instruments with them and were doing their best to bash out popular tunes on banjos and harmonicas, or blowing furiously on little paper trumpets they had purchased on their way to the park. The ground around them was littered with ticker-tape and confetti.

The spring day was an unusually hot one, but the soaring temperatures only seemed to increase the mood of elation – not just in Hyde Park, but all over London. In Trafalgar Square, revellers paddled in the fountains, gazing up at the bombers flying in formation over their heads. At Piccadilly Circus, there were bands playing, and a conga line snaked around the statue of Eros. From the windows of the nearby Rainbow Club, where American GIs had gathered throughout the war for a taste of home, toilet rolls were being thrown into the street in lieu of streamers.

The largest gathering was at Buckingham Palace, where more than 20,000 people arrived to see the royal family on their balcony. Seven times that day the King came out to wave at them, accompanied by his daughter Elizabeth in her ATS uniform. Meanwhile, at the Cenotaph, a more sombre crowd had gathered to admire the floral tributes and pay their respects to the fallen.

That afternoon Winston Churchill addressed the assembled masses in Parliament Square. 'This is your victory,' he told them. 'Everyone, man or woman, has done their best. This is not a victory of a party or of any class. It's a victory of the British nation as a whole.' When the jubilant crowd began singing 'Land of Hope and Glory', the Prime Minister joined in proudly.

On her plinth in Hyde Park, Kathleen was having a wonderful time just sitting and watching the celebrations around her, but after several hours up there she found she had grown desperate for the toilet. 'How are we going to get down again?' she asked Sally. The distance to the ground was too far for them to jump.

Luckily, a couple of naval officers who were sharing the plinth with them overheard Kathleen's words. 'We'll get down first,' one of them suggested, 'and then you jump and we'll catch you.'

'All right,' Kathleen agreed, a little nervously. She waited for the men to climb down from the statue and then, on a count of three, hurled herself into their arms. Sally followed suit a few moments later, laughing as she leapt from the plinth. It certainly wasn't the kind of ladylike behaviour that had been drummed into the girls by the WRNS, but on a day like this, who cared?

Looking over at the public toilets, Kathleen was horrified to see a line of women snaking all around them. 'Don't worry,' one of the sailors told her, 'I've got an idea.' He took Kathleen's hand and pulled her towards the front of the queue. 'Excuse me!' he shouted. 'My wife is pregnant and she needs to go immediately!'

Kathleen was promptly ushered into the next available cubicle and tried her best not to giggle, as the man called after her, 'You'll be all right now, darling!'

When she emerged a couple of moments later, she found the two sailors still outside, chatting to Sally. 'I hear you girls have never been on board ship in your whole time in the Navy,' one of them told Kathleen. 'Is that right?'

'I'm afraid so,' she replied ruefully.

'Well, we can't have that,' the officer replied. 'You'll just have to come to our frigate for some grub. It's moored down on the river at Chelsea.'

'Ooh, yes please!' Kathleen replied. With the war coming to an end, it could be her only chance to go on board a naval vessel before she was demobbed – and she wasn't about to pass up a free meal either.

The sailors led the girls out of Hyde Park, past the Albert Memorial and the Natural History Museum, and through the bustling streets of South Kensington until they reached the embankment, where, sure enough, a small battleship was moored. As they ascended the gangplank, one of the men motioned to a bosun standing on deck, who piped them aboard with his whistle as if they were honoured guests. Giggling, Kathleen and Sally followed the sailors onto the boat.

The two officers were evidently used to a much more luxurious lifestyle than Kathleen had experienced in the Navy. They led the girls into a dining room with snow-white tablecloths and perfectly arranged napkins. 'It's as good as the Ritz!' Kathleen whispered to Sally.

The girls were attended to by a pair of stewards, who were as well trained as waiters in a fancy restaurant, serving from the left and taking away from the right. And then there was the food – perfectly cooked steak, something the girls hadn't tasted in a long time, along with crisp roast potatoes and baby carrots. All in all, it was the best meal Kathleen had eaten for years.

Despite their impeccable manners, Kathleen thought she saw one of the stewards raise an eyebrow at the sight of her and

Sally. 'They think we've been picked up!' the other girl laughed. But the naval officers made it clear that they were both quite happily married, and were just tickled to see the two Wrens enjoying themselves so much.

Later that day, after they had thanked the sailors for their kind hospitality, the girls wandered the streets for a while, soaking up the atmosphere. By the early evening, Sally was feeling tired and decided to return to the YWCA hostel, but Kathleen wasn't ready to turn in just yet. Instead she walked into the West End, where amid the throng she was surprised to spot the familiar, ruddy-cheeked face of the master gunner from *Hornbill*. 'Wren Skin!' he called, making his way over to her. 'Fancy meeting you here.'

Kathleen's boss insisted that she join him for a drink at a nearby pub called the Captain's Table, a popular hangout for Navy personnel. There she followed him down a little flight of stairs into a room that was packed with naval officers. 'What'll you have?' he asked her, as they walked up to the bar.

'I'd love a shot of rum,' Kathleen said.

'And the same for me,' the master gunner told the barman, who was looking at Kathleen's uniform suspiciously.

'I'm sorry, sir,' the barman replied, 'but it's officers and NCOs only in here. I can serve you but not your friend.'

'Well, that's easily solved,' the master gunner replied, whisking Kathleen's hat off her head and replacing it with his own. 'There you go – now she's a warrant officer.'

The barman smiled. 'As you wish, sir,' he replied.

Kathleen was soon sharing a drink with some of the Navy's finest, for the second time that day enjoying perks that her lowly rank wouldn't normally entitle her to. VE Day had far surpassed her expectations, and she knew she would never forget it. By the time she got back to the YWCA that night she was so exhausted that she barely noticed the hard floorboards beneath her head.

When she arrived back at HMS *Hornbill* the following morning, however, Kathleen discovered that the celebrations there had been even wilder than what she had witnessed in London. Everywhere she looked, men and women were lying prostrate on the ground, empty bottles clasped in their hands.

'Ah, Skin, excellent!' a Wren officer called out to her from the passenger seat of a low-loader lorry. 'You can help me gather the troops.'

The order turned out to be more literal than Kathleen had imagined. As they drove around the camp, she came to realise that she and the officer were pretty much the only sober people there. Even the young sailor driving the lorry was still half-cut from the night before. Some poor souls were conscious but wandering about in a confused daze. 'I don't know where my cabin is,' one seaman moaned pathetically.

'Get on the back of the lorry!' the Wren officer told him sternly.

Gradually, they combed the roads of the camp until they had picked up all the stragglers they could find. Then Kathleen went off to inspect the Armoury hut.

What she found inside was a scene of utter devastation. There were rifles and magazines strewn all over the floor, and from the number of spent cartridges on the doorstep she deduced that they must have been fired in the air in celebration. Worse still, every single one of her pyrotechnics was gone. Someone had evidently decided to mark Victory in Europe with an improvised fireworks display.

*

It wasn't long before Kathleen received orders that she was to leave HMS *Hornbill* for good. With the war in Europe over, her skills as an armourer were no longer required, and she was now to learn the trade of a motor transport driver. 'Get your things together,' a warrant officer told her. 'You're off on the six o'clock train.' She barely had time to say goodbye to the other girls in her cabin before she was setting off for London again. Although she was sorry to leave her friends, Kathleen was excited at the prospect of a new start. Maybe, she thought, being a driver would be her ticket to an overseas posting.

For the next few weeks, Kathleen's new home was a medieval mansion on Chelsea Embankment called Crosby Hall, where trainee MT drivers were billeted. On arrival, she was rather alarmed to discover that many of her room-mates already had extensive driving experience. Like many of the Wrens she had encountered, most of them were terribly posh, and they talked about how 'Daddy' let them take the car out whenever they wanted. A few, meanwhile, had come from Canada or Australia, where it seemed everyone learned to drive at an early age. 'I've been doing it since I was nine,' a Canadian girl called Elsa informed Kathleen nonchalantly.

On the first morning of the training course, a row of vehicles of various sizes pulled up outside the hall, ready to collect the girls for their first driving lesson. They were told that they would have to master not just one but all of the different types if they were to pass their test, including 5-tonne lorries, 15-hundredweight trucks, smaller vans and staff cars.

The instructors were former London bus drivers, and it was clear that they weren't exactly thrilled about their new job. 'Here come another lot of idiots,' Kathleen heard one of them say as the group of new recruits approached.

A middle-aged man with a thin, worn face motioned for Kathleen to get into the driving seat of one of the 15-hundredweights. He hopped up next to her, while the Canadian girl, Elsa, sat in the back, waiting for her turn at the wheel.

The instructor took Kathleen through the different parts of the vehicle, explaining what the pedals did and how the gear-stick worked. 'Now, why don't you have a go?' he said.

Kathleen had been expecting the man to show her how everything was done first, but clearly this was to be a baptism of fire. Soon she was lurching her way along Chelsea Embankment, the truck stalling every few metres – much to the delight of a group of male students who were learning in one of the 5-tonners. 'Hello, Jenny!' one of them shouted, as they overtook her. 'Make sure you've got a firm grip on the gear-stick!'

Ignoring the young men, Kathleen turned in the direction of the Great West Road, and began crawling up it at a snail's pace. Luckily there weren't too many other vehicles about, or she knew she would probably have been hooted at for her slow driving. Yet to her even this glacial speed seemed dangerously fast, and she gripped the steering wheel anxiously, plagued by the thought that she might be the cause of an accident. Every minute on the road felt like an hour, and she silently prayed for the lesson to end before she killed someone.

When her turn was finally over and Elsa got into the driving seat, Kathleen was overwhelmed with relief. But she cringed at the thought of how much better the Canadian girl was bound to be.

It quickly became clear, however, that Elsa intended to make no concessions for the fact that she was in Central London now, and not the wilds of Saskatchewan. She set off at a roaring pace, and as she came up behind another vehicle going more slowly than she was, she began hooting the horn as hard as she could.

'Stop that!' the instructor told her.

'I know what I'm doing!' Elsa shouted, driving as close as she could to the other car until it pulled over to let her pass. 'There, you see!' she said victoriously.

'Let's take a left here, off the main road,' the instructor said wearily.

'Right you are,' Elsa replied, swinging the lorry round into the side road without even slowing, and proceeding to drive up it on the wrong side.

'Get on the left!' the instructor cried, as an approaching car began honking at them wildly.

'Oh, you English and your silly laws!' Elsa exclaimed, unperturbed, as the car swerved to make way for her. As it went past she turned her head to follow it with a string of swear-words, the like of which even the London bus driver had never heard.

'Just pull over as soon as you can,' the poor man said. Kathleen could see he was as shaken by the ordeal as she was. It was a relief to them both when she took the wheel again and they began their slow, lurching progress back to Crosby Hall.

At the weekends, while the other girls on her course went dancing at the Hammersmith Palais, Kathleen would go and visit Arnold's family, who lived across the river in Clapham. Even before their first meeting, she had heard so much about Mr and Mrs Karlen from her fiancé's letters that she felt as if she knew them already, and when Arnold's father opened the door he was exactly as she had imagined. Dark and handsome with a well-tended moustache, she could just picture him commanding the kitchens of the Mayfair restaurant where he worked.

Mrs Karlen, meanwhile, was a rosy-cheeked country girl from Lincolnshire, from whom Arnold and his brothers had inherited their blond hair and blue eyes. Even in middle age, she still had a fresh-faced beauty, and Kathleen could see why her Swiss husband had fallen for her.

The Karlens were warm and welcoming to Kathleen, and in Arnold's absence they treated her like an adopted daughter. They were all fascinated to hear about her experiences on the driving course, and when she told them the size of the trucks she was learning on they were astonished. 'I can't believe a girl your size can even turn the wheel of one of those things,' Arnold's mother told her, obviously impressed.

But Mrs Karlen had some news of a more sombre nature to share – Arnold had recently been demoted. 'I'm sure it's all a misunderstanding,' she told Kathleen. 'He and his men arrived at a concentration camp in Germany and he found a box of gold watches that had been taken from the poor souls in there. He took it away for safekeeping, but when his commanding officer discovered the box with Arnold's things he thought he must have stolen it. He said he had to punish him to set an example to the men.'

'Oh dear,' Kathleen replied, 'poor Arnold.' She knew how proud her fiancé was of his status in the Army, and how hard the demotion must have hit him. But privately she couldn't help thinking what a strange thing it was that he had done.

Back at the training centre, Kathleen was growing a little more confident in her driving, but she found the job physically exhausting. The vehicles had been designed with men in mind, not women, and as Mrs Karlen had suggested, just turning the steering wheel was hard work – Kathleen often had to stand up to get enough leverage. She didn't see herself as a natural driver by any means, but she reasoned that if she could only pass the test then perhaps she would be in with a chance of being posted somewhere exciting abroad.

The girls on the course continued to be pestered by the men training alongside them, and Kathleen found that ignoring their rude remarks only seemed to make them more determined to wind her up. One day, as she was setting off along the embankment, she heard one of them shout to his friends, 'I'm going to get her.' Before long, the man began tail-gating Kathleen's vehicle, forcing her to go faster and faster.

'Slow down!' the instructor shouted.

'I can't – he's going to hit me!' Kathleen cried.

The instructor turned and looked out of the window at the lorry behind them. 'Bloody hell, he is as well,' he exclaimed. 'What does that maniac think he's doing?'

In the back of the other lorry, the man's friends were cheering wildly, and, encouraged, he began honking his horn and swerving from side to side, trying to force Kathleen off the road. The girls sitting behind her began to scream, and above all the noise Kathleen couldn't make out what the instructor was trying to tell her.

'Turn left, turn left!' he bellowed, finally loud enough for her to hear it. Spotting a little path, Kathleen swerved at the very last moment. To her relief, the lorry behind didn't have time to follow, and continued speeding away up the road.

Moments later Kathleen realised that she had in fact turned into a private garden, and she was going too fast to stop herself from driving straight through it. The van careered through row upon row of carefully tended cabbages, which were sent flying up into the air, and Kathleen saw the poor owner of the house standing on his doorstep shaking his fist at her. She didn't even have time to shout an apology as she smashed right through a gate on the other side.

At long last the driving course was finally over, and one by one the girls submitted to a practical exam that took up most of the day, as they were put through their paces on the various vehicles they had learned to drive. Kathleen was convinced that she had failed the test, and was thrilled when the instructor told her that she had just scraped through.

When she got back to Crosby Hall, however, she found that not all her fellow trainees had been so lucky. Several of the girls who had been driving for years had failed, and they were bitterly disappointed. Their cockiness had led them to take too many chances on the roads, or to ignore what the instructor was telling them – and in the end their attitude had cost them dearly.

For the girls who had passed, orders soon went up on a noticeboard, detailing where they were being sent next. Kathleen quickly scanned the list, hoping that she would finally be going abroad.

But after all the trials and tribulations of the driving course, there was to be no exotic posting. Next to her name she found the words, 'HMS *Sanderling*, Scotland'.

HMS *Sanderling* turned out to be a former RAF airfield ten miles from Glasgow, which had recently been taken over by the Fleet Air Arm. Compared to *Hornbill* the camp had a rough and ready feel, but the surrounding countryside was beautiful.

The Wrens found themselves sharing the base with the local wildlife, most of which seemed to be indifferent to the presence of the military in their natural habitat. The airstrip had become a popular hang-out for hares, and at the height of summer hundreds of them were busy mating and fighting on it ferociously. Whenever a plane came in to land, the girls would rush out onto the runways with clappers, to scare away as many of the creatures as they could.

But the animals weren't the only ones in danger. One of Kathleen's tasks at HMS *Sanderling* was to direct the incoming planes to the correct runway, driving a van bearing a large sign that read, 'FOLLOW ME'. It was a terrifying job, and she could only cross her fingers and hope that the pilots didn't come in over speed and run her down along with the hares.

At *Sanderling*, the pristine country air rang with a noise that Kathleen had never heard before – a strange 'Crrrk, crrrk' that sounded like someone running their finger along a very large comb. But when she asked her fellow Wrens what was making the bizarre sound, nobody seemed to have any idea.

There was a little farm at one end of the airstrip, run by two ancient Scottish sisters, and Kathleen decided to ask them what kind of animal it was that she could hear.

'Ach, that there's a corncrake, lassie!' one of the old women told her when she described the distinctive call. 'Ye dinne get them in England?'

'No, never,' Kathleen replied. But later that day she finally saw the creature that had been making the astonishing noise, scurrying along the side of the airstrip. It was a dappled browny-yellow bird with extremely long legs, and was giving the hares a run for their money.

Encountering animals around the camp was one thing, but Kathleen dreaded meeting them on the roads. Some girls had already been unfortunate enough to accidentally run down wild deer, which had to be heaved into the back of their vehicles and reported to the authorities. After her first few weeks in Scotland, Kathleen counted herself lucky to have avoided any such encounters, but one day, finding herself lost on the way to the local post office, she drove into a farmyard to turn her van around and accidentally ran over a duck.

Kathleen jumped down in horror and rushed over to where the poor creature was lying, hoping that perhaps it had just been knocked off its feet. But the animal was completely lifeless, its eyes closed and its body perfectly still.

Ever since she had started driving, Kathleen had been gripped by the fear that she would run someone over in her vehicle. Now it had finally happened – the duck had become her first victim.

Wracked with guilt, she rushed over to the farmhouse and knocked on the door, which was opened by a burly farmer. 'I'm so sorry, but I've just run over your duck!' Kathleen told him, ringing her hands.

The stout man eyed the flustered Wren on his doorstep. 'How long ha' ye bin driving?' he asked her.

'Not very long,' Kathleen admitted. 'I'll pay for the loss myself.'

'It dinne look like ye'll have to,' the man said with a chuckle, pointing over Kathleen's shoulder.

She turned in time to see the duck miraculously get back on its feet, flap its wings and waddle off to join its friends.

'Oh!' Kathleen said, her cheeks turning red with embarrassment. She rushed away from the farmhouse and hopped back into her van as fast as she could, the farmer's laughter following her up the lane.

After the incident with the duck, Kathleen drove more cautiously than ever, anxious to avoid any further casualties.

The next time she set off to collect the mail from the nearby village of Paisley, she crawled along the narrow country lanes, keeping an eye out for wildfowl.

One of the perks of doing the mail round was getting to the post before anyone else at camp, and Kathleen made the most of it to rifle through the bag and see if there was anything from Arnold. She was delighted when she discovered a letter from him, and parking her van on the slope at the back of the post office she settled down to read it before heading back to camp. When she got to the end she started over again, treasuring every word.

Kathleen was so absorbed in her fiancé's letter that she didn't notice an old man stopping to lean against the back of her van as he got out his pension book. When she finally stuffed the envelope into her pocket and released the handbrake to reverse back down the slope, she knocked the poor fellow clean off his feet.

Oblivious, Kathleen continued reversing, and was astonished when the old man's body appeared from between her front wheels. She gasped in horror – could it be that, despite her careful driving, she had killed a man at just two miles per hour? She had checked both side mirrors before she released the handbrake, but the van had no rear window and she hadn't been able to see directly behind her.

To Kathleen's relief, her victim was soon back on his feet, unscathed but furious at the ignominy of being knocked down on the way to collect his pension. He began ranting and raving, and, hearing his shouts, the employees and customers of the post office rushed out to see what all the commotion was about. 'She's run me over, that's wha' happened!' the old man yelled. 'She tried to kill me, she did!'

The man was ushered inside, and the postmaster was summoned to arbitrate. 'I'm very sorry for knocking you over,' said Kathleen, 'but I can't see any marks on you.'

'Well, the wheels ne'er touched me, did they?' railed the man. 'But they might ha'! I'll have ye for this, I swear!'

At the man's insistence, the postmaster telephoned Kathleen's camp, informing the driving officer there of the accident and letting him know that they were holding on to her while they 'gathered evidence'. Thankfully, the officer persuaded the man to release her, assuring him that the matter would be thoroughly investigated by the Navy, and to the fury of the irate pensioner, Kathleen was allowed to go.

Luckily for her, the driving officer had taken a bit of a shine to her, and when she told him the full story, he was able to see the funny side. But from that day on, she always kept an eye out for pensioners as well as ducks.

Kathleen's regular misadventures on the roads soon became a popular topic in her Nissen hut. Every day, when she got back from her shift, the other girls would ask to hear the latest madcap tale, gathering around her bed excitedly. One evening it was the gear-stick that came out in her hand in the middle of a busy street in Glasgow, another time how she had used her starting handle to thwack a man over the head who she had seen mugging a sailor. But whatever the story, it was always met with awed gasps from her cabin-mates.

'Oh, Kathleen, you are utterly hil-*ar*ious,' a girl called Diana Featherington-Bingley exclaimed, wheezing with laughter. A fellow driver, she was one of those girls who had been borrowing 'Daddy's car' since she was a teenager, but despite her cut-glass accent there was nothing stuck-up about her. She was perfectly happy to take her turn entertaining the others in the hut with her own ridiculous tales, such as the time she 'came out' as a débutante and was presented at court wearing a bouffant dress and carrying a fan of ostrich feathers.

The girls' cabin was a complete cross-section of society, its inhabitants ranging from a minor royal who drove the staff cars to Cockney cooks who worked in the camp kitchens. Kathleen's work as a nanny had taught her how to talk to people from all walks of life, and she found she was able to get along with everyone.

Most of the girls at *Sanderling* were English, but a few were 'locally engaged' – Scottish girls who lived nearby and had joined the WRNS under the proviso that they wouldn't be posted far from home. Among the latter were a couple of young women called Kitty Burns and Alison Duffy. Alison was a slip of a girl, but at the slightest encouragement she would leap from her bed and perform an extremely energetic Highland Fling, treating the entire hut to a show-stopping performance.

When they had time off, the girls tended to stay at the camp, but one day Kitty came into the hut in a fever of excitement. 'There's a highland dancing competition happening this weekend,' she told the others. 'We canne miss it!'

Soon she had convinced Kathleen and several of the other English girls that their time in Scotland wouldn't be complete unless they attended, and the little gang agreed to hitch-hike to the event together.

The competition turned out to be just part of a whole roster of traditional highland events, with burly Scots in kilts competing against each other in running, shot-putting and tossing the caber, among other sports that Kathleen had never even heard of. And then there were the musical performances. She had never seen so many bagpipes in her life, and as they started to play she felt as if her ears were being blown out.

While the girls sat and watched the musicians, a man with a clipboard came round, taking names for the dancing competition. As he went past, Kathleen caught his eye and said, 'Here, put me down, would you?'

Kitty stared at her in astonishment. 'What are ye doin', Kath?' she asked. 'Dinne ye ken the best o' the world's highland dancers are here?'

But Kathleen was up for trying anything once. 'I've watched Alison do the Highland Fling enough times in the hut,' she said, shrugging. 'How hard can it be?'

Soon the dancing competition was underway, and the girls gathered round the stage with the rest of the crowd to watch the first few contestants. They gazed in amazement as, one by one, the performers leapt expertly in the air, raising their hands elegantly as they hopped from foot to foot, and twirling round on the spot in their kilts and matching socks.

'Ooh, they are terribly good,' remarked Diana. Kathleen gulped, wondering what she had let herself in for.

'Next up we have Kathleen Skin,' one of the judges called out suddenly.

'Wish me luck!' Kathleen told her friends, as she headed up to the little stage. A murmur went round the audience as they saw the young Wren taking her position. Kathleen held her right arm in the air, just as she'd seen Alison do, and nodded to the bagpiper to begin. But as soon as he struck up the tune she began to realise that the perfect coordination of limbs which had looked so simple when the other dancers did it was really rather difficult to emulate. She flailed about wildly as she bounced up and down on the spot, throwing arms and legs out at whatever angle she could, and trying her best to make up for her lack of expertise with sheer energy and enthusiasm.

At first the audience merely stared in shock, but after a

while they started clapping along in time with the music, evidently amused by the mad English girl in their midst. Encouraged, Kathleen responded by hopping around more vigorously than ever, causing the crowd to roar with laughter.

By the time her Fling was over, everyone in the room had been won over and they gave her a mighty round of applause – despite the fact that the official judges had just awarded her the lowest possible score.

She returned, red-faced and out of breath, to find her friends in fits of laughter.

'Oh, Kathleen, you are hil-*ar*ious,' Diana said, wiping the tears from her eyes.

19

Jessie

At the Royal Army Ordnance Corps depot in Antwerp, Jessie collected her next order list from a pile on the desk, and set off with her trolley in search of the required engine parts. She passed row after row of shelves before finally she spotted a box with one of the right numbers on it. Then she climbed up the ladder and retrieved the part, wondering what on earth it was for.

Jessie's battery had been disbanded just a couple of weeks after VE Day, and the girls had found themselves scattered to the four winds. Elsie Acres had been sent off to Holland to become an Army typist, leaving before Jessie even had a chance to say goodbye. The next day it was her own turn to depart, as she was transferred to the RAOC. Driving away from the gun-site in the back of an ATS lorry, Jessie had taken one last look back, and had seen one of the other girls crying her eyes out at the thought that their little unit was no more.

At the depot, Jessie missed the excitement and camaraderie of ack-ack, but she certainly didn't miss the war. She was content to continue wearing her ATS uniform for as long as the Army still needed her, doing her bit in whatever way she was told. Being stationed in Antwerp meant she was closer to Mac as well, and the two of them now spent most of their evenings off together, generally at a place called The 21 Club, where soldiers of all nationalities mingled.

Encircling the club's vast dance floor was a balcony which sported the flags of dozens of different British regiments, and since it was almost impossible to find anyone in the sea of uniforms there, Jessie and Mac always met under the banner of the 11th Armoured Division – a menacing black bull with bright red eyes.

As they danced the nights away, the young Scotsman always held Jessie close. But when he told her he loved her, as he frequently did, she could never quite bring herself to say it back. However much Mac made her laugh, and however much she enjoyed his company, the fact was that he just wasn't Jim.

Jessie's work at the RAOC depot was undemanding, certainly compared to the pressure of life on a gun-site, but she didn't mind. It was a peaceful time and she was enjoying herself in Antwerp, seeing Mac in the evenings and spending her days getting to know the Belgian girls who worked alongside her in the stores, and who were always keen to practise their English. One of them, Jessie learned, had served with the local resistance group, the White Brigade, and had spent the war hiding out in the woods, and even killing Germans in hand-to-hand combat.

Jessie knew that, as far as her own life was concerned, she was just treading water in Antwerp, but it suited her and she was happy not to think too much about what might come next. It was a long time ago now that she had stopped imagining a future for herself, but the habit had stuck.

One day, however, the limbo that Jessie had been living in came to an abrupt end. Orders went up on the RAOC notice-board announcing that she was being transferred to a depot in Hamburg, in northern Germany, and would be expected to leave the next day. Jessie only just had enough time to dash off a brief note to Mac, letting him know which train she would be catching.

They met on the platform at Mechelen station, which was crowded and bustling with people – clearly there would be no opportunity for a heartfelt private farewell. Mac gave Jessie a little kiss and began helping her up onto the train. Then he stopped, and looked into her eyes for a moment. 'We can't go on like this, you know,' he said thoughtfully.

The guard on the platform blew his whistle, signalling the train to depart. 'What about getting married?' Mac asked Jessie suddenly. 'I think we could make a pretty good go of it.'

Jessie could feel the train begin to move beneath her. She knew that the moment had come to make up her mind once and for all. Mac wasn't Jim, but then no one ever could be. Was it really worth throwing away a chance at happiness for the memory of a man who was gone?

'I think you're right,' she said after a moment. 'We could.'

Looking back, Jessie saw Mac beaming from ear to ear. 'I'm so pleased!' he shouted after her, as the train pulled out of the station.

Jessie spent the journey to Hamburg feeling more contented than she had for years. Finally, she had made a decision, and for the first time since Jim's death she had a future to look forward to again.

But before that future could begin, there was one more thing she had to do – serve out the rest of her commitment to the Army. And she would be doing it in a country that, until recently, she had been fighting to destroy. Staying the night in a German barracks in Belgium had felt eerie enough, but now she was entering the homeland of the enemy.

As the train slowed on its approach to Hamburg station, Jessie looked out of the window. Along the sides of the tracks she could see dozens of emaciated German children, their arms reaching up hopefully towards her. Despite the bitter cold outside, they were wearing little more than rags. She thought back to the hungry Belgian kids who had taken her friends' sandwiches in Ostend – compared to these urchins, they had looked well fed.

Under armed guard, the ATS girls were hastily transferred onto a lorry and driven eastwards out of the city. All around them loomed the ghastly spectacle of post-war Hamburg, a place so utterly devastated by bombing and siege that it was scarcely recognisable as somewhere that human beings had ever lived. As far as the eye could see, there was not a single building standing intact, just jagged fragments of walls surrounded by endless heaps of rubble.

Everywhere Jessie looked she saw desperate-looking people picking through the debris, while gangs of feral teenagers hung about on street corners, homeless, parentless and starving, staring menacingly at the Army truck as it made its way through the streets.

Hamburg had suffered one of the most devastating bombing campaigns of the war. In the space of a week, more than 40,000 people had been killed as the US Air Force pounded the city by day and the RAF blasted it at night, sparking a 1,500-foot tornado of fire that had engulfed hundreds of thousands of homes and factories. And as if that wasn't enough, in the final month of the war the city's streets had played host to a vicious two-week battle, as the German forces there fought to the bitter end.

Beneath the rubble, thousands of corpses still lay undiscovered, attracting rats and disease. As they turned a corner, the girls in Jessie's lorry saw a team of workers digging up body parts and putting them into black bags. The stench of rotting flesh was almost unbearable, and she covered her mouth with her sleeve.

When they finally left the city behind them, Jessie couldn't help feeling relieved. A little while later the lorry arrived at a large RAOC depot in the woods near the small town of Glinde, and as it came to a halt inside the gate a male corporal with fair hair and a friendly face held out his hand to help Jessie down. After four years of doing a man's job, she was rather taken aback at the unexpected act of chivalry, but she soon discovered that her cohort were the first ATS girls to arrive at the depot, where the mixing of the sexes was seen as something of a novelty. Men and women were not even allowed to eat together in the canteen, and over dinner that night the girls sat at their own segregated table.

The next morning, the new arrivals were lined up and given injections for typhus, which was rife in Hamburg as a result of all the rotting bodies. They were warned never to leave the camp without an armed guard, and to try to stick to groups of six or more even while they were there. 'The people here are in a desperate state,' an officer told them. 'They've been known to slit a man's throat just for a pair of shoes.'

The new girls were told that they would be working alongside German civilians in the stores, but that any fraternisation with them was forbidden. That was hardly going to be a problem, thought Jessie. After six years of war, she had no desire to speak to a German, and neither did any of the other girls.

Nonetheless, as the weeks went by and she got used to the sight of her German colleagues, dressed in rags and with bits of old tyres wrapped around their feet for shoes, Jessie couldn't help feeling sorry for them – and when she noticed odd supplies going missing from the depot she made the decision not to report it. After the wholesale devastation she had seen in

Hamburg, she could only imagine the dire conditions the women must be living in. Around the camp, she had heard some of the British soldiers talking about their 'bits of frat' – a term they used to describe girls who were so desperate that they would sleep with a man in exchange for coffee or cigarettes.

Perhaps sensing that Jessie was more sympathetic than most of her colleagues, one of the German women eventually came up and spoke to her. 'From your husband?' she asked, pointing to the ring that Jessie still wore on her left hand.

'Late husband,' she replied coolly. 'He was killed in the war.'

The woman nodded. 'My husband also was killed,' she replied sadly.

'Where?' Jessie asked, not entirely sure if she wanted to hear the answer.

'*Luftschlacht um England*,' the woman replied. 'I think you say, Battle of Britain.'

Jessie looked at her for a moment. Most of the German pilots she had helped shoot down had probably had wives at home, she realised – women who had missed them just as much as she had missed Jim. 'There are a lot of us, aren't there?' she said gently.

'Yes,' the woman agreed. Then she went back to her work.

For the girls stationed there, the RAOC depot was a strange and unsettling posting – they were cooped up in the middle of nowhere, and too scared to ever leave camp. After a couple of months a building in Hamburg was shored up to make them their own little cinema, but even so they had to visit it under armed guard and then come straight back as soon as the film had finished.

The men and women of the depot did their best to make their own fun, and as ever Jessie's piano playing was much in demand. The kind corporal who had helped her out of the lorry when she first arrived turned out to be a classically trained baritone, who performed with his local operatic society back home in England. He introduced himself to Jessie as Ralph, and asked if she would mind accompanying him on the piano so that he didn't get too rusty while he was out in Germany. They whiled away many happy hours singing and playing together while she waited for her demob papers to come through.

Finally, after several months in Germany, Jessie was told that her number had come up, and she gladly boarded a train headed back to Calais. After an uneventful voyage across the channel, she found herself back in England again.

At a depot in York, Jessie joined the other troops waiting to be demobbed. The girls were herded around like sheep from one end of a large hall to the other as they underwent the process of being turned back into civilians. One by one, they handed in all their kit except their service dress and greatcoats, and collected clothing coupons and railway warrants for their journeys home.

Among the crowd, Jessie spotted a girl she remembered from her basic training in Leicester. She rushed over to say hello, and soon they were trading stories of how life in the ATS had treated them. It was only when she heard the other girl's account of the last few years that Jessie realised just how incredible her own experience had been – while she had been shooting down enemy bombers and travelling to Belgium and Germany, this girl had spent the entire time at an office in England. Working on the ack-ack guns had been tough, but Jessie and her friends had been lucky to have a job that was so important, and she felt proud of what they had accomplished together.

Now, though, Jessie's career in the ATS was over, and a few minutes later she emerged from the hall as a civilian once again. For the first time in years she was a mere individual, no longer part of the great machine that was the Army. It was an uncomfortable feeling, and she wondered for a moment whether she should have signed up for another two years, as some of the girls had done. But she knew Mac was waiting to be demobbed too, and once they were both out of the Army they could begin their new life together.

Jessie caught the train down to Spalding, marvelling as she got out at the station just how little the town seemed to have changed. Back in Holbeach Bank too everything was exactly as she remembered it.

When she arrived home her father was out, so it was Mrs Ward who opened the door. 'Jessie!' she exclaimed. 'What are you doing here?'

'I've just been demobbed,' Jessie told her. 'I've come home.'

'I'm glad,' said her mother, with a softness that her daughter hadn't seen before. Jessie knew that they would never be close, but perhaps if her mother was willing to treat her with kindness they would get on all right after all.

To Jessie's relief, her mother's good mood seemed to last, and when her father came home she found herself showered with affection. 'Here she is,' Mr Ward declared proudly. 'The girl who won the war!'

The next morning, for the first time in years, Jessie opened her old wardrobe, staring uncertainly at the civilian clothes left over from her previous life. Somehow they didn't feel like they belonged to her any more. The colours all looked so bright and childish, and she couldn't bear to put any of them on.

Instead she slipped back into her service dress and set off for Spalding, determined to blow her clothing coupons on a new outfit. But when she got to the shops, she realised that she had no idea what to buy – she had got out of the habit of thinking about which clothes went together, and had completely lost track of what was fashionable. In the end she bought a handful of blouses in various shades of brown, and a large packet of green dye.

When she got home, Jessie transformed her ATS skirt from khaki to a muddy olive colour. Then she put it back on, along with a brown blouse and her old Army shoes. It wasn't exactly a new look for the recently demobbed Private Winkworth, but at least it was a start.

After a couple of weeks, Mac too was released from the Army, and before returning to Grantown-on-Spey he came to visit Jessie in Holbeach Bank. When she met him at the station she couldn't help laughing at the sight of his grey demob suit, which hardly matched his cheeky personality. Jessie realised she would have to get used to it soon, though, when he returned to his old job at the Bank of Scotland.

'Well, you might not like the suit, but I hope you'll like this,' Mac said, taking a little box out of his pocket. Inside was a gold engagement ring, set with opals.

Jessie gasped. 'They're my favourite stone!' she told him.

For the first time since she had married Jim, Jessie took her wedding ring off and put it in her pocket. Then she let Mac slide the beautiful engagement ring onto her finger.

She felt fairly confident that Mac would get on well with her father. Mr Ward had a lot of time for any man who arrived at his door bearing tales of Army life, and her new fiancé knew how to spin a good yarn. Back at the house in Holbeach Bank, she was pleased to see the two men dissolving in fits of laughter as they traded old stories.

It was her mother that Jessie was more worried about. But all through dinner that evening, Mrs Ward continued to behave herself, treating Mac with courtesy and respect. At the end of the evening, she came up to Jessie and said, 'I like him.'

Coming from Mrs Ward, who liked few people on this earth, it was a rare compliment. Jessie knew that, in her own way, her mother was trying to atone for the past.

That night Jessie put Jim's ring into a little box, and shut it away in a drawer. She knew that she would treasure it for the rest of her life, but it didn't need to define her any more.

At her aunt's house in Holbeach, Jessie stood in front of the mirror, carefully straightening her hat. It was a brilliant shade of blue, to match the dress, jacket and shoes that she had bought specially for the big occasion.

There was a knock at the door, and she opened it to find her father standing outside, offering his arm with a smile. Jessie took it, and they set off on the familiar journey to All Saints church.

The ancient building looked as magnificent as it had on the day she had married Jim there, and despite the sad memories associated with the place, Jessie's heart was filled with joy rather than sorrow. She was a different person now, and ready to write a new history for herself.

Waiting outside the church was her best friend Elsie Acres, beaming in a pale blue bridesmaid's dress. She had recently got married as well, and her new husband Jack had come along to serve as Mac's best man.

As she walked up the aisle, Jessie smiled at a couple of familiar faces on her right – Mac's father Willie and his youngest sister Betty, who had travelled down from Scotland for the wedding. They grinned back at her, with all the warmth and affection that she remembered from her visit to Grantown-on-Spey.

But no one in the church was smiling quite as much as Mac when she finally reached his side at the altar.

This time around, Mr and Mrs Ward insisted on hosting a reception after the ceremony. Back at the little house in Holbeach Bank, everyone joined in a toast to the happy couple and enjoyed a slice of their wedding cake – white, with a tartan band around it.

That evening, Jessie and Mac packed their bags and boarded the train to Scotland. They would be spending their first night as a married couple in a cramped sleeper cabin, but she didn't mind one bit. A new beginning was waiting for her at the other end of the journey, and she intended to make the most of it.

20

Margery

Since the end of the war, the Air Force had been doing its best to equip servicemen and women for civilian life before they were demobbed. The Educational and Vocational Training scheme had been designed to prepare airmen for jobs in Civvy Street, while WAAFs were taught skills that might come in handy around the home, from cooking and cleaning to reupholstering armchairs and wiring plugs.

In Britain, these classes – which were offered by all three of the services – were taught in local schools and colleges, with a teaching staff of 10,000 civilian instructors. But for men and women serving abroad the options were more limited. So it was that Margery found herself attending a course in home management, taught in a specially equipped bungalow that had been built in the desert.

After her years in the military, the idea of being trained up as a perfect housewife seemed faintly ridiculous to Margery, and she struggled not to laugh at some of the tips the girls were given. Their instructor was a dumpy little sergeant from Devon who had worked as a cook before the war. 'If you ever buy a packet of dates,' the woman sombrely warned the girls one day, 'make sure you shake them out on a plate before you eat them. That way you'll give the maggots a chance to wriggle away.'

Margery was relieved when the course finally came to an end, but returning to Turah didn't offer much in the way of excitement either. For months now she had been watching as men and women were sent back to England, wondering when her own time would come. She was growing tired of life in the strange limbo of the Egyptian desert.

When the news finally arrived, it was sudden and unexpected. Normally, dates of release were listed in the Air Ministry Orders posted on the camp noticeboard, but in Margery's case there was just a quick tap on the shoulder and an order to pack her bags at once. A spare place had been found on one of the boats heading back to England, and her name had been plucked from the list.

There was no time for a proper boat party to say goodbye, just a quick, tearful farewell with her friends at the camp. Elspeth, in particular, was heartbroken. 'I wish you weren't leaving me here,' she said, with tears rolling down her face.

'Don't worry,' Margery told her, 'you won't have long to wait. And we'll stay in touch back in England.'

She turned to the rest of the girls, determined not to give in to her own emotions. 'You're a rotten lot,' she joked, 'so I won't be upset about leaving you. I'm just happy to be going home, and I know you will be too when the time comes.'

Margery was driven by lorry to Port Said, where a ship was already loaded and waiting for her. It was a far cry from the palatial ocean liner on which she'd made the outgoing journey – this time she was travelling on a small cargo vessel, and it was crammed almost to bursting with returning WAAFs and airmen.

It wasn't until they hit open water that Margery really began to feel the difference. The ship was tossed about mercilessly, causing all its doors to swing wildly on their hinges. By the time they reached Malta, where they stopped to pick up some Wrens, the weather had taken a turn for the worse, and as the rain lashed at the little ship, the passengers were forced to remain below deck for days on end. Margery and the WAAFs she was bunking with kept themselves occupied with endless games of cards, but it was a pretty miserable journey for all concerned.

When they finally docked at Southampton, the girls were desperate to get off the boat, but they were told that they would have to wait another couple of days, until a train became available to take them up to RAF Wythall, an old barrage-balloon centre that was now being used for demobbing WAAFs.

Eventually Margery arrived at the dispersal centre, where a long queue of girls had already formed in the great hall. She worked her way from one table to the next, receiving her clothing coupons and ration card, her service and release book, and vouchers to spend on chocolate and cigarettes. She handed over the khaki drill uniform that she had worn out in Egypt, and in exchange she was given £12. 10s. for the purchase of civilian clothes.

The whole process only took about ten minutes – the demobbing machine was a well-oiled one by now, having already released almost 100,000 WAAFs. The final stage in the procedure was a quick handshake with a young officer, who thanked Margery for her service before sending her on her way.

When Margery left the great hall, it was as a civilian once more. After so many years in the service, it felt strange to be an individual again, and she felt a slight twinge of the old fears that had previously held her back in life. But she was far from the only former WAAF who was struggling with the sudden adjustment – back at Birmingham station more than a few of the women on the platform were quietly snuffling.

Margery took the first train heading south, but it was a long journey, and made longer by frequent delays. She spent the time gazing out of the window, contemplating the green fields and rolling hills of the English countryside. After her years in the desert it all looked alien to her now – there were too many trees, and not enough space between them. It didn't really feel like home at all.

Finally Margery arrived in North Wallington, where she was surprised to see that everything looked just as it had before she'd left. As she walked up the drive to the little maltster's house, the door flew open to reveal Mrs Pott. 'Oh good, I'm glad you're here,' she said hurriedly, 'because Peggy's home on leave and Jessie's booked us all tickets for *High Time* at the Palladium. The two of them are up in London already, but we should be able to catch them before the show starts.'

Margery couldn't believe it. Here she was, having just returned from Egypt, and all her mother seemed to care about was a trip to the theatre. Right now the last thing Margery felt like doing was getting on another train, still less going to watch a variety show in London – all she really wanted to do was collapse on her old bed.

Nevertheless, a couple of hours later, the whole Pott family were settling into their seats at the grand Edwardian theatre. Margery felt overwhelmed by the hyperactive performers in their colourful costumes, the blaring noise of the band, and the caterwauling of the audience as they tunelessly sang along. She blanched as 'Two Ton' Tessie O'Shea belted out 'Money is the Root of All Evil', with her blonde hair bouncing and her enormous mouth fixed in a gormless grin. Margery's mum and her two sisters were evidently enjoying themselves, but more than ever she just wished she could go to bed and hide under her pillow.

When the Potts got back to North Wallington, Margery perked up a little at the sight of a letter on the doormat bearing

Doug's handwriting. She had written to tell him that she was on her way home, and reading his reply she learned that his friend Norman from Kasfareet was currently staying with him in Bishop's Sutton. Doug asked if Margery would like to join them that weekend for a pub crawl.

Margery wrote back at once to say she would love to see them both, and when Saturday afternoon came around she brushed the cobwebs off her old bike, pumped up the tyres, and told her mother that she was going out for the evening.

The journey would normally have taken her an hour, but Margery managed it in 45 minutes, her legs propelled by the thought of recapturing a slice of her former life in Egypt. The address Doug had given her took her to a row of tiny farm-workers' cottages, and in the window of one of them she spotted his familiar, boyish grin.

Doug came to the door and greeted her with a kiss on the cheek. 'So you made it back to Civvy Street!' he said with a laugh.

Norman appeared behind him, looking as pleased to see Margery as Doug was. He was slightly less sun-kissed than she remembered – but then he was living in the Midlands now, she reminded herself, rather than in the desert.

'Well, what are we waiting for?' Doug said, cheerful as ever. 'Come on!'

They headed straight for his local, a cosy sixteenth-century pub called the Ship Inn. Doug bought the first round of drinks, and before long they were reminiscing about the old days in Kasfareet. As they talked about Egypt, Margery realised just how much they had crammed into their time there – the trips to the pictures, the dances, football matches and swimming parties, teas at the YWCA and the Tedder Club. It was a miracle they hadn't all dropped dead from exhaustion.

After they drained their glasses at the Ship Inn, the three old friends moved on to a pub called the Chequers, followed by a couple more establishments that Margery didn't catch the names of. She was just thrilled to be back together with Doug and Norman. She hadn't had so much fun in months, and when the landlord rang the bell at the end of the night it felt far too soon.

Doug offered Margery a lift back to North Wallington, and they all piled into his little car. Along the way he was still chatting away light-heartedly, and Margery was enjoying the relaxed, carefree feeling of being a little tipsy. But she noticed that Norman was rather quiet, and at one point she overheard him mutter to Doug, 'When are you going to tell her?'

'In a minute,' Doug replied, before quickly changing the subject. Margery wondered what on earth it was he was planning to say to her.

When they reached North Wallington, Norman pressed Doug again. 'You really ought to let her know,' he said, more firmly.

'Let me know what?' Margery asked, giggling. 'What's going on?'

Doug pulled up outside the maltster's house and turned to look her in the eye. She could tell that he was feeling embarrassed. 'I'm engaged, Margery,' he said finally.

'Engaged?' Margery repeated, as the word cut through her fuzzy-headedness. She couldn't quite believe she had heard him right. She and Doug had been writing to each other ever since he'd left Egypt, and he had never mentioned anyone else in his letters. Hadn't he cycled over to her mother's house when he first got back to England, telling her that he and Margery were going to get married?

But then Margery remembered the letter she had dashed off to her mother on VE Day, stating quite firmly that she had never made Doug any promises. Had her reply got back to him somehow?

'I – I could still break it off,' Doug offered, a little uncertainly.

Margery looked at his handsome, boyish face. For so long, she had kept him at arm's length, her wariness stopping her from ever letting him get too close. In the end he must have given up hope that they would ever be more than just friends. And how could she blame him?

While Margery was still out in Egypt, Doug had obviously met someone else – someone who had said yes when he asked her. She knew in her heart that she had no right to make a claim on him now.

'It's all right, Doug,' Margery said quietly, as she got out of the car.

After that evening, Margery knew she wouldn't see Doug again. But soon she got a letter from her friend Brownie, the sergeant who had worked in the metal-plating cave at Turah. He had promised to keep in touch with her when she left Egypt, and she ripped open the envelope excitedly, hoping to hear the latest news about Cairo and life at the Kasr-el-Nil barracks.

Brownie told her that, now the war was over, his wife Minnie had come out to Egypt to join him. Unfortunately, though, she had overheard some of the men in the mess asking her husband about Margery and had got the wrong idea about their friendship. It had made things difficult between them, he explained, and he had come to the decision that the best thing was to stop writing to Margery altogether. He hoped she would understand why this was the last letter she would ever receive from him.

Having lost her two closest male friends, Margery decided to try catching up with some of the girls she had grown up with in North Wallington instead. But whenever she looked someone up it seemed that they had either moved away from the village or moved on with their life. Her school friend Daisy was now living in Scotland, and all the local girls who were still around were now married with children. When Margery went to visit them, they barely paid her any attention, breaking off from the conversation to occupy themselves with their babies, and glazing over whenever she started telling them about her adventures abroad. It seemed that nothing Margery said meant anything to them, as they had never been in the forces, and there was a gulf between her and them.

Margery wasn't only feeling friendless but directionless as well. The Air Force had provided her with both a social life and a job, and now she had neither. Her sister Peggy, meanwhile, was having more luck adjusting to civilian life. She had trained as a health visitor as soon as she was demobbed from the Army and had recently moved to take up a position in Dorset, where by all accounts she was making a name for herself.

'Why don't you go back to old Dodge's?' Mrs Pott suggested one day, seeing Margery moping about the house. 'I spoke to the manager last week, and he said he's been keeping your job open ever since you left.'

Margery groaned. The last thing she wanted to do right now was step back into her old shoes. But then what other options did she have?

The following Monday found her seated once again behind the draper's cash register – as if the war, the WAAF and Egypt had never happened.

*

One afternoon, Margery was in Fareham on an errand when she spotted a face from the past – a dark-haired girl called Barbara who had worked in the stores at Titchfield. She was heavily laden with shopping bags and looking rather downcast, but as soon as she saw Margery her face lit up.

'Corporal Pott!' Barbara exclaimed. 'What are you doing here?'

'I only live up the road in North Wallington,' Margery replied. 'How about you?'

'Titchfield village,' she told her.

'How have you been?' Margery asked Barbara, wondering if all the ex-WAAFs were having as tough a time adjusting to Civvy Street as she was.

The story the other woman told made her feel incredibly lucky in comparison. Barbara had married a sailor shortly before the war, and had spent every day of the conflict hoping and praying that he would come home to her in one piece. When the war finally ended she was overwhelmed with relief, and waited impatiently for him to be demobbed so they could pick up their life together where they had left off six years earlier. At last she got word that he had been discharged from the Navy in Scotland, and was coming down to Titchfield. But Barbara's husband never arrived – on the way back home he was killed in a car accident.

Margery felt awful for Barbara, and she realised that there were people coming out of the war with much tougher things to deal with than she had.

Before going on her way, Barbara told Margery that she'd recently heard about a branch of the RAF Association in Portsmouth, which held monthly gatherings of former Air Force personnel. 'Maybe we could go together, since we're both local,' she suggested. 'It would be good to get out of the house.'

The letters 'RAF' were like music to Margery's ears, and she accepted without a second's thought.

A couple of weeks later, the two girls met up on the bus to Portsmouth. As it trundled along, Margery felt a buzz of excitement, something she hadn't experienced for a very long time.

The Air Force club was meeting in a room above a pub called the Cobden Arms, and as the two girls entered, Margery saw that there were around 30 people there already – mostly men but some women too – all standing around and chatting, with drinks in their hands. Everyone was wearing civilian clothes, but somehow she could tell at once that they were ex-service.

A jolly-looking former WAAF spotted the newcomers and headed over to them. She introduced herself as Peggy and had soon ushered them over to a mixed group who were reminiscing about their basic training when they first joined the Air Force. 'You girls had it easy,' Margery heard one of the men saying.

'Oh no we didn't!' the women standing next to him protested. 'We square-bashed just as hard as the boys. That's why we were better than you at marching!'

Margery laughed along with the others. Just hearing people talk about life in the Air Force was comforting to her – it felt like coming home, far more than returning to North Wallington had done. There was none of the standoffishness that she would have found in a group of civilian strangers suddenly thrown together – here, as soon as people met, it was as if they'd been friends for years.

That was what she had missed so much after leaving the WAAF, Margery realised – the camaraderie. By the end of the night, she and Barbara had paid up for a year's membership of the RAF Association, and were looking forward to their next meeting in a month's time.

With the regular get-togethers to look forward to, Margery found she didn't mind living back home with her mother in North Wallington, and even going to work at the draper's every day began to feel more bearable. Her friends and neighbours might not understand her, but it didn't matter any more – she had found her people again.

In particular, the RAF Association meetings offered something that Margery had missed ever since leaving the WAAF: male company. Among the former airmen who were regulars at the monthly meetings was a group of blokes who enjoyed playing on the pub's billiard tables and darts board, and increasingly she found herself joining them. Being the only woman in the gang didn't faze her – in fact if anything it brought back happy memories of her time at Kasfareet, hanging out with Doug, Norman and the boys.

Margery wasn't looking for anything more than friendship, but one evening Barbara asked her, 'Do you fancy anyone here?'

She surveyed the room thoughtfully. At the bar was an athletic-looking man who had evidently just arrived from some kind of sporting activity, judging from the beads of sweat dripping from his brow. He had just ordered a pint at the bar, and she watched as he downed it in one.

'I quite like the look of him,' Margery admitted. The man looked tough, solid, secure – the kind of chap you could rely on.

'Oh, a bloke like that's bound to be married,' Barbara told her with a sigh.

'Do you think so?' Margery asked her.

'Absolutely,' her friend replied confidently.

Just my luck, thought Margery – another married man! She put the man at the bar out of her head and went off for a game of billiards with the lads.

At the club's annual general meeting that year, the discussion turned to sporting activities. Peggy wanted to set up a Saturday netball team for the former WAAFs, who were keen to get a bit of exercise now that regular PT sessions were a thing of the past. 'But the only problem is, who would we play?' one of the other women asked. 'You've got to have two teams, haven't you, and I don't think we've got enough girls.'

'What about tennis?' Margery suggested. 'You only need two people for that.' At Kasfareet, she'd been given a few lessons by an airman who had played professionally in civilian life, and she quite fancied the idea of brushing up on her racket skills.

A tall, dark-haired chap in front of her turned around. 'I'll play tennis with you if you'll be a dance partner for me,' he said. 'I'm learning ballroom dancing, and I'm told I need a *lot* of practice!'

Margery wasn't about to pass up an opportunity like that. 'All right then, you're on,' she told him.

After the meeting, the man came over and introduced himself as Jack Harley, suggesting that he and Margery should meet the following Saturday at the South Parade Pier Ballroom in Southsea. 'You put me through my paces on the dance floor, and then next weekend I'll put you through yours on the tennis court,' he said, with a cheeky grin.

On Saturday evening, Margery caught the bus into town and she and Jack headed to the ballroom. It was a grand affair, with a stage at the front for the band to play on, and galleries around the sides so that people could get a good view of the dancers. As soon as Margery and Jack joined the couples on the dance floor, she saw his self-confidence begin to falter, and she realised that he hadn't been exaggerating when he said he needed practice. Jack's sense of rhythm was terrible and he was clumsy with his feet. Margery winced as he stepped on her toes over and over again.

'Can we just go outside so I can remind myself of the steps?' Jack asked after a while, clearly embarrassed.

They headed out onto the pier, with the music wafting after them, and practised the dance he had been struggling with. Somehow, outside in the semi-darkness, Jack's feet always knew where to fall, and he seemed to have acquired a sense of rhythm. 'I think you're ready to go back in,' Margery told him.

But once inside again, with spectators all around them, Jack was even more hopeless than before, stepping on Margery's toes more than ever.

Apart from the bruises sustained by her feet, Margery's arrangement with Jack worked pretty well though. One weekend he would come up to Fareham to play tennis, and the next they would go out dancing together. He was always the perfect gentleman, and generally bought her a nice meal afterwards.

At the next monthly meeting in the Cobden Arms, Margery arrived to find Jack at the bar, chatting to the athletic chap she'd noticed before. Once again, the man was dripping with sweat, as if he'd come from some kind of sporting event.

When Jack spotted Margery, he came over to greet her. 'Who's that man you were talking to?' she asked him, trying her best to sound casual.

'Oh, that's my big brother, Alistair,' Jack replied.

'Your *brother?*' Margery repeated, in disbelief.

'That's right,' Jack said, proudly. 'He's a brilliant racing cyclist. He's just come back from the track.'

Margery stared for a moment at the man by the bar. Barbara's words floated back into her mind and she couldn't resist asking, 'Is he married?'

'Oh, God no,' said Jack with a laugh.

Margery's face brightened. But then Jack added, '*He* won't ever marry.'

Every year, the RAF Association held a dance at a place in Portsmouth called The Kimbles. Margery was looking forward to showing the other members of the club how much progress Jack had made with his dancing, but when she suggested they meet up beforehand and go in together, he told her he'd rather meet up with her inside.

Margery couldn't help wondering what had prompted the change to their usual arrangement, but she shrugged it off. Perhaps he was just nervous about putting his new skills to the test in front of all their friends, and wanted a bit of time to compose himself.

On the day of the dance, Margery arrived at The Kimbles alone and headed straight for the cloakroom, but before she could get there Barbara came running up to her. 'I think you'd better watch out around Jack,' she said. 'He's got a girl on his arm, and she looks like she's gunning for somebody!'

'Don't be silly,' Margery told her. 'I'm sure it's a misunderstanding.'

But moments later, after Barbara had headed back into the dance hall, a pretty young woman marched up to Margery in the corridor. 'I'm Sheila,' she announced. 'Jack's *girlfriend*.'

Barbara was right – the girl looked furious, as if she might throttle Margery then and there.

'Oh – well – how do you do?' said Margery, backing away

and hurrying into the cloakroom. But to her dismay, the other girl proceeded to follow her, glaring angrily at Margery as she took off her coat and hat.

Margery rushed into the dance hall, with Sheila hot on her heels. The first familiar face she saw there was that of Jack's brother, Alistair. 'Can I talk to you?' she asked in desperation.

'What's the matter?' he asked, seeing the troubled look on her face.

'It seems as though Jack's got a girlfriend all of a sudden,' Margery told him, 'and apparently she's gunning for me!' From the corner of her eye she could see the girl approaching again. 'Perhaps we could have a dance?' she asked quickly.

'Oh yes, of course,' Alistair replied, whisking her onto the dance floor and out of Sheila's reach. Within moments they were spinning across the room together.

Unlike his brother, Alistair was a wonderfully graceful dancer, and his sense of rhythm was impeccable. For the first time in ages Margery found she could enjoy being led, instead of having to shove her partner around the dance floor.

'I've taken lessons,' Alistair explained, when she complimented him on his footwork. 'That's why Jack started going to classes – he tends to follow everything I do!'

After they had been dancing and chatting for a while, Margery asked Alistair about the sudden appearance of Jack's 'girlfriend'.

'Oh, that's Jack all over,' he laughed.

Margery thought it was pretty poor of Jack not to have introduced her to Sheila, or even to have explained the situation when they'd first started going dancing together. But she certainly wasn't going to worry about that now. Thanks to Jack's ireful girlfriend she had found herself in the arms of the man she really wanted – his bigger and better older brother.

Margery and Alistair danced together all night, swapping stories of their time in the Air Force as they twirled around the room. He told her that he had been an electrician before the war, and in the RAF he had been put to work as a 'ground grabber', taking apart crashed German planes and trying to work out their strengths and weaknesses.

'But what if something you touched exploded?' Margery asked him, enthralled.

'Well, it didn't,' Alistair replied with a laugh. 'You tried to see what was connected to what, and if you couldn't work it out you'd just have to push a button and see what happened!'

Margery's opinion of Alistair was rising by the minute. He must have had nerves of steel, she told herself.

Towards the end of the evening, as the event began drawing to a close, Alistair turned to Margery and asked, 'Do you cycle?'

She nodded, enthusiastically.

'Only my club is going for a ride next Sunday,' he continued. 'We meet at 9 a.m. outside the bike shop down the road if you'd like to join us.'

'I'd love to,' Margery told him, privately wondering how she was ever going to keep up with someone as fit as Alistair. 'I'll see you then.'

On Sunday morning Margery rose early and made a packed lunch for herself before setting out on her bike. She was running a little late, so she pedalled as fast as she could, determined not to miss out on her chance to see Alistair again.

She arrived at the bike shop sweaty and out of breath, but the cycling club were nowhere to be seen. Anxiously, she ran inside and asked the man behind the counter if he had seen them.

'Oh, they set off a while ago,' he told her. 'I think they were heading for Funtingdon.'

'Thanks!' Margery said breathlessly, rushing out of the shop. She jumped back on her bike and began pedalling harder than ever.

Margery knew the group would stop for a mid-morning pint somewhere along the way, so every time she passed a pub she slowed down to check whether they were inside. But again and again she saw no sign of them. She was beginning to worry that she would never be able to catch them up – after all, the club was made up of fit and experienced cyclists who were probably whizzing along at 100 miles an hour.

Just as she was on the point of giving up and turning back towards home, Margery spotted a pub with a row of racing bikes lined up outside. She threw her own tattered old bike on the ground and rushed through the door, doing her best to smooth down her windswept hair.

Inside, she spotted Alistair draining the end of a pint. 'She made it!' he called out to the rest of the group he was sitting with.

One of the other men clapped Margery on the back. 'We didn't expect to see you,' he declared. 'Alistair thought he'd been stood up!'

'Well, I knew where you were heading, so it wasn't too difficult to find you,' Margery said shyly. If they only knew how frantically she had pedalled for the last two hours!

The group were all finishing up their drinks, and there wasn't much time for Margery to catch her breath before they were back on the road again. The day's ride was pretty tough for her and she struggled to keep up over the 50-mile course, but to her delight Alistair cycled next to her all the way. Margery was too breathless and exhausted to make much in the way of conversation, but the fact that he was there meant a lot to her.

When the group finally got back to Portsmouth, everyone went their separate ways, promising to meet up again the following week for what sounded like another epic outing. Margery's legs and back were aching, but she wasn't able to rest them just yet – she still had to cycle all the way back home to North Wallington.

'I'll ride with you, if you like,' offered Alistair, when she told him she ought to be on her way.

Margery was touched. She knew he lived in Portsmouth, and accompanying her would mean a 15-mile round trip. 'That's very kind of you,' she told him. 'I'd be delighted.'

Now that it was just the two of them, they rode at a more leisurely pace and were able to chat properly. The more Margery got to know Alistair, the more she liked him. He was more serious than his brother Jack, and had all the good qualities that she had imagined when she first clapped eyes on him at the Cobden Arms – steadiness, reliability and a manly bearing.

Despite her weariness, Margery felt the last leg of the journey fly by, and before she knew it they were pulling up outside the maltster's house.

Alistair dismounted from his bike and leaned in to kiss her, and Margery didn't pull away.

From then on, Margery became a regular at the cycling club. She didn't mind being one of the few women in the group – in a way it was like being back in the Air Force, where girls were expected to keep up with boys, not treated as delicate little creatures who needed looking after. As her stamina grew, so too did her enjoyment of the long rides, and she found she was able to tackle even the toughest routes with ease.

Every week, after the group got back to Portsmouth, Alistair would escort Margery home to North Wallington. She would make him a hot drink before he cycled all the way back in the dark, taking a kiss with him for the journey.

After a couple of months, Alistair was standing on the doorstep one evening, about to hop back on his bike, when he suddenly turned to Margery. 'You know, it would be a lot easier if I didn't have to do this every week,' he said.

'What do you mean?' she asked anxiously. She had always felt guilty about him coming so far just for her sake. Was he about to put an end to their arrangement?

'I mean,' replied Alistair slowly, 'do you think maybe we could get married?'

Margery looked into his eyes for a moment. Finally, she had found someone she truly trusted, and she wasn't going to let him slip through her fingers.

'Yes,' she told him. 'I think we could.'

21

Kathleen

With the war over, Kathleen had come to accept that the chance of an exotic overseas posting had passed her by – she might have joined the Navy, but she wasn't going to see the world. She took the realisation in her stride, though, counting her many blessings. The terrifying uncertainty of six years of conflict had finally come to an end, and her beloved fiancé Arnold had survived it, ready to be reunited with her at last. Her four siblings, in their various armed services, had made it through in one piece as well, and Kathleen knew that many families were not so lucky. As a driver at HMS *Sanderling* one of her responsibilities was fetching mail for the camp, and she had brought back plenty of the dreaded War Office telegrams, and seen the blood drain from her colleagues' faces as they opened them.

Right now, Kathleen's priority was that she and Arnold should finally be married. She had waited so many years for the war to end so that they could be together at last, and she didn't want to wait one minute longer.

First, though, she would have to get herself demobbed. As a rather late addition to the WRNS, Kathleen was liable to be kept in the service for a while, unless she could make a case to her superiors that she was needed elsewhere. She had given some thought to what she might like to do in civilian life, and had decided to try her hand at teaching. A new government scheme had been introduced to pay for trainee teachers' accommodation and course fees, and she dutifully sent off her application forms. Since many young teachers had been killed in the war, there was a national shortage, and before long she was accepted on a course in Warrington. In the circumstances, the Navy were more than willing to let her go.

Kathleen's last day at *Sanderling* was a tearful one. In her short time at the camp she had already made firm friends, and as she went to pack up her kit for the last time she found her bed covered with cards and presents. Kitty Burns rode the bus with her to the local station. 'I'll noo ferget ye, Kath!' she called, as Kathleen got off to catch the train down to London.

Once officially demobbed, and back in civilian clothes for the first time in years, Kathleen had a little free time before she was expected to begin her teacher training course, so she set off to her mother's house in Cambridge. Mrs Skin was thrilled to see her, but it felt strange being back at home after so long away.

One day, Kathleen was coming back from a bike ride along the river when she saw a group of German prisoners of war walking into town. They had come from a POW camp in the nearby village of Trumpington, where they were still employed as farm labourers.

She gazed in fascination at the rows of young faces – men and boys who, up until recently, had been her mortal enemies. Now they looked entirely peaceful, friendly even, as they laughed and joked among themselves. Despite their country's defeat, perhaps these young men shared the relief everyone in Britain felt that the war had finally come to an end.

As Kathleen watched the group of Germans go by, she was stunned to spot a familiar face in the crowd. It was Konrad, the boy whose family she had stayed with in Kiel, just weeks before war broke out in 1939.

Konrad had evidently recognised Kathleen too, because he immediately rushed over to speak to her. 'You remember me, don't you?' he asked.

'Yes, of course,' Kathleen replied. 'What are you doing here, Konrad?'

'I was in the Luftwaffe,' he replied. 'My comrades and I were sent to join the Army in Libya and I was taken prisoner there. Three years ago, we were brought over to England.'

Kathleen could scarcely believe it. All this time Konrad had been living only a couple of miles away from her mother's house. She thought back to the kindness his parents had shown her when she visited them, and how Konrad's father had rushed her to the Dutch border just in time for her to return to England. 'When you get home, do give your parents my regards,' she told him warmly.

A shadow fell over Konrad's face and he stared at Kathleen with sorrowful eyes. When he spoke, his voice sounded different. 'My family are dead,' he told her. 'Your people killed them. My mother, my father, my brothers. You smashed everything we had to pieces. There is no home any more.'

Kathleen was shocked. 'I'm so sorry, Konrad,' she replied, unsure what else to say. She was deeply saddened to hear that his family had been killed, especially since they had been so kind to her. But didn't he know that the Germans had bombed her country too?

The young man clearly had no wish to talk further. He turned around and went to join the other prisoners before Kathleen could even say goodbye.

*

Although Kathleen's family had been lucky enough to survive the war, they were gradually beginning to scatter. Her brother Cecil had decided to take up the Australian Government on their post-war immigration scheme and become a 'ten-pound pom', leaving Britain for a new life Down Under. Mrs Skin had begun to get itchy feet too, and before long she was on a boat for South Africa, hoping to reconnect with her family there. Meanwhile, Kathleen's sister Lila had married a Norwegian sailor she'd met while stationed with the Navy at Scapa Flow, and they were planning to emigrate to the United States.

Kathleen's own long-awaited wedding, however, was still on hold. She had assumed that after he was demobbed, Arnold would go back to his pre-war job selling furniture at a department store in London, and they would be able to see each other more frequently as they began to plan the big day. But he turned out to have something else in mind. 'I'm going to stay in Germany for a while and work on the reconstruction,' he told her in a letter. 'There's lots of work for ex-servicemen here.'

Kathleen was disappointed that Arnold's decision meant they would be parted even longer, but at least, she reasoned, he would be earning good money. The sooner they scraped together enough to put down a deposit on a flat, the sooner they could start their life together.

In the meantime, Kathleen had her teacher training to focus on. Before long she was off to Warrington to begin her course, living in nearby student accommodation. Thanks to the teacher shortage caused by the war, most of her fellow recruits were older than the usual trainees, and like her many of them had already spent years in the services. The instructors, used to handling young people fresh out of school or university, struggled to assert their authority over this new cohort, who balked at some of the rules, especially when they were told they had to be in by 10 p.m. every night. 'I've been fighting a war,' one of the men remarked. 'No one's going to tell me when I'm supposed to be tucked up in bed!'

As it turned out, Kathleen was able to provide a crafty solution for her fellow students. Her bedroom backed onto an alleyway which ran along the back of the accommodation block, which meant that anyone who wanted to stay out past the curfew could get into the building by climbing through her window, without having to use the main gate. Although this meant that her room was essentially a thoroughfare any time up until about 1 a.m., she was willing to pay the price in order to keep her new friends out of trouble.

By the time Christmas rolled around, it was time for the trainees to have a go at teaching for real. They went to a nearby school, where Kathleen watched as, one by one, her fellow students struggled with the task of commanding a whole classroom of children. Some overreacted to any disobedience and became tyrannical, throwing their weight around in an attempt to gain authority, while others couldn't assert themselves at all and simply crumbled when put in front of a class.

When Kathleen's turn came she was relieved to find that she had been assigned to a relatively young age group, who all seemed rather sweet and quiet. She enjoyed the experience of teaching them, and quickly formed a good relationship with the class.

But while discipline didn't seem to be an issue, what Kathleen found harder to deal with was the evident poverty of the children. The whole country was experiencing a tough period of austerity, and for these kids it had clearly begun to bite. One little blond boy sat wearing a ripped jumper over a stringy old vest, and a pair of hand-me-down trousers cut off at the knees to fit his short legs. Instead of shoes, he had only wooden clogs, which he wore without socks, and the skin on his feet had been rubbed raw.

But despite his pitiable appearance, the boy seemed cheerful, and when Kathleen asked the class if they would like her to tell them a story, his little face lit up. 'Please, Miss,' he called out, 'can we 'ave the one wiv the lad an' the cow?'

'I'm not sure I know that,' Kathleen replied, casting a quick glance at the boy's regular teacher.

'He means Jesus in the manger,' the other woman whispered.

Dutifully, Kathleen launched into the nativity story. The boys and girls sat attentively as she told them all about the bright star in the night sky, and the wise men and the shepherds visiting baby Jesus.

At the end of the class, Kathleen went up to the teacher and asked her about the little blond boy. 'It's terrible, isn't it?' the other woman told her. 'He comes in like that every morning, and he's never had a bite to eat. I've started sending him home with sandwiches and cake, so at least he has something for his supper.'

Kathleen felt more strongly than ever that she had found the right profession.

With her course coming to an end, and Arnold's stint in Germany almost over, Kathleen was looking forward to the day when they would finally be reunited back in England. So she was a little surprised to receive a letter from her fiancé announcing that he was moving to Switzerland instead. His parents had recently retired to his father's hometown of Zurich, and Arnold himself had been offered a job with an airline in Geneva. It was an excellent opportunity, he said, and he didn't want to go back to his old life selling furniture. 'There's an Anglican church near my apartment that would be perfect for a wedding,' he added.

Kathleen felt excited by the idea of moving abroad, and she was sure there would be an English-speaking school in Geneva where she could get a teaching job. Most importantly, the wedding plans finally seemed to be going somewhere – all they needed to do now was settle on a date. She wrote back and told Arnold that as soon as her course was over she would come and visit him, and they could discuss the arrangements for the big day. She would be bringing one of her teacher training friends with her, a girl called Peggy, who had agreed to be her maid of honour.

Arnold wrote back full of enthusiasm for the idea, and promising to take Kathleen and her friend to the best restaurant in Geneva when they visited. Since it wouldn't seem proper for the girls to sleep at an unmarried man's apartment, they arranged that they would stay with his parents in Zurich, and come over on the train for the day to see him.

As they boarded the plane at London's new Heathrow Airport, Kathleen and Peggy were full of excitement. Peggy was thrilled at the prospect of flying for the first time, and Kathleen was in high spirits too, convinced that when she came back from Switzerland she would finally have a date for the wedding. She was also looking forward to catching up with her future in-laws, who had been so kind to her when she was doing her driver's training in London.

The Karlens' new flat was very near the airport, and when the girls arrived they served them a delicious dinner. Arnold's mother was as friendly as ever and seemed keen to do all she could to ensure the two young women were comfortable. But there was a stiffness to her manner that Kathleen hadn't noticed before, almost as if she felt awkward around her.

In fact, when she came to think about it, the whole family were acting a little strangely. Arnold's younger brother was also visiting at the time and kept making odd remarks that Kathleen couldn't quite make sense of. 'Every time I go to Geneva I have to take more baby clothes with me,' he told his parents over dinner, casting a meaningful look in her direction. But no one picked up on the strange comment, and the conversation soon turned to something else.

The following day, the two girls caught the train to Geneva. It was a journey of almost three hours, and for Kathleen – who was desperate to be reunited with her fiancé – every one of them felt like days. At long last they pulled into the Gare de Cornavin, where Arnold was waiting on the platform.

Kathleen rushed over to him, and he swept her up in his arms. 'My darling!' he exclaimed. 'It's been so long.' Before she had a chance to reply they were locked in a passionate kiss.

'This is my friend Peggy,' Kathleen told him, once she had prised her lips away from his.

Arnold turned to the young woman, and took her hand. 'Delighted to meet you,' he said, as charming as ever. Then he turned back to Kathleen. 'I've booked us in for dinner at a fabulous restaurant in the Cologny district,' he told her. 'I know you're going to love it. But first why don't you two come to my apartment for a drink?'

Kathleen felt her fiancé slide his arm around her waist. Gently, he led her along the platform, while Peggy followed a couple of steps behind. Even after so long apart, it was easy to slip back into their old familiarity. And yet, just as everything felt exactly as it always had before, something about him was different. Perhaps it was just that he seemed more worldly, which she supposed was to be expected – after all, he had led a hundred men into battle, with all the triumphs and horrors that entailed. But his appearance had altered subtly as well – he didn't just look older, but held himself differently too. Looking back, Kathleen felt that the Arnold she had got engaged to had been little more than a boy in comparison, but she liked this new Arnold, who was strong as well as charming. She felt she would be utterly safe with him.

The two girls got into Arnold's car, and soon they were speeding through the streets of Geneva. Before long they arrived at a smart modern building, and Arnold led them up a few flights of stairs. He opened the door and gestured for the girls to enter, but as they stepped into the open-plan living area, all three of them suddenly froze, rooted to the spot in astonishment. In the middle of the room, sitting in a metal bathtub, was a young woman with jet black hair – and she was completely naked.

Kathleen glanced over at Arnold and saw his face contort with fury. 'I told you to get out of here!' he yelled at the girl in the tub. Kathleen had never seen him angry before and it scared her.

The girl quickly grabbed a towel, gathered up her things and rushed out into the corridor, muttering some kind of an apology to Arnold in French.

Looking rather shaken, Arnold gestured Kathleen and Peggy towards a couple of sofas. 'I'm sorry about that,' he said, as he turned his back to fix them a couple of drinks. 'She's one of the stewardesses from work and I said she could use the bath.'

By the time he brought the drinks over, and came to sit down next to Kathleen, he was cool and collected once more, asking them all about their journey as if nothing had happened. Kathleen was too stunned to know what to say. In her embarrassment she couldn't bear to acknowledge what she had just seen, so she just answered Arnold's questions and did her best to smile. Much as she wanted to give her fiancé the benefit of the doubt, the explanation he had given hadn't sounded very convincing. But then, she reasoned, he had been on his own for a long time. So what if there had been other girlfriends? Kathleen was the one he was planning to marry, and once they were together for ever, all that would be in the past.

When the girls had finished their drinks, Arnold took them out for dinner at the classy restaurant he had mentioned. It was the most stylish and elegant establishment Kathleen had ever been to in her life, and she gazed in awe at the chandeliers hanging from the ceiling, the little orchestra playing in the corner, and the women dressed in dinner gowns, adorned with furs and pearls. She had worn her best dress for the occasion, but now it suddenly seemed rather shabby and she couldn't help feeling awkward surrounded by such rich people.

Arnold, however, was in his element, confident and self-assured. He chose the wine and helped the girls pick out the fish they wanted from a huge tank, to be taken into the kitchen and cooked by the five-star chef. As they ate, he discoursed on every topic under the sun – apart, that is, from the one subject Kathleen had come to Geneva to talk about: their wedding. Every time there was a lull in the conversation, she hoped that he would turn to their forthcoming nuptials, but again and again he moved on to discuss the state of the airline industry, or the reconstruction efforts in Germany, or the weather.

Kathleen felt too embarrassed to bring up the topic herself – after talking so confidently to Peggy on the journey over about how they were finally going to set the date, she couldn't bear to be seen to nag Arnold about it now.

After dinner the three of them went back to Arnold's flat. When they arrived, he turned to look at Peggy. 'You know, there's a beautiful arcade just down the street from here,' he told her. 'You could go and look around the shops while Kath and I have a little chat.' Kathleen could feel his arm sliding down behind her on the sofa. Something about the way he moved let her know that he wanted her.

Peggy shot Kathleen a concerned look. 'No, I think perhaps I should stay,' she said, clearly embarrassed.

'I really need to talk to Kathleen alone,' Arnold replied, a little testily. 'But if you don't want to go out, why don't you stay here and we'll go for a drive together?'

'It's all right, we can talk here,' Kathleen told him. 'Let's just go in the next room if you want to say something in private.'

Arnold led Kathleen into the bedroom, and she waited to see what he was going to say. But instead of talking he pulled her into another passionate embrace. 'I love you, darling,' he told her, sweeping her up in his arms. 'You know that, don't you?' She could feel his hands moving all over her body.

But to Kathleen, it just didn't feel right any more, and she wriggled free from his embrace.

'What is it, darling?' he asked her.

'The wedding,' Kathleen replied defiantly. 'Why haven't you talked about the wedding?'

'Don't worry, my darling,' Arnold told her. 'The wedding will happen in good time.'

'No,' Kathleen told him. 'I've been waiting long enough already. Why can't we get married now?'

'I'm afraid I haven't had a moment to look into the arrangements,' he said. 'But as soon as I do, I promise I'll write to you.'

'Arnold, you know I've been waiting for you – I've been faithful to you – all these years,' Kathleen said. She felt like asking, 'Have you been faithful to me too?' but then the image of the girl in the bath flashed into her mind.

Arnold was silent for a moment. 'Why should we wait any longer?' Kathleen asked him imploringly. 'What's in the way?'

But to that question he didn't seem to have an answer. 'I'd better take you back to the station,' he replied, the passion suddenly cooled. 'You don't want to miss your train.'

The short drive back to the station passed in awkward silence. As the girls got out, Peggy whispered to Kathleen, 'I think it's a good thing we're going. I can't make out what the matter is, but something here isn't right.'

On the railway platform, Kathleen and Arnold said a brief goodbye before he turned and walked away. But just as the two girls were about to get onto the train, Kathleen noticed a young woman with blonde curly hair striding up to them. She was wearing a smart fawn coat and ordinarily would have been considered pretty, but right now her eyes were narrowed in rage. For some reason, Kathleen couldn't help thinking of Medusa.

'Is one of you Kathleen?' the woman demanded in a heavy Swiss accent.

Kathleen nodded slightly, and the woman fixed her with a look of purest hatred. 'You leave my husband alone!' she spat at her.

'Your husband?' Kathleen repeated, confused.

'Yes, my *husband*,' the woman replied slowly, as if she was talking to an imbecile. 'Don't you know Arnold and I have a child together?'

For a moment, Kathleen stood rooted to the spot, feeling as if the wind had been knocked out of her. She couldn't speak, could barely think even, so she just stared at the woman, dumbstruck, as the horrifying truth washed over her. All her years of love and devotion had been for nothing. Arnold had played her for a fool.

Kathleen felt a hand on her arm. 'We've got to go,' Peggy was telling her, pulling her gently towards the open door of the train. She allowed herself to be guided inside, barely conscious of what was happening.

Slowly, the train began to pull away, but Kathleen's eyes remained fixed on the platform. The woman with the blonde hair had stormed off, and in the entrance to the station she could see Arnold standing alone, as motionless as a statue. Kathleen continued to watch as the little figure shrank to the size of a pinprick, and then he was gone for ever.

That night, the girls stayed once again with Arnold's parents in Zurich. When they arrived, Kathleen was too upset to talk to them, and she shut herself away in the bedroom, leaving Peggy to explain what had happened. But she knew she had to face them eventually, and after a few hours she emerged from her room.

Now that the secret was out, Mr and Mrs Karlen seemed relieved, and their former awkwardness was replaced with pity. 'I'm so sorry for what has happened,' Arnold's mother told Kathleen. 'I could barely believe it of my own son. I've never been so embarrassed in all my life.'

She explained that when he started work at the airline, Arnold had got his boss's daughter pregnant, and had been left with no choice but to marry her. 'We only found out recently ourselves,' Arnold's father added. 'He invited us to come to Geneva for a special meal, and told us to make sure we dressed smartly. It wasn't until we got there that we realised it was his wedding breakfast.'

As the firstborn, Arnold had always been the golden boy of the family, and Kathleen could see that his parents were struggling to cope with what he had done. Now she realised that his younger brother's odd remarks about buying baby clothes had been a way of trying to warn her.

'You know,' Mrs Karlen said, patting Kathleen's hand, 'I think you might have saved yourself a lot of trouble in the long run.'

Kathleen thought of the girl she had seen in the bath that morning. Perhaps Arnold's mother was right. For a moment she even felt a flash of pity for his wife – the woman was shackled to a cheating husband for good.

But the thought didn't make Kathleen feel any better about herself. Her entire world, and all her hopes for the future, had just come crashing down around her.

Back home in England, Kathleen had never felt so down in all her life. But now that her teacher training was finished she had to support herself, and that meant going out and getting a job. She took a position at a girls' school in Middlesex, from where she wrote a heartfelt letter to Peggy, apologising for bringing her into such an embarrassing situation. But the other girl never replied, and Kathleen realised that her intended maid of honour was now lost to her too.

She did, however, receive a letter from Arnold. He wrote to her cheerfully, almost as if nothing had happened, asking if she would be willing to meet him in London. He wants me for another bit on the side, Kathleen thought, her heart burning with shame. She felt such a fool for ever falling for Arnold's charms in the first place. But her anger and frustration was mixed with another feeling too – despite everything he had done to her, as she read over his words she could feel herself drawn towards him. She wasn't sure that she could trust herself if they ever did see each other again.

Kathleen didn't reply to Arnold's letter. Instead she told her landlady to keep a look-out for any more post from Switzerland, and to put it straight in the bin without telling her. Then she did her best to force herself to forget about the man on whom she had wasted so much of her youth. For the most part, she was able to push him to the back of her mind, but one day, when she was riding through Clapham on the top deck of a bus, she caught a glimpse of his parents' old house. In an instant all the hurt and humiliation washed over her once again, and the experience left her reeling. 'You're a fool, Skin,' Kathleen kept telling herself. 'Why didn't you see what he was like?'

The school Kathleen taught at was in a rough part of Hayes – so rough, in fact, that the taxi drivers refused to go near it. It was close to a stretch of factories that included not only Cadbury's chocolate and Quaker Oats but the home of the Fairey Aviation Company. It was here that many of the aircraft Kathleen had worked on as an armourer had been built – the Swordfishes, Fireflies, Albacores and Barracudas. After everything that had happened to her since she had left the WRNS, it felt strange to be just a stone's throw from the production line.

Kathleen threw herself into her teaching, doing her best to distract herself from what had happened by putting everything she had into her job. The harder she worked, the more she got back from the children, and far from being rough and unruly, as everyone around her kept saying, she found them to be intelligent and receptive as long as they were inspired in the right way. Many of them were behind in their lessons because their education had been so disrupted by the war, but Kathleen excelled at finding new, inventive ways to engage them. She would take them to a graveyard and let them make rubbings of headstones to teach them about history, or break open rocks so that they could see the geological layers inside them. Every Christmas she wrote a pantomime for the kids to perform, and composed her own carols for them to sing.

In teaching, Kathleen had truly found her vocation, and she was popular with staff and students alike. But as time went on, she began to feel that there must be more to life than what she was making of it. When one of her colleagues retired, Kathleen attended the party thrown in her honour, and was shocked to discover that the woman had worked at the same school all her life. To a girl who had always longed for adventure, the idea of staying in one place for so long seemed stifling. Arnold's betrayal had dented her natural self-confidence, but that didn't mean she was willing to settle for a life of caution and limited ambitions.

That Sunday, Kathleen went out and bought a copy of the *Times Educational Supplement*. Over breakfast she scanned the recruitment pages and saw that a number of organisations were looking for teachers to volunteer for postings abroad. There were schools opening up in Uganda, Malaysia and Chile, and Kathleen felt a long-forgotten spark of excitement reignite inside her. She hadn't had the opportunity to go overseas with the Navy, and her plans to move abroad with Arnold had come to nothing, but perhaps she could fulfil her dream in a different way.

Kathleen wrote off straight away, applying for all three of the foreign postings. She had experienced too many rejections during her years in the WRNS to risk trying just one of them.

A few days later, she received a trio of replies – and each one contained an invitation to come for an interview. Fortunately, the three organisations were all based within a couple of hours' train ride of each other and she was able to schedule them all on the same day, so there was no need for her absence to attract too much attention at work.

In the end all three of the organisations offered Kathleen a job, and as she looked over the various acceptance letters she could scarcely believe what she was seeing. Finally, she would be going abroad after all.

The only thing that remained was to choose which of the postings to accept. She decided to place the decision in the hands of her class at school – they picked Malaysia, so Malaysia it was. Kathleen handed in her notice, and her colleagues threw a farewell party in her honour.

Soon she was back at Heathrow, boarding a plane once again. There was no man at her side, but by now she had come to realise she didn't need one. Life in the WRNS had taught her the value of independence and self-confidence, and had shown her that every new beginning brought with it opportunities for friendship and adventure.

The girls from Kathleen's school had come to see her off at the airport, and as the plane began to soar into the sky, she gazed out of her window at the little figures smiling and waving on the ground. In a few moments they were gone and all she could see below her was green fields. Then they too gradually receded from view.

As she bade England farewell, Kathleen's regrets about the past seemed to fade away too. All she saw now were blue skies, stretching for ever, as the whole world opened out in front of her.

Epilogue

In the Malaysian jungle, Kathleen finally found the exotic adventure she had been dreaming of since childhood, when reading *Swiss Family Robinson* had first kindled her desire to travel. She lived in a small hut in a village 20 miles away from the nearest road – so remote that supplies had to be air-dropped in. The jungle was home to leopards and tigers, as well as plenty of poisonous snakes, and the locals instructed her in how to defend herself with a blowpipe.

Still somewhat scarred from her experience with Arnold, Kathleen enjoyed living out in the middle of nowhere, and she loved her work. But after a couple of years, the small jungle community was beginning to feel a bit limiting, so she applied for a posting at an Army school in Kuala Lumpur.

In the city, she found love for a second time, with an English doctor called Raymond who she met through a local Gilbert & Sullivan society. She had been cast as the captain's daughter in a production of *HMS Pinafore*, and the young medic was in the band, playing the oboe. He was meant to give her the first note of her solo, but every time they rehearsed the song, somehow he managed to get it wrong. 'I'm ever so sorry,' he told her, after one particularly frustrating rehearsal. 'Do you think I could take you out for dinner to make amends?'

The two of them hit it off immediately, and before long they were engaged to be married. Their friends in Malaysia threw them a party to celebrate, but as Kathleen and Raymond took to the dance floor, his legs suddenly gave way and he collapsed. His sister told Kathleen that it wasn't the first time it had happened, but none of his doctor colleagues had been able to work out what was wrong with him.

The couple decided to postpone the wedding while Raymond flew to Australia, hoping that the doctors there would be able to help. But they too could find nothing to explain his strange symptoms, and he returned to Malaysia seemingly recovered.

Kathleen went back to planning the wedding, hoping that the problem had gone away for good this time. But when Raymond was shopping for his wedding outfit he collapsed again, and was rushed to a local hospital. This time, it was clear he wasn't going to recover.

Kathleen obtained special permission for the two of them to be married at his bedside. A few days later, Raymond was dead.

The autopsy revealed that his body had been riddled with cancer, and it was a miracle he had survived so long. Instead of organising their wedding in Kuala Lumpur, Kathleen found herself helping to arrange her new husband's funeral.

After Raymond's death, Kathleen stayed in the Far East, determined not to give up on the two remaining loves of her life: travel and teaching. For the next few decades she moved from one far-flung location to another, working in schools not just in Malaysia but Uganda and Japan as well.

She never married again, but she felt that her life was a full one. Everywhere she went, she was adored by the children she taught, and soon earned the respect of her neighbours. In one posting she became known for rescuing orphaned animals, after helping to raise a baby tiger and a crocodile until they were old enough to be released. In another, she fostered local girls who needed a home.

In between her foreign postings, Kathleen returned now and then to England. During one visit, she was walking around London when she saw a man selling fruit from a stall by the side of the road. 'Please don't touch 'em, lady,' he told a customer who was fingering some pears. 'I've gotta sell 'em afterwards, you know.'

The man had his back to her, but there was no mistaking that voice. 'Can I touch them, Ginger?' Kathleen asked, sweetly.

Her old friend spun round and flashed her the same cheeky smile she remembered from their days at HMS *Hornbill*. 'You can touch anything you like, mate!' he told her cheerily.

Kathleen learned that Ginger was now married with three children, and he proudly whipped out his wallet and showed her photos of all the family. She was pleased to know that everything had turned out so well for him. All those years ago the two of them had been ships that passed in the night, but Kathleen had never forgotten him.

In later life, Kathleen returned to Cambridge, where she still lives today. She is a member of her local Wren Association chapter, which meets regularly to reminisce about old times in the Navy. Many of the other women there share tales of their exotic postings during the war – how they travelled with fellow Wrens to Colombo, Australia or Singapore.

But while Kathleen's own wartime service never offered her the same opportunities, in the years after they were demobbed none of the other women in her group have lived lives that match hers for adventure.

*

Margery's marriage to Alistair was a happy one, and together they brought three children into the world – two boys and a girl. While he worked for the council as an electrical engineer, she put her book-keeping skills to good use at the Co-op, travelling from store to store doing audit work. With the help of a loan from the Royal British Legion, they were able to buy their first home together.

When their children left, the couple moved to Alresford and Margery took a job helping out in the shop of a local golf club. One day, when the golf tutor died, she was tasked with ringing round all his pupils to let them know. To her surprise, one of the names on the list was her old friend Doug from Kasfareet. 'I don't believe it!' he exclaimed, when he heard Margery's voice on the other end of the line, and he immediately rushed round to see her.

It turned out that Doug was living just up the road, and he told Margery he had been approached by somebody from their Kasfareet days who was organising a reunion up in Yorkshire. His wife wasn't keen on making such a long journey, so he asked Margery to accompany him instead. Alistair came along too – and to Margery's relief, he and Doug got on famously.

The reunion was a great success, and Margery enjoyed the chance to reminisce about her days as a WAAF in Egypt. Soon it had become an annual event, and in between meet-ups she received a monthly newsletter called the *Kasfareet Kronicle*, full of stories and photographs of the camp.

After Margery and Alistair retired, she joined her local WAAF Association, a group of women who would meet at a church hall in Portchester to share stories of their experiences during the war. She also attended the AGMs of the national organisation, and in 2008, when the old committee decided to step down, she was asked if she would consider standing as

Assistant Treasurer. 'As long as the accounts are done manually,' Margery insisted. At nearly 90, she had no intention of learning how to use a computer.

Margery was duly voted in, and when the Association's Treasurer died, she stepped up to take her place. Soon she had devoted herself to a major campaign to raise funds for a permanent WAAF memorial. Thanks in large part to Margery's efforts, more than £10,000 was brought in, and on 11 June 2011 the memorial was officially dedicated at the National Memorial Arboretum. Inscribed with the various jobs that WAAFs took on during the war, it stands as a proud reminder of the great contribution made by the women of the Air Force.

In 2013, the WAAF Association chairwoman died, and with no one else willing to take over, Margery decided to put herself forward. Now in her mid-nineties, the once-timid girl from North Wallington runs an organisation with more than 700 members, helping to organise their grand reunion every summer, when the former WAAFs meet up – dressed in their smart navy blazers and skirts – for their AGM and gala dinner, complete with a sing-along of old wartime songs.

Jessie and Mac remained together for almost 20 years, and between them they raised a beloved son, Neil. But as time went on they began to drift apart, and eventually, when Neil went off to university, they parted.

Jessie did find love again, and funnily enough with an old friend – the polite young baritone who she had got to know in Hamburg. It turned out that Ralph had been carrying a torch for her all through the intervening decades, and hadn't so much as looked at another woman.

Jessie and Ralph shared 30 years of blissful happiness, singing and dancing through their life together until they were separated by his death a few years ago.

She continued to keep up with other Army pals as well. Her dear friend Elsie Acres died of breast cancer at the age of just 47, but Jessie and Elsie Windsor remain in touch to this day. The two old friends have never quite lost their old ack-ack skills either. Whenever Jessie sees a plane flying overhead she can't help estimating its height, while Elsie can make a pretty good guess at the length of fuse required to shoot it down.

Despite Jessie's father's insistence that she had single-handedly won the war, she had never thought of her work in ack-ack as particularly heroic or significant. She was a small cog in a giant machine, she had always told herself – and if it made even a tiny difference then that was enough.

One day, as she was buying some fish and chips in a shop in Aberdeen, she felt sure she recognised the accent of the woman behind the counter. 'Are you from Hull originally?' Jessie asked her.

'That's right,' the woman replied. 'Do you know the city?'

'I was there during the war,' Jessie told her.

The other woman looked at her for a moment. 'You weren't on one of them guns, were you?' she asked.

Jessie nodded, and a broad smile spread across the woman's face. 'Oh, you don't know what they meant to us in the city,' she told her. 'Whenever we heard the guns open up, it gave us a bit of hope to hold onto.'

The woman's words had a powerful effect on Jessie. Suddenly it was as if she was back on the gun-site in the middle of a raid – she could hear the captain's orders, smell the cordite and feel the whoosh of air as the guns blasted their shells into the heavens. As the flashback faded, she realised there were tears streaming down her face. 'I'm just glad it helped somebody,' she said quietly.

Today, Jessie is a committed member of the Royal British Legion. She attends a local meeting every month and always wears her beret with pride. Until a few years ago, when she broke her hip in a fall, she joined in the annual parade on Remembrance Sunday, marching along enthusiastically with the other former servicewomen, just as she learned to do all those years ago during her basic training in Leicester.

It is the one day of the year when Jessie's emotions always seem to get the better of her. As soon as she hears the words, 'They shall grow not old, as we that are left grow old,' a lump forms in her throat, and she struggles to get out the final line – 'We will remember them' – without choking. The passage of time has only made the words harder to bear.

Every November, Jessie lays a poppy down for Jim, the husband who never had a chance to grow old with her. A few years ago, when she was standing by the Cenotaph, an Army chaplain walked up beside her. 'It's a long time ago, dear,' he said. 'But your heart never quite mends, does it?'

'You're right,' Jessie told him, blinking away a tear.

These days, at the age of 92, Jessie can no longer march in the parade, but she still does her bit for the Legion, standing out in the cold for hours at a time, selling poppies by the entrance to her local supermarket. She always wears her old medals for the occasion – meticulously polished and buffed up, just like they taught her in the Army.

As the crowds of busy shoppers pass by, every so often someone comes up to her and asks, 'What did you do in the war?'

'I was one of those bloody ATS tarts,' Jessie replies with a smile.

Acknowledgements

First and foremost, our thanks go to our core interviewees – Jessie Denby, Margery Harley and Kathleen Skin – who were generous enough to share their stories with us, and to put up with many hours of detailed questions. We are grateful, too, to all the other women who kindly gave up their time to speak to us about their experiences in the WRNS, WAAF and ATS.

As always, we have done our best to remain faithful to what our interviewees have told us, although after more than 70 years some memories are understandably incomplete, and where necessary we have used our own research, and our imaginations, to fill in the gaps. Some names have been changed for the sake of anonymity.

For help in finding subjects to interview we are grateful to the British Legion, the WAAF Association, the WRAC Association and the Association of Wrens. Many individuals also provided assistance in our research, and in particular we would like to thank Barbara Bennett, Linda Hamill and David Hunt.

For help with transcription, we are grateful to Becky Barry, Reni Eddo-Lodge, Sarah Ellis, Catherine Gerbrands, Terry Hearn, Becky Macnaughton, Isabelle Schoelcher, Alexandra Wieck, Alex Young and Aurella Yusuf. Michèle Barrett provided feedback on an early draft of the manuscript and Gilly Furse built the book's website.

Our thanks go to Anna Valentine, Natalie Jerome, Kate Latham and Simon Gerratt at HarperCollins for seeing the book through to production, and to our brilliant copy-editor Steve Dobell for his hard work and patience. As ever, we are grateful to our agent Jon Elek for his support and encouragement throughout the process.

To see photographs of the girls who went to war,
and read more about them, visit:
www.girlsatwar.com

About the Authors

Duncan Barrett grew up in London and studied English at Jesus College, Cambridge. In 2010 he edited the First World War memoirs of pacifist saboteur Ronald Skirth, published as *The Reluctant Tommy*, and in 2014 his book *Men of Letters: The Post Office Heroes Who Fought the Great War* was nominated for the People's Book Prize.

Nuala Calvi also grew up in London, and trained as a journalist at London College of Printing. She has written for *The Times*, *The Guardian*, *The Independent*, the BBC and CNN, as well as numerous *Time Out* guides.

In 2012, Duncan and Nuala's book *The Sugar Girls* shot into the *Sunday Times* top ten, spending eight weeks in the chart and finishing as the second-highest history bestseller of the year. It was followed in 2013 by *GI Brides*, which was both a *Sunday Times* and *New York Times* bestseller. Both books are currently in development for television.